Modern Critical Interpretations

Modern Critical Interpretations

Kurt Vonnegut's
Cat's Cradle

Edited and with an introduction by
Harold Bloom
Sterling Professor of the Humanities
Yale University

CHELSEA HOUSE PUBLISHERS
Philadelphia

Printed and bound in the United States of America

10 9 8 7 6 5 4 3 2 1

∞ The paper used in this publication meets the minimum
requirements of the American National Standard for
Permanence of Paper for Printed Library Materials,
Z39.48-1984

Library of Congress Cataloging-in-Publication Data

Kurt Vonnegut's Cat's cradle : modern critical interpretations /
Harold Bloom, ed.
     p. cm.
Includes bibliographical references and index.
  ISBN 0-7910-6337-2
  1. Vonnegut, Kurt. Cat's cradle. I. Bloom, Harold.
  PS3572.O5 C335 2002
  813'.54—dc21
                                         2002001818

Chelsea House Publishers
1974 Sproul Road, Suite 400
Broomall, PA 19008-0914

The Chelsea House World Wide Web address is
http://www.chelseahouse.com

Contributing Editor: Matt Uhler

Produced by Publisher's Services, Santa Barbara, California

Contents

Editor's Note

My Introduction ponders the nature and limits of Vonnegut's irony in *Cat's Cradle*.

The novelist Terry Southern, who had authentic affinities with Vonnegut, begins the sequence of critiques with a review of *Cat's Cradle* that sees the satire as fantasy of a high order.

In a note on names in the novel, William S. Doxey traces Felix Hoenikker to the greeting: "Happy Hanukkah," a Jewish salutation for the Feast of Lights.

Jerome Klinkowitz records a public appearance of Vonnegut which exemplified a refinding of a "karass" or group destiny, out of his own past.

For Richard Giannone, *Cat's Cradle* is all a digression, from Hoenikker's fatherhood of the atomic bomb, to his more destructive invention, ice-nine. This digression is seen as being very much in the spirit of two apocalyptic satires, Jonathan Swift's *A Tale of a Tub* and William Blake's *The Marriage of Heaven and Hell*.

In a seriously playful reading, John L. Simons invokes Dante's *Inferno*, but affirms, with Vonnegut, an anti-Dantesque philosophy of flow.

Jerome Klinkowitz reappears with a comparison of *Cat's Cradle* and *God Bless You, Mr. Rosewater*; after which Leonard Mustazza finds another variant in *Cat's Cradle* of Vonnegut's obsessive image of Eden.

To Zoltán Abádi-Nagy, Bokononism is an authentically ironic gospel, one that cancels itself, after which Jerome Klinkowitz considers *Mother Night* and *Cat's Cradle* as ways of viewing man's place in the world, while Peter Freese emphasizes instead that Vonnegut's invented religion is a benign humanism.

Gabriel García Marquez's Macondo in *One Hundred Years of Solitude* is contrasted to Vonnegut's San Lorenzo by Wendy B. Faris, who points out that both imaginary lands end in an ice-apocalypse.

Vonnegut's visionary satire of a cosmos is seen by David H. Goldsmith as a serious absurdism, after which James Lundquist gives us a general survey of Vonnegut's many cosmic variations.

The symbolism of the Book of Jonah and its effect upon *Cat's Cradle*, is seen by Lawrence R. Broer as a very personal matter for Vonnegut, while Peter J. Reed examines the singular blend of pain and comedy in *Cat's Cradle*.

In this volume's final essay, Loree Rackstraw meditates upon the Faustian element in Vonnegut, one that casts the novelist as Mephisto in relation to his Faustian protagonists.

Introduction

Bokononism, a religion that freely acknowledges its status as a fiction, is one of the two lovely ironic inventions of *Cat's Cradle*. The other is "karass," the doctrine of hidden soul families, which curiously resembles the Kabbalistic notion of *gilgul,* Isaac Luria's idea of the transmigration of souls. In Lurianic Kabbalah, soul families are united by the root of a common spark.

As an ironist, Vonnegut is too kindly to sustain comparison with Jonathan Swift, whose *A Tale of a Tub* is one of the ironic masterpieces of the ages. I prefer *Cat's Cradle* to Vonnegut's other fictions precisely because it seems so well aware of the limits of its irony. Barely below the surface of the book one can discover many of Vonnegut's nostalgias: a longing for the earthly paradise, an exaltation of an ideal familial love, and the hopeless hope for a rational utopia, a redemptive reversal of the Faust myth, and a profoundly personal identification with the ironically successful prophet, Jonah.

Bokononism is necessarily more an ironic humanism than it is a spirituality. Vonnegut, in my view, does not intend Bokononism as another pragmatic nihilism. Its secret is in *karass,* with the implication that almost anyone can belong to one's soul-family. "Ye must love one another," is Vonnegut's authentic belief, which transcends irony.

An author who has been rewriting the Book of Jonah all his life is probably aware that it is read aloud complete on the afternoon of the Jewish Day of Atonement. *Cat's Cradle* may seem too funny to be an atonement, but that is the achievement of Vonnegut's art. A Jonah who can move us to laughter is a valuable resource, perhaps our final ironist.

TERRY SOUTHERN

After the Bomb, Dad Came Up with Ice

The narrator of *Cat's Cradle* purports to be engaged in compiling a responsibly factual account of what certain interested Americans were doing at the precise moment the atomic bomb was dropped on Hiroshima. Through correspondence with the three children of the late Felix Hoenikker, Nobel Prize winner and so-called "father of the atomic bomb," he evolves a portrait of the man in relation to his family and the community.

We learn that at the eventful moment in question Dr. Hoenikker was, in fact, "playing with a bit of string," having made of it a "cat's cradle"—and that his youngest son, to whom he had never previously spoken, was frightened when Dad came up to him, jerking the string back and forth, saying: "See the cat! See the cradle!"

We further learn that on the night of his death, years later, he was again "playing around"—in the kitchen this time, with some water and bits of ice. With his characteristically pure-science approach ("Why doesn't someone do something about mud?" the Marine Corps general had asked him) he has isolated crystals of ice in such a way that water can now be caused to freeze at a relatively high temperature. "Ice-9" it is called. The family dog laps at a bowl of water which has been touched with a piece of Ice-9 and is promptly frozen stiff. The Hoenikker children carefully divide this last gift to mankind from Dr. Hoenikker.

From *The New York Times*, June 3, 1963. © *The New York Times*.

Following the doctor's death, the story devotes itself to what happens to the three children and to Ice-9. Frank, the eldest, has become the right-hand man of Manzano, the President of a Caribbean island. The daughter and the younger brother visit the island to celebrate the forthcoming marriage of Frank to the regional sex-goddess; we soon learn that he has bought his position of power with a piece of Ice-9—which President Manzano then uses to commit suicide, thereupon naming Frank his successor.

Frank declines the responsibility and offers the post to the narrator. As the two of them try discreetly to dispose of the President's frozen corpse, the narrator realizes how extensive the spread and acquisition of Ice-9 has become. The younger brother, Newt, a midget, has exchanged his share for a few mad nights with a Russian circus performer, also a midget. The unmarriageable daughter, a six-foot bean-poler, has used hers to buy a handsome physicist. Finally events reach their inevitable conclusion—the freezing of all the earth's waters, and life itself.

Cat's Cradle is an irreverent and often highly entertaining fantasy concerning the playful irresponsibility of nuclear scientists. Like the best of contemporary satire, it is work of a far more engaging and meaningful order than the melodramatic tripe which most critics seem to consider "serious."

WILLIAM S. DOXEY

Vonnegut's Cat's Cradle

While some attention has been given to Vonnegut's use of names in *Cat's Cradle* (see Stanley Schatt, *Kurt Vonnegut, Jr.* [Boston: Twayne, 1976]), several important names remain unexamined, specifically those of Felix Hoenikker, Lionel B. Johnson, and Earl McCabe.

In Latin, "felix" means happy. "Hoenikker" may be pronounced the same as "Hanukkah," which is a Jewish holiday (also known as the "Feast of Lights") celebrated for eight days beginning on the 25th day of Kislev (3rd month of the Hebrew year corresponding to November-December). Hanukkah is marked by the exchange of gifts. The holiday commemorates the Jews' victory over the Syrians led by Judas Maccabeus, who reconquered Jerusalem and restored the temple in 165 B.C. "Hanukkah" is derived from the Hebrew *ḥānakh*, to be dedicated. Nobel Laureate Hoenikker is most certainly that, though it is through game-playing and following his curiosity that he makes his great discoveries.

Felix dies on Christmas Eve, and ice-nine—his most recent, and most lethal, formulation—is his gift to his children. "Some Happy Hanukkah!" Vonnegut seems to be saying.

As Bokonon, Lionel B. Johnson is a spiritual leader for the inhabitants of San Lorenzo. His message, cast in the form of calypso verses, is based upon his admonition that, "'All of the true things I am about to tell you are

From *The Explicator* 37, no. 4 (Summer 1979). © 1979 by Helen Dwight Reid Educational Foundation.

shameless lies.'" The significance of his name seems to be in the fact that as "Johnson" he is a "son of John" who offers spiritual leadership as did his namesake John, author of the Book of Revelation which deals with "last things." It is Johnson-Bokonon who makes the last gesture of the novel by stating that were he a younger man he would "write a history of human stupidity" and then go up on the mountain and freeze himself into a statue "thumbing" his nose"—but at whom? Surely God; but rather than speaking the name of the unnamable, he says "'at You Know Who.'"

The name of Earl McCabe—a deserter from the U.S. Marine Corps who, with Johnson, took control of San Lorenzo in 1922—may have no significance beyond itself. It may, however, contain an ironic reference to the Judas Maccabeus who, by leading his people to victory over the Syrians, caused the occasion for which the Hanukkah celebration was created. A parallel in *Cat's Cradle* may be seen in Felix Hoenikker's Hanukkah gfit to his children eventually being used in San Lorenzo to freeze the world solid. The connection between the two characters seems to exist only on the level of names, but in accordance with Bokononist belief this in itself may be good evidence that the scientist and the deserter belonged to the same *karass*, a structure analagous to the checkerboard yet "as free-form as an amoeba."

Vonnegut's humor is of a cosmic type which, ultimately, enables the reader to smile at fate and perhaps even laugh. The extended significance of the names of Felix Hoenikker, Lionel B. Johnson, and Earl McCabe adds to one's realization of the comedy that is *Cat's Cradle*.

JEROME KLINKOWITZ

The Private Person as Public Figure

When on November 1, 1993, Kurt Vonnegut spoke to an overflow crowd at Heritage Hall in the Civic Center of Lexington, Kentucky, he was almost certainly motivated by a principle drawn from *Cat's Cradle*, his novel published thirty years before.

At the beginning of *Cat's Cradle* the narrator describes how life has become less nonsensical to him after learning about an honestly bogus Caribbean religion called Bokononism, the central belief of which concerns the notion of karass. Humanity, it is said, is organized into teams who fulfill God's Will without ever knowing what they are doing. Such a team is called a *karass*—and having any intimation of who else may be in one's karass gives a sense of deep purpose to the otherwise chaotic nature of life.

The comic nature of this novel derives from how unlikely and apparently disparate the membership of a karass can be, stretching across generations, geographies, and cultures to form surprising but ultimately necessary connections. As a thematic device, it allows Vonnegut to introduce and synthesize themes as dichotomous as war and peace, hate and love, absurdity and meaning. Philosophically, his prototypical religion lets him explore how people can derive benefit from a belief system based on its own self-evident fabrication. The greatest benefit, however, is to his novel's structure. Modeled as it is on the notion of karass, *Cat's Cradle*

From *Vonnegut in Fact: The Public Spokesmanship of Personal Fiction* by Jerome Klinkowitz. ©1998 University of South Carolina.

ranges as far and wide as a jazz musician's solo, dipping and weaving through
apparent impossibilities to form what in the end is as coherent as a harmonic
pattern's resolution. The method can be found not just here but anywhere in
Kurt Vonnegut's fiction. And shortly after the publication of *Cat's Cradle* in
1963, it became apparent in his essays and public addresses as well.

In connection with his 1993 appearance in Lexington knowledgeable
journalists made reference to this notion of karass. It was a seeming contradiction, after all, that an acknowledged atheist should appear on behalf of
Midway College, supported as it was by the Disciples of Christ. And how odd
that this religiously affiliated school, raising funds for its new college library,
should seek the help of our era's most frequently banned author, his
Slaughterhouse-Five having been the target of Christian militancy since its
publication in 1969. Yet here he was, this figure of postmodern innovations
and sophistications, entertaining and instructing an audience of fourteen
hundred in the heartland and advising them that their library would
encourage a subversion of dogmatism more effective than eastern mysticism.

What brought Kurt Vonnegut to Lexington was his perception, at age
seventy, of the workings of his karass. Not that one needs a technique of
innovative fiction to explain the track of one's footprints in the sands of life.
But having one had given this author a handle on otherwise perplexing ideas,
on the whole notion of a latter twentieth century in which conventions and
values themselves had been eclipsed by as yet inexplicable forces. As a
survivor of one of these catastrophies, the World War II firebombing of
Dresden, Germany, Vonnegut would have asked the question anyone beating
such 1-in-100,000 odds would ask: why me? As a novelist, he had come relatively late to such ponderings, not beginning his career until 1952, at age
thirty, with *Player Piano*. It would take another decade and a half before the
matter of Dresden was first addressed, about the same time as his personal
fictions began expressing themselves in public spokesmanship. Now, as a
man in his seventies, Vonnegut would respond enthusiastically to elements in
his past, delighting in fortuitous connections and marveling at ironies of
correspondence still apparent from distances of fifty years and more.

For Lexington, the first connection was Ollie Lyon. As chair of
Midway College's Development Council, Lyon found himself reaching back
to the late 1940s for a resource in raising funds. As a publicist for General
Electric in Schenectady, New York, Lyon had worked side-by-side with
another young World War II veteran who'd begun responding to the brave
new world of technology around him with sardonically satirical short stories.
When on February 11, 1950, *Collier's* magazine published this fellow's
"Report on the Barnhouse Effect," Lyon helped celebrate his friend's good
fortune, for Kurt Vonnegut was the first among them to break out of the

corporate tedium into something hopefully bigger. So many years later that success would have a happy payback in helping Lyon's work with Midway's fund drive.

Yet for Vonnegut the benefits would be even greater. Reuniting with Ollie Lyon was both a joy for reminiscences and a helpful benchmark for measuring just what purposes had been served in the interim, just what sense life may have made in that half century since these two men had returned from the war and gone to work rebuilding a bombed-out world. They did this work at General Electric, a company so taken with the idealism of such effort that its motto became "Where Progress Is Our Most Important Product." Lyon and Vonnegut were at the forefront of this idealism, publicizing the achievements of GE's Research Laboratory, itself a scientist's dream where investigators could follow their every whim. From civilization's most devastating war, these two young men had returned to embark on not just massive reconstruction but, in technological terms, a virtual reinvention of what humankind could make.

Does the novelist reveal himself when he sits down over morning coffee at a dining room table in Lexington, Kentucky, to talk about the past with a friend of fifty years? In Kurt Vonnegut's case, the answer would be yes, because his artistic talent all these years had been to draw on autobiographical elements in constructing a fictive approach to a world evolving well beyond the old conventions. For the first one-third of his writer's career, these novels had seemed so radically innovative as to defy comfortable explanation; in despair, critics had dismissed them as science fiction, even though their few science-fiction elements existed only as devastating satires of the subgenre. Then, beginning in the late 1960s and corresponding with his first serious recognition, Vonnegut had introduced more discursive elements in his work, references to a history he had shared and which the reader could reliably recognize. From here the author's work would include more and more autobiographical elements, his fiction being supplemented by a growing body of discourse which in the forms of essays and public addresses made instructive use of specific components in that vision. Finally, in what Vonnegut would self-consciously describe as the conclusion of his effort, he could be seen clarifying the importance of these elements—revisiting them, as it were, before taking leave of his spokesman's duty. At Lexington, beginning with Ollie Lyon, one can see much of that clarification taking place.

The novelist as public figure involves himself in much more than speech making. The nature of his booking, as has been seen, is an important part—not just an anonymous invitation from a bureau or committee but, as so often happens, a connection from the past that involves the whole business of coming to speak, meeting old friends, making new ones, and refining one's own view in the process. Sitting around the table with Ollie Lyon and others, Vonnegut could feel transported back over half a lifetime to the publicity office at GE, where he and his colleagues would seek relief from the loneliness of writing by socializing around the coffee pot or water cooler. In such circumstances it is enlightening to see ideas from Vonnegut's speech not just interweave with notions from his fiction, as listeners could hear the night before, but mix as well with comments about his and Ollie's experiences as beat reporters for one of the world's largest and most inventive corporations at the very start of what would become the postmodern era. Here themes from *Player Piano* and *The Sirens of Titan* seem far less science-fictionish than commonly middle-class, as two friends remark how what began as a technological miracle meant to free people from drudgery wound up relegating them to the emptiness of having no meaningful, rewarding work. Yet life's dimensions inevitably outstrip those of simple ideas, whether of philosophy or fiction, and from these same years with GE, Vonnegut and Lyon could also appreciate the joy of their bonding—of how these young professionals away from home and separated from the nurturing culture of their prewar lives drew on each other's support to form a true extended family, not just another idea in Kurt Vonnegut's fiction but an antidote of sorts to the dead end of scientific progress.

Here are not just components being checked off but a fictive vision being constructed. As Vonnegut and Lyon chat over morning coffee one sees the progress of novels taking shape, from the technological satire of *Player Piano* to the coy invention of *Slapstick* and the deeper understanding of *Bluebeard* and *Hocus Pocus*. And it happens among neither the claptrap of low-grade space opera or the intricacies of intellectual metafiction but rather in the context of two eminently familiar men whose backgrounds and subsequent careers have followed the pattern so common to their generation: being educated for the bright world of scientific modernism, seeing it challenged first by wartime destruction and then again by the nature of postwar development, quitting the corporate ideal to strike out more rewardingly on their own, and—after long, successful careers in these endeavors—taking stock of how it had all turned out.

A karass, *Cat's Cradle* suggests, includes someone like Ollie Lyon, bringing Kurt Vonnegut back to ideas and experiences of half a century before. But there are many other players as well, and the author's Lexington visit identified two more. Appearing with him at his press conference were Louis Grivetti and George Bloomingburg, older friends whose bond to the author was sealed by an experience even deeper and more profound than those formative years at GE. Grivetti and Bloomingburg had been prisoners of war with Vonnegut in Dresden and survived with him what has been called the largest massacre in European military history. With him they descended into their underground meat-locker quarters, where on the night of February 13–14, 1945, they listened while one of the world's most architecturally and artistically treasured cities was destroyed above them—destroyed with scientific brilliance and precision for virtually no strategic or tactical purpose. Today Vonnegut is fond of saying that the firestorm raid, controversial even at the time, turned out not to end the war one minute sooner, not to have saved one Allied life or freed one person from a concentration camp. Only one person on earth drew any benefit from the massive bombing, but for him it was a windfall. That person was Kurt Vonnegut, whose *Slaughterhouse-Five* as novel and movie earned him upwards of a million dollars—about five dollars for every man, woman, and child killed that night.

Yet in his reunion with Grivetti and Bloomingburg, Vonnegut would be reminded once again how history itself offers no simple explanation, how as in his General Electric experience the fiction writer's synthesis is needed to contain such apparent contradictions as good and evil, hope and despair. Vonnegut's response had been to dedicate himself to a life of pacifism, speaking on its behalf and writing a novel considered to be a classic of antiwar literature. Yet this type of response need not be the only one, not even the only successful one, for in reuniting with Lou Grivetti he had to confront the fact of one POW colleague's opposing strategy, that of continuing in a twenty-year military career and achieving the rank of colonel. Asked whether this bothered him, Vonnegut answered no, not at all—that what mattered was the bonding when he and Grivetti were very young men. That bonding, after all, was what brought them back together today. What happened in between might well appear inexplicable, but in the workings of this world their reunion was obviously necessary. In fretting about discrepancies between the one's pacifism and the other's military professionalism investigators might well be looking for answers in the wrong place.

The war business, in fact, had come to interest Vonnegut more in his advancing years. It had always been a quiet influence on his personal life, showing itself in affinities with writers totally unlike him except for the service life they had shared. Teaching at the University of Iowa in 1966, for example, he had begun a close friendship with Writers' Workshop colleague Richard Yates, a mannerist with a style as fine as Flaubert's and as far removed as possible from the jerky, almost brittle experiments with prose that Vonnegut was crafting into the first draft of *Slaughterhouse-Five*. Yet the two became at once like brothers, simply because they were both infantry privates from World War II's last phase, a phase fought mostly by half-trained, confused youngsters. Afterward, as an internationally famous author, Vonnegut would meet the German novelist Heinrich Böll, the two finding common sympathy as infantry veterans, albeit of opposing armies—having recognized that the immediate enemies of each were officers and that the larger struggle was one against war itself. The Dresden firebombing made its first appearance in Vonnegut's work about this time, in a 1966 introduction (written from Iowa City) to a new edition of *Mother Night*, just at the time Vonnegut was meeting Yates, reviewing Böll's *Absent without Leave*, and making plans for writing *Slaughterhouse-Five*. Yet even through his war novel's best-seller fame the author was loath to credit too many historical specifics, making clear that protagonist Billy Pilgrim was not Kurt Vonnegut himself but rather an Everyman figure in the children's crusade that the latter days of World War II had become.

As time moved on, however, and half-century anniversaries of the conflict turned up on the calendar, Vonnegut joined the trend of reminiscence and began talking in detail about his experiences in the war. Fifty-year commemorations serve a purpose, for they coincide with new phases in the lives of their participants, recently retired as they are with time to look back on these events and measure their importance even as a look forward implies that there might not be too much time left. In May of 1990, while television ran documentaries on the Nazi blitzkrieg five decades before, Kurt Vonnegut spoke at the Smithsonian's Air and Space Museum as part of a series on strategic bombing. Representing the victim's perspective, he repeated many points from his basic public addresses of the time—but also mentioned, in an offhand manner and in response to the news that another POW colleague was in the audience, that one of their buddies had not been so lucky, dying of malnutrition and virtual despair a few weeks before the war ended. This individual Vonnegut identified as Joe Crone, and from the description of his character listeners might have supposed that here was a model for Billy Pilgrim.

POW Tom Jones's reunion with Kurt Vonnegut at the Smithsonian that night provided another contribution: a set of photographs from their final prisoner-of-war days back in May of 1945, when the author and seven buddies wandered free from their quarters, searching the countryside for Allied units. Vonnegut recalled the horse and wagon they had commandeered, and also the peaceful valley through which they'd traveled. Indeed, he had just recently described it at the end of his novel *Bluebeard*. Now he was reminded that one of their group, Bill Burns, had found a camera with film and had, with Jones, clicked off several snapshots. Given copies, he would use them next year as documents concluding his book of essays *Fates Worse than Death*, a technique reinforcing his position as witness. In this same section Vonnegut reprints a page from an Allied intelligence document outlining beforehand the importance of Dresden as a target, which was nil.

Having first established the importance of his wartime experience for the artistic imagination, something he had waited twenty-five years to do, the author of *Slaughterhouse-Five* now, another quarter century later, would speak with candor in a more documentary fashion. Not that he had to research these materials. Rather they would be brought back to him by other longtime partners in his purpose, all of whom had taken different paths to these days fifty years later. Lou Grivetti stayed in the service to become a colonel; Bill Burns went into broadcasting; Kurt Vonnegut wrote *Slaughterhouse-Five*. Now, a lifetime afterward, Vonnegut was pleased to look back through all that past for fragments of what they'd shared in common; for each of them a snapshot of the war could speak volumes.

With the fiftieth anniversary of the war's end approaching, Kurt Vonnegut found that memories long disregarded or trivialized were taking on great importance. And so for the commemoration of the Dresden bombing and then for V-E Day itself he declined invitations to speak as the author of *Slaughterhouse-Five*, preferring to focus attention on the veterans whose stories had for too long not drawn many listeners. That had been his own experience when returning home in 1945, wishing to write a great war novel but finding that no one cared for such a topic just then. When he did get around to it in 1969, the result was read as something as pertinent to Vietnam as to World War II, successful as *Slaughterhouse-Five* was in its methods of fragmentation and indirection. But by 1995 those veterans who remained, whose stories were now more comparatively rare, for the first time took center stage. And as he did with Bill Burns's and Tom Jones's photographs, this was what Vonnegut chose to tell.

Thus the revelation, made in public addresses and correspondence with the association of his old prisoner-of-war colleagues, that the "Joe Crone" recalled so casually with Tom Jones that night in 1990 was more than just an offhand model for Billy Pilgrim. The POW group, whose directory prided itself on tracing careers and listing addresses of those surviving from the group of 121 prisoners housed in Dresden's slaughterhouse number 5, could now hail the literary celebrity of Edward Reginald "Joe" Crone Jr., a quiet young man who had enlisted in the army so he could finish one more year of college (after which he hoped to enter the religious ministry), who'd been trained in the service for work with an engineering battalion but then, in November 1944, had rushed as an ill-prepared infantryman to help fill the massive need for fresh troops on the Ardennes front. Gangly and awkward, innocent and confused, images from his 1940 high school yearbook and snapshots from army boot camp show him to be the perfect picture of what Kurt Vonnegut had in mind for a hapless participant in the children's crusade his war had become. Real-life details and points of character sought out from those who remembered him complement the portrait of Billy Pilgrim in both novel and movie—not historical correspondence as such but rather a reminder of how art and life enhance each other when good narratives work especially well.

From Vonnegut's Dresden group a remarkable number survived the war, and an even more remarkable number lived on through the postwar decades to become honored septuagenarians on the fiftieth anniversary of V-E Day in 1995. According to the list compiled by former POW Ervin Szpek, only two died in the slaughterhouse number 5 prison itself, and both are commemorated in *Slaughterhouse-Five.* Michael D. Palaia is listed as having died in prison, executed by a firing squad—not for stealing a teapot (in the novel) or a Dresden figurine (in the movie) like character Edgar Derby, but for taking food, as Lou Grivetti would clarify during the meeting at Lexington. The other was Joe Crone, who—having despaired of surviving and given away his meager rations of food—virtually willed himself to death on April 11, 1945, just four weeks before the war would end. This was how Kurt Vonnegut recalled Joe's death when chatting with Tom Jones in 1990; to both of them it was a reminder of how odd and yet how necessary the workings of our lives happen to be.

Thus Kurt Vonnegut's public spokesmanship would reflect the quirky nature of that necessity. His message at Lexington and elsewhere would include simple bits of folk wisdom meant to correct misapprehensions and put people more at ease, from such things as understanding the seasonal change of weather to lightening the burdens of misconstrued responsibility. He would speak on major social issues and address himself to concerns as specific as gun control, classroom size, and the need for people to identify in groups. But his approach was anything but dogmatic or deductive. Rather his listeners could hear him amass points of information with the seeming randomness that they had come to him in life—this from General Electric, that from the war, another piece from back home in Indiana—and follow with amused pleasure how the speaker could knit them together into a surprising inevitability that not only resolved the issue but did so with the shock of unsuspected necessity. It was the same unsuspected necessity that had the author sharing coffee one hour with Ollie Lyon from GE and the next swapping POW stories with Lou Grivetti and George Bloomingburg, regretting only that Kentuckian Bill Burns, who'd found that camera forty-eight years before, was sick today and couldn't be with them to reminisce over his photographs.

Did this reunion mean that the author's karass was complete? Not at all, for life was continuing and with it humankind's need to discern a sense of import. By now Vonnegut knew that the act of coming to deliver a speech could influence its subject—seeing Tom Jones in his Smithsonian audience and learning now that Lou Grivetti had become a military careerist were just two more examples. But the business of arranging a speech at the Lexington Civic Center's Heritage Hall meant more than crossing paths with Ollie Lyon and Lou Grivetti. It involved helping with a poster for the event, not just to advertise his speech but to be sold for additional Midway College fund-raising. For this he was brought together with a local printmaker, Joe Petro III, with whom Vonnegut prepared a design similar to the line drawing of himself on the last page of his 1973 novel, *Breakfast of Champions.*

Since introducing such drawings into his work Vonnegut had continued dabbling with other semiabstract renderings, going so far as to have a small show in 1980 at New York's Margo Feiden Galleries. But in meeting Joe Petro the author discovered both a new medium and a congenial printer with whom to work. With Petro, Vonnegut could apply india ink to acetate and have anywhere from a dozen to fifty prints pulled with fine detail in exceptionally brilliant color. Stimulated by the poster-making experience and delighted with Petro's work habits, Vonnegut began an association that would occupy his future while once more gathering purpose from his past. His father and grandfather, while working as architects, had been artists, and the entire Vonnegut family, especially Kurt's sister and his daughters, enjoyed great talents for drawing and painting. He himself appreciated how working with Joe was a relief from the isolation of writing, and also a reprieve from the task of producing work that bore the responsibility of articulated meaning. Yet even in their self-apparency his artworks shared a similarity with his novels and his speeches: that correspondences need not be one to one, and that in the spontaneity of radically combined elements could be found a pattern to life not otherwise so readily discerned.

It is the need to find such patterns, Vonnegut believes, that distinguishes humanity as a species. Men and women, he has learned—both as a trained anthropologist and practicing novelist—are the only creatures in nature whose lives seemed bedeviled by having to find a purpose for things, a meaning for existence that in natural terms would rather follow its own rhythms of being. Such self-imposed responsibility is itself vexing and can distract one from the pleasures of life. But the drive becomes problematic when humans attempt to impose their own notions on the nature of existence. On the one hand, such impositions cause one to focus on what might be unimportant things; on the other, they almost inevitably lead to frustration when life itself refuses to work out according to plan.

Not just Kurt Vonnegut's work but all postmodern thought addresses this problem. A more useful endeavor is not to impose assumptions but rather deconstruct them, revealing the arbitrary side of what has been assumed to be natural. Once this deconstruction has taken place, one's thoughts can then be restructured to accommodate what may have been otherwise censored out. Vonnegut's own method, implicit in his fiction and explicit in his public spokesmanship, is to organize ideas and images so that a space can be opened for a freedom of fresher thought. Thus does he loosen the claims of convention and open the possibilities for surprise, all the while keeping himself ready for innovations of the occasion—whether they be Ollie Lyon raising funds for a church-supported school or Lou Grivetti turning out to have retired as a colonel.

Sometimes criticized as an apparent nihilist, Kurt Vonnegut in fact brings a message that is hopeful. If life seems without purpose, perhaps it is because we have tried (and failed) to impose a purpose inappropriately. The quest for meaning can be self-defeating, especially when pursued with the rigidities of conventions that in truth no longer apply. The radicalness of the author's own propositions seem so only because of the persistence of those conventions he so successfully interrogates.

Kurt Vonnegut's first such interrogation was in the form of a short story, "Report on the Barnhouse Effect," written with the encouragement of Ollie Lyon and his other coworkers at General Electric in 1949. For the next two decades he would write in obscurity and seeming anonymity. But from those conditions arose both the need for and the techniques of a public spokesmanship that would influence his manner of expression in fiction and nonfiction alike. Once perfected, that manner would make Kurt Vonnegut one of the most popularly received and happily heeded novelists of his age.

RICHARD GIANNONE

Cat's Cradle

> I think the Commonwealth of
> Learning is chiefly obliged to the
> great *Modern* Improvement of
> *Digressions.* . . .
> —Jonathan Swift, *A Tale of a Tub*

The story of *Cat's Cradle* is told by a free-lance writer called, quite simply, John, whose recent project is a book about the day Hiroshima was bombed—August 6; 1945—to which he has given the working title *The Day the World Ended*. In order to get background material, John decides to research the private life of Dr. Felix Hoenikker who was, in the grim familialism we have adopted toward our nuclear progeny, one of the fathers of the atomic bomb. Gathering details about Hoenikker involves John with the man's three children, whose lives lead John through a chain of events culminating in a disaster surpassing the Hiroshima calamity he intended to write about. John never does get back to his original subject. The Hoenikker side of the project drifts, or literally digresses, from the main issue and takes on a narrative importance of its own until the Hiroshima material disappears and the digression becomes the novel.

Cat's Cradle, then, is a digression about the Hoenikker family, and this displacement of the narrator's proclaimed topic by a subsidiary one alerts us to Vonnegut's intention in his fourth novel. His meaning lies precisely in the

From *Vonnegut: A Preface to His Novels* by Richard Giannone. © 1977 by Kennikat Press Corp.

book's narrative detour; for swerving reflects Dr. Hoenikker's deviation from responsibility in his scientific research, a deviation which brought about the Hiroshima disaster in the first place and then yielded *ice-nine*, which finally destroys the entire world.

John survives to tell about the later calamity and changes his name to one more in keeping with trial he has endured. "Call me Jonah," are his first words. His phraseology pointedly aligns Vonnegut's narrator with Melville's storyteller Ishmael in *Moby Dick*, and by extension with the classical American artists who are, as William Carlos Williams terms them in *Paterson*, "Ishmaels of the spirit." Having narrowly escaped in their pursuit of the great white whale of knowledge, such people survive to tell us of the world's incomprehensibility. The spirit of Ishmael is that of prophecy born of affliction. Vonnegut makes of his spiritual Ishmael a darker figure who shadows forth the dire warning that we must change our ways if we are to avoid universal annihilation. The bearer of cosmic news is as familiar a figure in Vonnegut's books as is the conflict between "know-how" and "know-what." The threat of technological advancement without regard for ethical purpose necessitates the omens issued by the messenger. By placing the pursuit of knowledge in the atomic age under the sign of Jonah, Vonnegut in *Cat's Cradle* has extended the responsibility of the envoy and, therefore, the character of his news. The Old Testament context brought into play through Jonah warrants our attention because it provides guidelines for understanding Vonnegut's artistry.

The little Book of Jonah is an anomaly among the prophetic books of Israel. It foregoes the customary collection of oracles in favor of humor to convey God's word; its artistry is matchless in prophetic literature. The story of Jonah is a comic novella about a prophet who hardly fits the traditional picture of those disturbing men whose voices rock the world. Prophets usually cry out God's word with brave disregard of consequences; but when God commands Jonah to go to Nineveh to announce his intention to destroy the city for its wickedness, Jonah hops a ship to Tarshish, which lies in the opposite direction. God reacts to Jonah's evasion with a storm, imperiling the lives of all the sailors on the ship Jonah has boarded. They are saved only when Jonah is thrown into the sea, where, as we know even without reading the Old Testament, he is swallowed by a large fish in whose belly he spends three days and three nights. God rescues Jonah and orders him again to go to Nineveh. At this point in the narrative, after three distressful days in the belly of the fish, Jonah is back where he started. This time he obeys God and proclaims Nineveh's destruction with such power that the city repents. The people's turning away from evil moves God to spare Nineveh, meaning, of course, that Jonah's prophecy is not realized. In fact, God's change of plan dejects Jonah. He feels trapped. When he tries to avoid delivering the message, he is punished horribly; when he obeys, the message is negated and Jonah is made to appear foolish. His displeasure gives rise to the legitimate question of just how reliable God is. The Book of Jonah seems to answer that the Lord's word is not firm, that his anger is not absolute. Jonah cannot comprehend this ambiguity. He prefers to see Nineveh wiped out for the sake of his need for certitude. Besides, he rationalizes, he knew that God would be merciful and that is why he made haste to Tarshish. In light of this bafflement, Jonah prefers death to confusion. "I beseech thee," he says to God, "it is better for me to die than to live" (Jonah 4:3). God responds to Jonah's amusing self-righteousness and despair with a question: "And should not I pity Nineveh, that great city, in which there are more than a hundred and twenty thousand persons who do not know their right hand from their left, and also much cattle?" (Jonah 4:11).

God's question concludes the Book of Jonah, and strikes the crucial theological note of the text, emphasizing compassion for the repentant Nineveh over Jonah's desire for justice at any cost. Jonah values the completion of his task as God promised it over the continuance of human life. For God such consistency seems unimportant. God's pity for Nineveh effectively undermines any hope Jonah might have of finding a settled, predetermined order behind God's plan. God is free to change his word as he chooses without regard for what humans might have in mind about God's keeping his word. God does not even permit the prophet of his choice smugly to count on the infallibility of his word. In such a theology, clarity of purpose from the human perspective gives way to the splendid mystery of divine compassion. It is a theology of mystery.

From a résumé of the Book of Jonah and from a brief analysis of its meaning, we can see its appeal to Vonnegut's moral imagination. Comedy in the service of prophecy expresses the two modal energies of levity and gravity that he works through. Moreover, uniting comedy and prophecy enlarges our sense of both forms. Within the Jonah story, neither the events nor the story's large meaning moves in a straight line: Jonah's purpose comes about through digression; his obedience is arrogant; his success brings despair. But the theology of the Book of Jonah has an even deeper appeal to Vonnegut's sympathy. God's purpose is hidden behind contingency, which from the limited human view easily accommodates the absurdity of the universe. Here God incorporates the ambivalence experienced by the modern person at every moment. The Book of Jonah closes with a question from God, and that question leaves matters suspended in reflection rather than in dogma. Here is the God who shows us that deliverance—and not mere actualization—is the fulfillment of prophecy. The sign of Jonah is precisely such deliverance achieved through preaching. Vonnegut implies through his novelistic use of Jonah that science has led us so far astray that the enormous cry of Old Testament prophecy is needed to correct the course of life. *Cat's Cradle* is a sharp appeal for deliverance from the incursions of science, which Vonnegut before was satisfied merely to deride. As with its masterly ancient model, Vonnegut's little book of Jonah calls for special appreciation of the literary form in which its message is clothed.

The setting of Jonah's search marks the religious character of his mission. The pivotal events occur during Christmastide. There is "that fateful Christmas Eve" when Dr. Hoenikker dies—fateful because on that holy evening his three children received the direful gift of *ice-nine*. Their father's plaything, *ice-nine*, was all he had to give his children, and his last Christmas is the nativity of the world's end. Years later, Jonah begins his search during Christmas, and his experience shows how the hope once promised by the season has been overtaken by an unfolding doom. Meanwhile, the atomic bombing of Hiroshima has intervened, placing Hoenikker's idling on a different level of accountability.

This new Jonah does not sojourn in a fish's belly; instead, he is swallowed up by two social monsters. The first is the technocracy for which Hoenikker worked, the Research Lab of the General Forge and Foundry in Ilium, New York, Vonnegut's ubiquitous spawning ground for American industrial monstrosities. The information Jonah receives about Hoenikker from his associates is valueless because they neither knew him nor understood his work; but the way his colleagues live and, especially, how they speak define perfectly the way Hoenikker developed as a scientist. They speak in memos, using a fatuous and bland language that exposes an inability to make moral discriminations. When they do try to make judgments, they come up with slick public relations salutes to the company. The place is peopled by versions of the vacant Miss Pefko, who takes dictation as though the English they use were Ethiopic. Mechanical speech seems to be the only communication available to those who surrender their sovereignty to a corporate leviathan. The famous passage from Hobbes's *Leviathan* which Julian Castle cites late in the novel applies to Ilium. "'The truth was that life was as short and brutish and mean as ever.'" Jonah sinks into the world of materialistic absolutism where pure research is a cover for profiteering and militarism and where no one questions what is going on. It is an ugly place, for Jonah describes the city as blanketed by a motionless smog. Befouled and stagnant, Ilium's atmosphere is the climate of Hoenikker's mind: a moral vacuum.

When Dr. Asa Breed, who runs the lab, boasts to Jonah that "'new knowledge is the most valuable commodity on earth,'" he exposes the abuse by which science operates. It practices a reverse alchemy whereby truth is debased into gadget. *Ice-nine* epitomizes such an inversion of truth. The Marines wanted a way to get out of mud, and Hoenikker came up with a way to freeze liquids at higher temperatures than usual. *Ice-nine* allows the Marines to suspend the law of nature and to play God by walking on water. "*Ice-nine* was the last gift Felix Hoenikker created for mankind before going to his just reward."

As Jonah goes deeper into this social beast, he sees that the absence of morality in the lab extended into Hoenikker's family life, where there was authority without feeling. His three children led loveless lives. Newt, the youngest, writes tenderly of his father's efforts to play with his small son; but the recollection reveals the pathos of the child's single contact with his father, for Dr. Hoenikker never played with Newt, and "'he had hardly ever even spoken to me.'" Franklin, or Frank, the older son, had almost "no experience in talking to anyone" as a child. The horse-faced daughter Angela was obliged to be mother to her brothers and servant to her father when Hoenikker's wife died from lack of love at Newt's birth. The physical appearance of Hoenikker's offspring displays the destruction their father fostered in the world: the midget Newt, the giantess Angela, the morbidly silent Frank. A Hoenikker family portrait blends the grisly elegance of a Charles Addams cartoon with the hideous exaggeration of *Mad* comics.

Not long after the Ilium expedition, Jonah gets caught up in the political deformity of San Lorenzo, a Caribbean island republic. San Lorenzo recalls its notorious namesake, Lorenzo the Magnificent of Florence, who exercised absolute authority tempered by appearances of republican equality. Lorenzo's dictatorship (from 1469 to 1492) taught Machiavelli a few things about political corruption. Vonnegut's mythical island bears a more immediate resemblance to Haiti under Papa Doc Duvalier, whose duplicity was less subtle than Lorenzo the Magnificent's, but equally despotic. When Jonah arrives on San Lorenzo, he finds that Franklin Hoenikker is serving as the Minister of Science and Progress—a political fact which confirms the inauspicious hints in the island's name.

San Lorenzo's highest mountain, Mount McCabe, is described in a way to indicate that Jonah-Ishmael is again meeting the elusive whale of unknowability. "It was a fearful hump, a blue whale, with one queer stone plug on its back for a peak. In scale with a whale, the plug might have been the stump of a snapped harpoon. . . ." The wounded leviathan is a defunct utopia where idealism has disintegrated into cynicism. In this banana republic without bananas, Jonah encounters tyranny, misery, deceit, and hopelessness. San Lorenzo is the earth stripped of its possibilities, for "God, in His Infinite Wisdom, had made the island worthless." Its history is the history of people's futile effort to correct God's wisdom. Lionel Boyd

Johnson and Earl McCabe, who discovered the place, in 1922 (the year of Vonnegut's birth) set about applying their economic and legal skills to found a utopia. They fail. "Everybody was bound to fail, for San Lorenzo was as unproductive as an equal area in the Sahara or the Polar Icecap." It develops only by accident—one shipwreck brings the discoverers, yet another brings Frank, and Jonah himself "didn't feel that purposeful seas were wafting me to San Lorenzo." Born and sustained by chance, San Lorenzo is a terminus for human strays.

Where Ilium practices reverse alchemy, San Lorenzo engages in reverse theocracy. The state is governed by diabolic untruth. Johnson, whose name becomes Bokonon in the local dialect, establishes a religion to allow the inhabitants to endure their horrible life. Bokononism is a blatant opiate to blind people to the misery around them; and to ensure its success, McCabe and Bokonon forbid the practice of Bokononism and outlaw Bokonon himself, thereby giving the religion a kick and a scapegoat. Religion is but a distraction; good and bad are artificial distinctions concocted to oppress.

Jonah gradually becomes assimilated into San Lorenzo's corrupt politics and belief. The moment he arrives, Papa Monzano, the dictator, collapses in great pain and unexpectedly names Frank his successor; but Frank has no taste for rule and convinces Jonah to assume the presidency. Jonah agrees, mainly because marriage to the gorgeous Mona Monzano goes with the job. Mona is a debased Venus whose symbolic standing as a national shrine suggests Vonnegut's notion of politics as a derangement of sexual energies, which is the paradigm of the political order on San Lorenzo. Jonah's relationship with Mona is an expedient of power, unloving and entirely beyond the control of either party.

On San Lorenzo Jonah learns the process of victimship, or reverse self-hood. During his inauguration, when a plane crash brings the castle and Papa's frozen body into the sea (Papa had swallowed a vial of *ice-nine* to spare himself the misery of cancer), Jonah is engulfed by human bungling. "I opened my eyes—and all the sea was *ice-nine*." He is trapped inside a glaciated planet, which is Vonnegut's version of Moby Dick's terrifying white blankness. He survives "the blue-white poison" physically by descending into an oubliette bomb shelter; and spiritually he lives with all he has been through by adopting the useful untruths of Bokononism. This Jonah emerges from the leviathan's interior to rail against human stupidity but not to promise deliverance from it. As a disciple of Bokonon, he tries to schematize a cynicism to cope with such omnipresent unthinking.

II

This account of Jonah's adventures shows how *Cat's Cradle* develops from the three novels preceding it. Resumed are the attacks on technology and the utopian aspiration registered in *Player Piano*. Where the managers run people's lives in the first book, in *Cat's Cradle* science wipes out the world; and where human efforts to set up a mechanized commonwealth resulted previously in an uprising against the synthetic community, they now harden into dictatorship. What holds the corrupt political order together on San Lorenzo is Bokononism, an elaborate version of the religious scheming in *The Sirens of Titan*. Rumfoord's Church of God of the Utterly Indifferent, however, is a benign pilot project in dealing with a godless universe next to the inquisitional cruelty of Bokononism. If the subjects come from the first two novels, the technique in *Cat's Cradle* derives from the third, *Mother Night*. Vonnegut's first-person narration makes *Cat's Cradle* a personal testimony to the warning of *Mother Night*, namely, that pretense and lies can overtake truth; for in *Cat's Cradle*, as Jonah tells his tale, lies systematically overtake actuality.

Critics have recognized the affinity among Vonnegut's first four novels; and seeing no advance in technique or change of theme, they tend to put *Cat's Cradle* aside. "Compared with the two preceding novels," Reed says, "it seems thinner in plot, more superficial and fragmentary in characterization, weaker in its ability to evoke emotion or concern, and consequently less substantial." It is simply another of Vonnegut's parodies of the truths by which one lives, according to Max Schulz. "The satire is there," Goldsmith allows, "but it is Horatian," by which he presumably means tame. With few exceptions, critical reaction has placed *Cat's Cradle* in Vonnegut's development as a résumé of what came before.

Repetition, however, can also refine meaning; and in observing the deepening of earlier interests in *Cat's Cradle*, we can see how this novel intensifies the attacks on politics and religion. This change in degree of treatment also makes for a change in kind of novel, and the kind of art Vonnegut aspires to in his fourth book is that of great satire. *Cat's Cradle* belongs in the tradition of grand censure along with Swift's *A Tale of a Tub* and Blake's *The Marriage of Heaven and Hell*. Now, Swift and Blake are writers to whom Vonnegut admiringly alludes; and looked at by their lights, *Cat's Cradle* does shine, as Tanner says, as Vonnegut's "brilliant little fiction."

Cat's Cradle shares in the mission of Swift's treatise and Blake's poem: all three show how the official teaching of religion is merely a rationalization toward the end of enduring a corrupt world and of gaining as much personal power as the venal world affords. For Swift the culprit is

Christian Puritanism; for Blake, Swedenborgianism; for Vonnegut, the imaginary Bokononism, or any institutionalized belief. And in all three an intellectual corruption parallels the moral erosion. Swift takes on a gamut of learned fopperies that subvert truth. Blake goes after the false wisdon that artificially distinguishes between good and evil to subdue the human spirit/The intellectual abuse of our age for Vonnegut is science, which has gone beyond endangering the abstract ideal of truth to threaten everyday survival. When learning overcomes truth, it becomes sophistry; but when science overrides responsibility, it blasphemes life. These perils make it necessary to expose the "numerous and gross corruptions in Religion and Learning," as Swift phrases it, to protect humanity. The ugly images of the human form pervading *Cat's Cradle*, the *Tale*, and the *Marriage* embody the havoc already caused by these abuses. The body manifests soul; Swift's filth, Blake's tortured figures of contained energy, and Vonnegut's cartoon grotesques are the nauseating aspects of the human spirit calling for correction.

Blake will be valuable later in the discussion in understanding the apocalyptic ending of *Cat's Cradle*. For the total design of the novel, however, *A Tale of a Tub* offers an illuminating analogy. Two qualities of Swift's satire bear on Vonnegut's strategy. In the *Tale*, Swift puts on a false mask and allows his Author to take on attitudes opposed to his own. This opposing figure allows Swift to work against his own fabrication. The disguise creates a parody of the attitudes it speaks for. A second technique enhances the first; the story of the *Tale* shows the Author imitating the very corrupt intellectual habits that he sets out to censure. Swift's skill in fashioning this ironic reenactment brings all the disparate parts of the treatise into an instructive whole. Disparateness is what the reader experiences in the *Tale*, and with disparateness the *Tale* progresses. The elaborate introductions, the double dedication, the self-conscious apologies and haughtiness, and above all the prodigious digressions *are* the form. In the *Tale* the reader is made to see that formlessness is a deliberate principle of design. The fragments collectively reveal how some human minds work. For Swift the mind goes by digression. By the time the *Tale* ends, digression overtakes the story (which incidentally is about three brothers), and robs the story of dramatic impact by reducing it to insignificance. Swift's assult on the form of the *Tale* carries an attack on our intellectual assumptions. Human wisdom, for instance, pretends to arise through systematic thinking but actually unfolds from randomness. What we mean by Swiftian satire—which is the high-water mark of the genre—is making the subjects of ridicule into organizing principles of form.

Vonnegut proceeds in the same way in *Cat's Cradle*. Jonah is not a character in the customary sense so much as he is a mock author. He is not a narrator with a personality developed from inherent qualities, for his several names tells us that he is a reduction to narrative expedient. Whether he is John, as he once was, or "had been a Sam, I would have been a Jonah still" because the name evokes the disaster that determined his being. In the post-apocalyptic void all identity is adventitious. He stands a fool before forces that propel him from project to project, from place to place, from monster to monster. He wants "to examine all strong hints as to what on Earth we, collectively, have been up to" and rightly regards himself as more qualified "to answer those tough questions than any other human being," and yet he acknowledges that he can only rephrase the jumbled questions he raises. Though Jonah says that "nihilism was not for me," he becomes its unwitting spokesman. For all his unique experience teaches him, Jonah's life remains "meaningless." He tries to believe that love will make sense amid vast disorder and resigns himself to a loveless universe. "And no love waiting for me anywhere. . . ." Passive resignation allows Jonah to live in the fallen world but it also allows him to be absorbed by the cynicism that destroyed the world. By becoming a Bokononist after his trip to San Lorenzo, Jonah rationalizes all that is irrational and doctinizes irresposibility; for the business of Bokononism, Julian Castle explains to Jonah (using language reminiscent of the Works's slogan in *Player Piano*) is "'to provide the people with better and better lies,'" to keep them from the truth, which is "'that life was as short and brutish and mean as ever.'"

Through its sustained digressions the novel follows Jonah's ineluctable reduction to the hopelessness he seeks to transcend. Beneath the surface event we can read the history of modern science and religion shifting from their original purpose—to provide knowledge and faith—to their harmful effects of destruction and deception. Vonnegut, however, writes more than allegory; he provides an account of Jonah's personal encounter with the false claims of science and religion—or to stay with the Old Testament myth, an account of his two ordeals within the modern leviathans. This frame gives Vonnegut the opportunity to study Jonah's individual vulnerability to the abuses that he is studying for hints about the meaning of life.

While the planet Earth in the novel falls apart completely, Jonah's world divides neatly into two parts. (The Book of Jonah is designed in halves—Jonah on the ship and at Nineveh.) Ilium and San Lorenzo fabulize the novel's double subject. One is the city of science; the other, the island of belief. Though each arises out of a separate intellectual system, they are twin states of being. Both have a facade of harmony that obscures a hideous life. Ilium's affluence compensates for its spiritual poverty; San Lorenzo proffers spirituality to fill its material want. Together they school Jonah in the futility of aspiring to improve or even to understand the human condition. Ilium presents him with the proudest achievement of the modern century, science, which finally is nothing more than the tinkerings of a Nobel laureate in a moral vacuum. Then on San Lorenzo he learns that the loftiest of human intentions, philanthropy and political idealism, are rooted in power play. Each adventure leads Jonah to a discovery that reverses his thinking. These dramatic reversals state the condition of inversion that Vonnegut closes in on.

Though the two setbacks parallel each other, they show a change in Jonah. His recollection of Ilium is shaded by Bokononist detachment, so it is difficult to know Jonah's mental stance when beginning his investigation of Hoenikker. We do know that his aborted project was "'to emphasize the *human* rather than the *technical* side of the bomb,'" so he has only a limited fascination with science. In fact, his sardonic responses to the staff of the lab suggest a healthy skepticism about the pretensions of pure research. After Hiroshima he is not likely to be taken in by the mythology of scientific disinterestedness. But he does have expectations, however minimal, about human feeling, and he respects achievement. What he learns about Hoenikker would raise the eyebrows of a misanthrope, however. This Nobel physicist not only worked in a moral void; he lived in it. "'People weren't his specialty,'" explains Newt; and on this score everyone agrees. His wife died for lack of love and understanding. "'Family things, love things,'" not even living held value for Hoenikker. Only truth did. But just what truth means to a man who once asked, "'What is sin?'" defies understanding. The best Jonah can make of such inanity is a Swiftian exercise. As Swift dismisses his treatise on learning as "a tale of a tub," which readers of his day would know signifies a cock-and-bull story, Jonah entitles his study of modern science *Cat's Cradle* to mock the mind of the acclaimed Nobel laureate as a mechanism for heightening triviality. Making a cat's cradle with string and waving the tangles before his kids was Hoenikker's one pastime, driving Newt, for one, crazy while schooling him in nihilism. "'A cat's cradle is nothing but a bunch of X's between somebody's hands, and little kids look and look and look at all those X's. . . .'" When the tension holding the string in shape is relaxed, "'*No damn cat, and no damn cradle*,'" complains Newt. The string game suggests to Jonah that truth for Hoenikker is a mere fabrication, a game, a whimsy momentarily poised over nothing. When he sees Newt's painting of a cat's cradle he wonders if the lines "might not be the sticky nets of human futility hung up on a moonless night to dry." Jonah's descent into the belly of Ilium shows him that the human side of the bomb is an emotional abyss, but Jonah's detachment allows him to handle this discouraging revelation.

Before descending into San Lorenzo, Jonah's capacity to resist a fatally negative view of the world is severely tested. He returns to his New York apartment from Ilium to find that a poet acquaintance named Krebbs left everything "wrecked by a nihilistic debauch." He burned the couch and killed Jonah's avocado tree and "sweet cat." Around the slaughtered cat's neck hangs a sign, "'Meow.'" It is the painful cry of a real cat treated as though it were the fake cat in the string game. The scene literalizes the abstract rules of the game. By literalizing language—a Swiftian master stroke—Vonnegut confronts Jonah with the nihilism implied in Hoenikker's leveling life down to idling. And Krebbs's pointless savagery momentarily dissuades Jonah from surrendering to the ethical anarchism he has been drawn to by the horrors he witnesses. Bokonon has a word for this event, as he has for everything: Krebbs is a *wrang-wrang* or "a person who steers people away from a line of speculation by reducing that line, with the example of the *wrang-wrang's* own life, to an absurdity."

San Lorenzo tests Jonah's turning away from nihilism. The island's abject misery would challenge the faith of a blind optimist; for Jonah, whose affirmation is tentative, the voyage is an insuperable ordeal. The irresponsibility of Ilium would be a luxury on San Lorenzo since there is nothing here to be irresponsible about. Everyone has thrown up his or her hands in despair. Questions of conscience that are raised about Ilium are beside the point of life on San Lorenzo because conscience implies moral choice, which is rendered nugatory by the people's having nothing to choose. "'Nobody objects to anything,'" Frank Hoenikker says. "'They aren't interested. They don't care.'" Even power, the cynic's protection, seems undesirable, and is unwanted, at any rate by Frank. His unprincipled refusal of San Lorenzo's rulership traps Jonah in the island's affairs. Like father, like son; authority entails the very duty that Frank cannot accept. The difference between the two episodes of moral renunciation is that with the son's, Jonah becomes implicated by agreeing to govern the forsaken island society. His motives are mixed with his sexual desire for Mona, to be sure; but Jonah still feels that he can improve the quality of life on San Lorenzo. His rising moral responsiveness is set against the refusals of moral accountability by the Hoenikkers.

Two strategies shape Jonah's San Lorenzo voyage: reduction and inversion. Their significance is most apparent in the series of ceremonies that unify the San Lorenzo adventure. The first ceremony is a rite of protocol for the new arrivals, among whom is the new American Ambassador, Horlick Minton. Formality requires that Papa Monzano himself greet the emissary. When Papa climbs from his Cadillac, the emaciated, rickety natives strike up the national anthem proclaiming that they are "Where the living is grand" to the tune of "Home on the Range." The anonymous Homesteaders of *Player Piano*, who became Rumfoord's motley believers in *The Sirens of Titan* and Campbell's duped listeners in *Mother Night*, reappear in malignant form.

They are living repudiations of the anthem they utter and of the island's governance, which their agony exposes as self-aggrandizement. The welcome is really a repulsion, which is the appropriate greeting for this isle of alienation. The observance salutes deception. But the pain that seizes Papa during the entertainment marks the limit of people's vast powers of fabrication. ("When you're dead you're dead," reads the Introduction to *Mother Night*.) Papa's final decree of willing the presidency to Frank turns the proceedings into an investiture. Within the day Frank turns his ascendancy into an abdication—casting aside political power as he squandered the chemical power of *ice-nine*. Appalled by the populace's plight, Jonah is shocked and angered by Frank's turning away "from all human affairs."

The day after Jonah's arrival is The Day of the Hundred Martyrs to Democracy, the national holiday in honor of San Lorenzo's negligible contribution to World War II. That the martyrs were conscripted and immediately killed by a German submarine just outside the island's harbor does not matter. On San Lorenzo the botch is honorable because failure is all the islanders have. The actual celebration involves several rituals—the military memorial service, the engagement of Frank to the stunning Mona, who goes with the office of the presidency, to which is added the proclamation of Jonah as president after the wreath ceremony and the air show. There is a great deal of holiday-making but no pleasure. These ceremonies do not reset the stage of human life to give dignity and mystery. They are macabre dramas that shuffle the pawns around clumsily to trivialize their conduct and to impoverish them anew.

Jonah's inaugural reflections show how he is drawn more deeply into the deceptions he seeks to escape. At first, he thinks of having "the awful hook," which is used to kill people for rejecting Bokononism, removed; but then he realizes that he has nothing to put in its place to keep order through fear. Jonah acquiesces in despair because circumstances are too hopeless. His defeatism is more benign in tone than Krebbs's defilement, yet is finally just as culpable. Vonnegut tips the reader off to Jonah's moral hardening through his mounting egoism. "So I put my speech in my pocket and I mounted the spiral staircase in my tower. I arrived at the uppermost battlement of my castle, and I looked out at my guests, my servants, my cliff, and my lukewarm sea." His becoming boss does seem to be "my apotheosis," as Jonah revealingly calls it; and as a god he will be exempt from the human misery he is incapable of alleviating.

Rhetoric begins the inauguration but cataclysm ends it. Again, Vonnegut reduces words to fact. After the flatulent greetings from the American ambassador, the air raid sets off the explosion that brings Papa's *ice-nined* body cascading into the sea. This is not a memorial to the one hundred martyrs to democracy but the very martyrizing of humanity to tyrannical stupidity. All but a few perish—consumed in the belly of the whale. "My lukewarm sea had swallowed all." The whale again defies its hunters. Doomsday aptly commemorates life in this void in the Caribbean. That this sweltering tropical nowhere should freeze over into the gulping whale-like monster is right because ice epitomizes the emotional coldness that allowed Dr. Hoenikker to invent *ice-nine* and then selfishly to barter it as Frank does to Papa for personal gain and as Angela does for a husband. In novel after novel, Vonnegut warns of the intellect's potential destructive power, showing us how its discoveries can prompt a person to try to rule over life, and death, and nature as would God. The world locked in ice depicts creation captive to arrogant intellectual error. The image looms satiric yet prophetic, insisting that we take this outcome into moral account while it entreats for the liberating heat of wisdom and the creative fire of the imagination to thaw creation back to life.

III

The day the world ends is also a day of betrothal in the novel. Frank's marriage to Mona Monzano is to be announced. This is nullified when Frank refuses to accept the presidency and asks Jonah to be president. Jonah agrees and gets the hand of Mona who, as "the national treasure," goes with the presidency. The unexpected juxtaposition of these bizarre nuptials and doomsday is part of Vonnegut's aim for grand satire.

In the Bible the end of the world is often compared to a wedding to symbolize the lasting union of humanity with the universe. *The Revelation of John* foretells the relation of the soul and the church to Jesus as that of bride and bridegroom. Blake in *The Marriage of Heaven and Hell* prefigures the oncoming world as the marriage of desire with cosmic light and heat. In Blake's scheme, when fiery human passions subsume the restraints of prudence, the God within us is released. The apocalypse, then, has a creative aspect since it brings about a lasting transformation of the momentary into the eternal. And so the wedding.

Vonnegut's apocalypse does not anticipate transcendence in this way. One engagement is nullified and the other, with Jonah, aborted by Mona's suicidal kissing of *ice-nine*, her true, demonic groom. The novel's ending fulfills these negations with a divorce of life from the earth by *ice-nine*, which holds the world in abiding irrelation. A super-feverish boil of 114.4° Fahrenheit would melt the ice but we are left with no sense of potential restoration of the world's parts into a whole. Much of the novel's meaning is manifested in the image of divorce. In a disjoined world people exist in loneliness.

Appropriately, then, Jonah's post-apocalyptic writing of the story expresses no interest at all in establishing human relationships. He accepts living in ultimate disespousal. All along the reader has sensed, in the made-up calypso jiving, that meaning has separated from the words we use, indicating that a new language is needed. The mind-reeling rapidity of the clipped chapters (127 chapters in 191 pages) registers the divorce of thought from feeling as the segments of the novel flow apart—never again to be joined in conventional printed narration in Vonnegut's subsequent books.

Cat's Cradle describes a hell divorced from its redemptive spouse, heaven. Blake's Marriage bears closely here. His poem shows that "there is a real hell in the human mind, and it achieves the physical form of dungeons, whips, racks and all the miserable panoply of fear." Ilium has a prison and it is the lab's "cloister of cement block," but San Lorenzo is a total penal colony. Mug shots and fatal warnings greet arriving passengers at the airport. The state emblem is a huge iron hook on a beam between two telephone poles which keeps the decrepit citizenry in line. "It was low and black and cruel." There are torture chambers, too. Finally, there is the day-to-day torment of being alive on San Lorenzo. The oubliette under Papa's residence best expresses the life of the place. Here Jonah and Mona take refuge during the apocalypse while the others make it to a dungeon. In doing so, they descend into the very structure of the human mind of our age. Survival, like life, is an oubliation. These refugees from ice-nine, trapped in mental bondage, duplicate the dungeoning of creation above them. The double image of imprisonment above and below is Vonnegut's counterpart of "infinite Abyss" in the Marriage. The image signifies the torture of self-annihilation.

The last part of Blake's poem presents, as Harold Bloom puts it, "an emblem of the negation of vision." Blake sees a Devil in a flame rising before an Angel who is seated on a cloud above. The Angel, outwitted in a moral argument, embraces the flames and emerges again as the prophet Elijah or Devil. The transformed Angel becomes Blake's friend. Together they read the Bible "in its infernal or diabolical sense," which they will pass on to the world if the world "behave well."

Cat's Cradle concludes with a comparable encounter between Jonah and a swami leading to a promised infernal text about life. Like Blake, Jonah at the End sees a visionary, Bokonon, who was something of a prophet and now, by calculated inversion, becomes an outlawed devil. He is not consumed in flames but is dying slowly of ice-nine. Jonah and Bokonon talk of their text, The Books of Bokonon, which shares in the diabolical irreverence of Blake's "The Bible of Hell." Dazed, Bokonon proffers Jonah the final sentence of The Books of Bokonon, which is an urging that Jonah write "a history of human

stupidity." This is to be written in untruth because in a world of radical insta-
bility and deception, inverted language is all that is left for communication.
Accordingly, the epigraph to the complete novel runs: "Nothing in this book
is true." We are left in *Cat's Cradle* not only with the negation of vision but
also with the negation of communication. Solipsism, the final divorce of relations, among persons, is the ruling condition in the novel.

The satirist's job is to poke fun at things, and Vonnegut's ceremonial
Author cannot be faulted in this work. Jonah has everyone making fools of
themselves and mocks his own attempt to clarify things. This was aptly indicated in the hardcover edition (but not in the Dell paperback) by the math-
ematical sign for logical conclusion (∴) that he put at the beginning of each
chapter to claim a deductive connection that he does not make. Reason
necessarily resists the idea of a planet freezing over with *ice-nine*. In his
bafflement Jonah develops a scorn for those who take the world's end
solemnly. He teaches the reader how to take a joke, which is not only a way
of describing how to read the book but also a way of telling us how to live
wisely in the universe. But the great satirist does more than rip things apart;
he is, Frye says, "an apocalyptic visionary . . . for his caricature leads us irre-
sistibly away from the passive assumption that the unorganized data of sense
experience are reliable and consistent" and invites us to see (and now I cite
Blake's *Marriage*) "the infinite which was hid." A change in our perception
affords a new kind of contact with the world.

Vonnegut goes about his task in *Cat's Cradle* in the same way. He
does not stay with Swift's unattainable idealism. Nor does he posit Blake's
glorious mythology of man's resurrection (though he does show the beyond
in other books). His view is personalist and immanent. "'Think of what
paradise this world would be if men were kind and wise.'" Unfortunately
what the novel dramatizes does not share this cheerfulness but rather
encourages a judgment that a scientific and utopian belief in the limitless
power and perfectibility of human nature is one of those evil illusions by
which humankind tries to make life easy and wonderful while actually
causing great pain. The proclamation of Vonnegut's Jonah points toward but
does not reveal deliverance. He directs us to laugh at the disasters brought
about by our scientific and political egotism in order that we may turn away
from a prideful death-wish to appreciate what is good in the world and dear
in other persons. As Jonah of the Old Testament became a sign to the people
of Nineveh, so stands his self-appointed namesake before this generation. In
reviving this ancient mode of addressing the human situation, Vonnegut
expands his conception of his fiction into an instrument of prophetic reform,
a purpose that subtly shapes his forthcoming experimentation.

JOHN L. SIMONS

Tangled Up in You: A Playful Reading of Cat's Cradle

> . . . the two most potent spiritual
> forces in contention today have
> nothing to do with nations, political
> parties or economic philosophies.
>
> The opposing forces are these: those
> who enjoy childlike playfulness when
> they become adults and those who
> don't.
> —Kurt Vonnegut

*C*at's *Cradle* (1963) remains one of Kurt Vonnegut's least understood achievements. Sometimes the novel's complexity is underrated, as when Peter J. Reed writes, "Compared with the two preceding novels, it seems thinner in plot, more superficial and fragmentary in characterization, weaker in its ability to evoke emotions or concern, and consequently less substantial." Sometimes the novel's implications are misconstrued, as when Richard Giannone speaks of "the inquisitional cruelty of Bokononism." These problems are related, for it is necessary to grasp Vonnegut's stance toward his Bokononist materials if one is to appreciate the complexity of his fictional argument.

From *Critical Essays on Kurt Vonnegut*, edited by Robert Merrill. © 1990 by Robert Merrill.

The crucial question is whether Vonnegut embraces the virtually nihilistic views on life expressed by a number of his characters. Vonnegut's narrator, John, originally intends to write a book about what the rest of civilization was doing on the day the first atomic bomb was dropped on Hiroshima. This book was to be entitled *The Day the World Ended*. Eventually, however, John, who is clearly his author's alter ego, chooses a different title, one that is emphatically antiapocalyptic: *Cat's Cradle*. He does so because everything in Vonnegut's fictional universe resists the impulse toward fixity, finality, or "ends" in general. As Kathryn Hume has remarked, Vonnegut sees the world as flux, involving metamorphoses, instabilities, exaggerations, and distortions. The essential "elasticity of Vonnegut's universe," Hume notes, "is just one more way of focusing attention on underlying ideas. His cosmos, consisting of endless transformations provides him with many of his literary techniques for guiding the reader's attention." What the reader is guided to see here is a fragmented world poised at the edge of chaos but potentially responsive to the far from nihilistic view of life embodied in John's and Vonnegut's title.

It is surprising how little attention has been paid to the cat's cradle as a crucial symbol in a novel of the same name. In fact Peter Reed, whose reading of *Cat's Cradle* remains the best single treatment of the book, seems to view the cat's cradle pejoratively, seeing it through the disillusioned eyes of Felix Hoenikker's midget son, Newt, as a kind of betrayal of any symbolic or meaning-making possibilities. "All incomprehensible X's. No cat. No cradle. That sums up man's dilemma as the novel shows it," writes Reed, echoing Newt's cynical observation about the string figure his father makes for him: "*No damn cat, no damn cradle.*" But both critic and character have missed the point about the importance of cat's cradles in the novel. It is not the string figures themselves that Vonnegut vilifies, but rather Felix's willfully thrusting a cat's cradle at his terrified son instead of allowing the boy to play with it, in his own way, by himself.

Cat's cradles are children's playthings, but in primitive cultures they are also very popular among adults. In her book *String Figures and How to Make Them: A Study of Cat's Cradle in Many Lands*, Caroline Furness Jayne makes a number of striking observations that would seem to address the interests of a writer who received his master's degree in cultural anthropology from the University of Chicago. (Indeed, Vonnegut's thesis was *Cat's Cradle* itself.) A cat's cradle is an "endless string," that is, a cord tied together at the ends, usually about six feet long and circular. Often depicted as a symbol of infinity, it has no beginning and no end, and can be constructed into innumerable designs. Primitive cultures use cat's cradles to give shape to their own mythologies, in particular their creation tales. For example, a cat's cradle is called "Maui" in New Zealand, and as one ethnoanthropologist writes of the many string figures the natives construct, "these are said to be different scenes in their mythology, such as Hine-nui-te-po, Mother Night bringing forth her progeny, Maru and the gods, and Maui fishing up the land." *Mother Night* is, of course, the title of Vonnegut's third novel (directly preceding *Cat's Cradle*), and "Maru" recalls the foot-touching rite of "boku-maru," which is considered one of the most sacred and sensual acts of the Bokononist religion that Vonnegut invents in *Cat's Cradle*.

Foot-touching may be seen as analogous to tribesmen playing cat's cradle with each other, using two pairs of hands and often reenacting "a whole drama . . . by means of changing shapes." Groups such as the Eskimos, mentioned in *Cat's Cradle*, attach "magical" properties to their cat's cradle games, while others seem to regard them far more lightly. Vonnegut, who laments the death of magic in the modern scientific world, understands both the serious and the playful sides of cat's cradle construction. He would be charmed by the notion that ethnologists, who are after all "scientists" of culture, do not agree about the ultimate significance of string figures.

For Jayne the real interest of cat's cradles lies in "the methods employed by different races in making the figures and a comparison of those methods," not in "the study of the relations between the finished patterns." She is more concerned with the ways in which particular string figures are conceived in the minds of their makers than with the final product. How close she comes to Jerome Klinkowitz's description of the way in which Bokononism "structures" the lives of the pitiful inhabitants of Vonnegut's Caribbean island, San Lorenzo: "Here is *Cat's Cradle*'s aesthetics of belief: meaning lies not in the content of a novel or the materials of a religion, but rather in the business of dealing with them. Once that process, that act of play, is complete, content should be forgotten. If not, it becomes the stuff of great mischief." Klinkowitz follows Jayne in valuing form over content, method over pattern, process over product.

This does not mean that patterns are utterly unimportant, only that they are subject to perpetual alternation and can never be hypostasized into fixed absolutes. Nevertheless, Jayne does attempt to define three different kinds of string games that offer uncanny insights into Vonnegut's fictional creations:

1. "those figures whereof the purpose is to form final *patterns*, supposed to represent definite objects;
2. "those which are *tricks*, wherein, after much complex manipulation of the strings, the entire loop is suddenly drawn from the hand by some simple movement; and

3.   "those which are *catches*, wherein, when certain strings are pulled, the hand or some of the figures may be unexpectedly caught in a running noose."

Jayne concludes, "Of course, there is no hard and fast rule of classification; several very pretty patterns may be converted into catches." As she implies, it is possible to combine "patterns," "tricks," and "catches" within a single cat's cradle, thus offering a sense of stability while at the same time undermining the stability, or trapping it in the web (cradle) of one's own creation. All of these allotropic elements are playfully at work in Vonnegut's own literary cat's cradle, as we see most clearly in the chapter called, appropriately, "Cat's Cradle." But before we look at that chapter we should first consider the crucial scene when little Newt Hoenikker is frightened by his father's sudden appearance bearing a string figure.

In chapter five Newt Hoenikker describes the day Dr. Felix Hoenikker plays (or so it seems) with his six-year-old son for the first and last time. By chance Dr. Hoenikker has just received the manuscript of a novel tied with mailing string. This novel was written in prison by a convicted fratricide named Marvin Sharpe Holderness. Holderness's novel concerns how "mad scientists made a terrific bomb that wiped out the whole world"; he writes to Felix Hoenikker, the inventor of the atomic bomb, because he wants to know just what to put into the bomb to make it sound authentic. Unfortunately for Marvin Holderness, Felix Hoenikker, who has never, according to his son, "read a novel or even a short story in his whole life, or at least not since he was a little boy," sets aside the manuscript and, momentarily fascinated by the loop of string he holds in his hands, "started playing with it. His fingers made the string figure called a 'cat's cradle.'" The scene is poignant because Newt, the essentially orphaned son of a living father, realizes that it was probably through a human tie, perhaps with his tailor father, that Felix learned to build cat's cradles. But Felix has long since abandoned imaginary "made-up games" for what he calls "real games," with all too real consequences for his family and for humanity. "He must have surprised himself when he made a cat's cradle out of that string," Newt continues, "and maybe it reminded him of *his own childhood*. He all of a sudden came out off his study and did something he had never done before. He tried *to play with me*. Not only had he never played with me before; he had hardly ever spoken to me" (my emphases). This towering figure, impersonal and abstract as a god, then went down on his knees, showed Newt his teeth, and waved that tangle of string in his face. "'See? See? See?' he asked. 'Cat's cradle. See that cat's cradle? See where the nice pussycat sleeps? Meow. Meow.'"

The scene appears to be harmless, even charming. But within the larger structure of the novel, and in direct relation to a particular day when nuclear Hell was unleashed on Hiroshima, it looms as darkly sinister in a book in which another kind of Hell is let loose upon the nuclear family typified by the Hoenikker children, but also the book's other physically and spiritually maimed families—the Breeds, the Mintons, the Castles, even the twice-divorced, booze-and-cigarette surfeited narrator himself.

As Felix draws nearer, Newt recoils, terrified. At a distance the father may seem a remote deity, but up close he resembles some satanic monster out of a science-fiction film. "His pores looked as big as craters on the moon," writes Newt. "His ears and nostrils were stuffed with hair. Cigar smoke made him smell like the mouth of Hell. So close up, my father was the ugliest thing I had ever seen. I dream about it all the time." Here we have what may be a gruesome parody of Joyce's description of little Stephen Dedalus, "Baby Tuckoo," gazing up at his father at the beginning of *A Portrait of the Artist as a Young Man.* Joyce's scene represents, as Hugh Kenner has written apropos of the "father with the hairy face," "a traditional infantile analogue of God the Father." But here in Vonnegut we witness the devil's almost Moloch-like appearance, his smoky rictus akin to the malodorous "mouth of Hell." The reference may be more deeply Dantean than we initially suspect. Considering that Felix Hoenikker is a form of anti-Christ, inflicting on man both nuclear war and perpetual winter, his actions as a scientist echo the words of Dante's Charon, ferryman to the underworld, who tells Dante and Virgil that he comes to lead them "into eternal dark, into fire and ice." The journey through the Inferno parallels Felix Hoenikker's inventions of the atomic bomb and *ice-nine.* In the initial stages of Dante's descent Hell's circles are generally hot, but when Dante arrives in the last circle, the ninth, he finds instead a "huge frozen lake," filled with those sinners whose sins involved "denials of love and of all human warmth," which is another way of defining Felix Hoenikker's relationship to his late wife, his children, and people in general.

At the very center of Dante's final circle of Hell, immobilized and up to his neck in ice, is Satan, perpetrator of the most destructive of all impulses, nihilism. In this vein he resembles the more comic but no less nihilistic Felix Hoenikker. Seemingly childlike and often referred to as "innocent," Felix nevertheless wreaks the same kind of doomsday havoc as Satan. In fact Vonnegut makes one of his strongest anti-nihilistic statements by pairing a would-be artist named Krebbs, who destroys John's apartment, with Hoenikker himself. As his final act of devastation Krebbs kills a cat by hanging it on the refrigerator door handle and placing under it a sign written in excrement that reads "Meow." This, of course, is no cradle but a cat's gallows, and Krebbs, like Hoenikker, is a man who really believes in nothing. Krebbs destroys a cat, Felix Hoenikker a cat's cradle (symbol of imagination). Felix's insistent "Meow, Meow" is really no less nihilistic than Krebb's sign. Neither science nor art can function without some respect for humanity, as both Felix (whose first name ironically evokes a famous cartoon cat) and Krebbs illustrate.

Felix Hoenikker's nihilistic egotism is fully in evidence in the scene with the cat's cradle. The father puts a tangled mass of string before his cowering child, who sees through it into Felix's horrific face. The father then proceeds to hold up *his* version of a cat's cradle and to sing *his* version of the nursery rhyme lullaby "Rockaby Baby," where a baby's cradle or human arms as a cradle figure so importantly. In the conceit of the cat's cradle metamorphosing into the baby cradle, Newt becomes the cat (or baby) falling when the wind blows, but with no one there to catch him. No wonder the boy "burst into tears" and "jumped up and ran out of the house as fast as I could go." For Newt, no cat's cradle means no "catch" and no catcher for the falling boy. The image is Salingeresque, the experience a nightmare; when he "grows up," Newt continues to paint that traumatic nightmare in the form of black "blasted landscapes," post-nuclear in their evocation of a ruined world. Newt's cynical "*No damn cat! No damn cradle*" underscores his sense, screened and deflected of course, of his own personal damnation before his father's indifference.

Any knowledgeable student of child psychology or of play therapy knows that Felix Hoenikker is not really *playing* with his son because it is he and not Newt who is manipulating the string figure. Devoid of a proper "mother," whom Alice Miller defines as "the person closest to the child during the first years of life," someone who can properly "mirror" the child's emerging identity and allow that child to grow *as a self,* Newt can only blame the cat's cradle for holding no cat and being no cradle. In essence he negates his own imagination, though the real cause of this crippling loss is not the string figure but his father, the absent "mother," the missing cradle rocker. What Newt fails to understand is that cat's cradles are not meant to be "real" in a scientific or factual sense. Rather they are games for us to play with and to act upon. They are useful fictions. Without them we cannot "invent" our own lives, are doomed to repeat endlessly (as Newt does with his paintings) our moment of loss.

What does "play" accomplish for a child, and why is its absence felt so profoundly? As defined by Bruno Bettelheim, play "refers to the young child's activities characterized by freedom from all but personally imposed rules (which are changed at will), by free-wheeling fantasy involvement, and by absence of any goals outside the activity itself." Remove play and games from a child and he or she loses the "chance to work through unresolved problems of the past, to deal with pressures of the moment, and to experiment with various roles and forms of social interaction in order to determine their suitability for himself." Bettelheim emphasizes that *real play* (a delicious Bokononist paradox) is "a child's true reality; this takes it far beyond the boundaries of its meaning for adults." Without play a child is shaped, formed, carved—like a statue—by the adult world. With play the child develops an "inner life," a fluid self that nevertheless begins to explore, to experiment "with moral identities." Games like "cops and robbers" are salutary, even if they deal in mimed violence, because "such conflicts between good and evil represent the battle between tendencies of the asocial id and those of the diametrically opposed superego," and they permit as well "some discharge of aggression either actually or symbolically, through conflict." Once again "play" sounds acutely Bokononist in its acting out of both sides of a moral struggle. And while Bettelheim seems to identify the formation of an ego with the forces of the superego gaining "ascendancy to control or overbalance those of the id," both Bettelheim and Vonnegut are conscious of the need to play in order to become a self. Nor would Bettelheim dispute Bokonon's exhortation to this followers to become "actors in a play they understood, that any human being anywhere could understand." Little wonder then that Bokonon describes growing up as "a bitter disappointment for which no remedy exists, unless laughter can be said to remedy anything." It is a tragedy for an adult to lose the ability to play, but unlike a child, and unlike the infantile, narcissistic Felix Hoenikker as well, the adult who plays can only be a good Bokononist if he realizes that he is playing, that his actions may have negative consequences (the A-bomb, *ice-nine*), and that if this is so they should be abandoned. That is what Vonnegut means by the epigraph to *Cat's Cradle*, where he instructs his audience to "Live by the foma ("Harmless untruths") that make you brave and kind and healthy and happy." The key word here is "Harmless."

    A discussion of play is important to art because creativity is an aspect of play and functions only when the artist-self exists in what D.W. Winnicott calls an "unintegrated state of personality," a condition in which the artist is able to act upon the "formless experience" of his or her life and to play with it, make something mysterious, flexible, and free out of it. Like Bettelheim and Vonnegut, Winnicott believes that without play the child's growth process is stunted and self-making cannot take place. As Winnicott writes, "To get to the idea of playing it is helpful to think of the *preoccupations* that characterize the playing of a young child. *The content does not matter.* What matters is the near-withdrawal state . . ." (first emphasis Winnicott's, second emphasis mine). Play is one of the "transitional phenomena" that Winnicott has explored so extensively in his work. It inhabits a mediating middle ground between the empirical and the invented worlds: "This area of playing is not inner psychic reality. It is outside the individual, but it is not the external world." Once again play is very Bokononist because, while Bokononism refuses to blink at the hard truth of a reality it cannot alter, it nevertheless fictionalizes that reality. Bokonon's principle of "Dynamic Tension," which derives from Charles Atlas and has appeared in children's comic books for years, closely follows the double vision (internal and external) of play. "Dynamic Tension" also resembles the making of string figures: "It is the same principle whereby if you hold your hands apart, pulling in opposite directions, you can string a cat's cradle on them; with no tension, of course, you would just have a muddle of string." Just as Bokononism is tough work for its followers, a point that few critics seem to note, play is tough work for its earnest youthful adherents. This is so because in play a child attempts to give constructive form to the world's fundamental disorder. That is what makes it, in Winnicott's words, "inherently exciting and precarious."

It is no happenstance that Winnicott himself employed string therapy games, analogous offshoots of cat's cradles, in treating disturbed children. And it is no chance occurrence that in one of those string games a boy named Edmund took a mound of tangled string, placed it "at the bottom of [a] bucket like bedding, and began to put [his] toys in, so that they had a nice soft place to lie in, like a cradle or a cot." Or a cat's cradle. What Edmund learns, and what both Bettelheim and Winnicott have taught us, is the vital necessity of play in the development of a child's psychic life. Without it we have the blighted freakish children of Felix Hoenikker, father of the atomic bomb, father of *ice-nine*, but failed father to his own children. This leads us, finally, to the most important section of *Cat's Cradle*.

In the chapter called "Cat's Cradle" Newt describes one of his scratchy morbid paintings as the depiction of a cat's cradle. John asks if the scratches are string. Newt responds, "One of the oldest games there is, cat's cradle. Even the Eskimos know it! . . . For maybe a hundred thousand years or more, grownups have been waving tangles of string in their children's faces." John's only response is "Um," but Newt proceeds, obviously anxious to make his point. He holds out his black painty hands (a gesture John himself unconsciously imitates throughout the novel) as though a cat's cradle were strung between them: "No wonder kids grow up crazy. A cat's cradle is nothing but a bunch of X's between somebody's hands, and the little kids look and look and look at all those X's." "And?" John asks. Newt replies, "*No damn cat, and no damn cradle.*" For Newt, then, cat's cradles represent lies, betrayals, perfidy, the end of imagination rather than the beginning. "X" equals nothing, and all possibility for creation is denied. It is a nihilistic image and functions in direct relation to other forms of closure or death in the novel, specifically the dropping of the atomic bomb and the end of the world through *ice-nine*.

Everything about Vonnegut's fictional world rebukes closure and confutes endings, apocalyptic or otherwise. Thus Vonnegut begins to deconstruct Newt's pointed observations at the same moment Newt makes them. Vonnegut does so initially through a description of the fantastic house built by Mona Aamons Monzano's father, Nestor, one of the few good fathers in any of Vonnegut's novels. Understanding this house is vital to understanding how the cat's cradle figure (itself architectural) dominates this chapter. The house resembles in part Coleridge's stately pleasure dome, for it is clearly a Bokononist home, grounded in physical reality but transcending that reality at the same time. Built on the side of the putatively mythic Mount McCabe, highest point on the island of San Lorenzo, and rising through ethereal mists, the house is formed out of "a cunning lattice of very light steel posts and beams," with interstices "variously open, chinked with native stone, glazed or curtained by sheets of canvas." Such terms as "cunning lattice," "variously open," "curtained," and "canvas" seem deliberately to evoke the structure's clever design, its freedom (openness), its artfulness (curtain and canvas allude to both drama and painting), as well as to cat's cradles themselves (the criss-crossed lattice), and are all used to undercut Newt's debunking of string figures. Of Nestor Aamons John writes, "The effect of the house was not so much to enclose as to announce that a man had been whimsically busy there." Like the house, Vonnegut's fiction defies definition, shows a man "Busy, busy, busy," or what "we Bokononists say when we feel that a lot of mysterious things are going on." The real mystery, sourceless, inexplicable, and "measureless to man," as Coleridge would put it, is the mystery of creation or play, the magic of cat's cradles themselves, fragile and fantastic forms, stretched delicately over an abyss (here the mountainside), yet infinitely free.

Asleep in a butterfly chair on that improbably poised "giddy terrace," itself "framed in a misty view of sky, sea, and valley," making it a part of nature and yet different from it, Newt dreams his grim dreams, then wakes to describe for John his spooky, grotesque paintings. And they *are* repellent, "small and black and warty," consisting of "scratches made in a black, gummy impasto." "The scratches formed a sort of spider's web," continues John, "and I wondered if they might not be the sticky nets of human futility hung up on a moonless night to dry." Here is the opposite image of a cat's cradle, which liberates the mind, for this cradle is a sticky "spider's web," image of human futility, that which entraps us in our own natures and finally kills us. There can be little doubt that Vonnegut himself identifies in part with this vision. But only in part. This is a vision halved, unfinished, all darkness without light, evil without good, despair without hope. It is, in short, an anti-Bokononist perception of the world, the specter of a fallen cradle, a blighted childhood (like Newt's), lacking the "Dynamic Tension" that precariously balances its paradoxical oppositions so that human life is possible despite our pathetic condition.

Appropriately Newt, whose dreams are violent, wakes to the sound of gunfire, an explosion not unlike a bomb blast, that propels him into the previously cited "reading" of his own painting. But there is little difference between Newt and what he paints. Here is Newt putting "his black, painty hands to his mouth and chin, leaving black smears there. He rubbed his eyes and made black smears around them too." His painting may be "something different" to others who see it, as a work of art should be, but to Newt it is one thing only, the objectification of his father's betrayal of Newt's childhood, symbolized by the destruction of a cat's cradle. In an important sense Newt has not yet been born because he has not been allowed to experience his childhood. We see the little man "curled" prenatally (perhaps even like a cat!) in that big butterfly chair, still waiting to metamorphose, to fly himself.

Everything that surrounds Newt and John on that wondrous terrace seems to symbolize the fertile life-affirming impulse. The mountain, whale-shaped and hump-like at the top, may also have connotations relating it to Mona Aamons Monzano, the would-be earth goddess with whom John is in love and whom he marries. Surely Vonnegut intends the pun on "a mons," as in "mons veneris." But if the mountain represents in part female fertility, then the stream and waterfall that flow down its side imply the opposite or male potential for life. These two forces, male and female, unit in Nestor Aamon's house, which, in a sexually charged image, "straddled a waterfall." In addition the mountain and the waterfall share the Bokononist oppositions of fixity and flow, what might be called the novel's flexible form, its ceaseless mediation between chaos and order.

Having suffered at birth the loss of his natural mother, little Newt cannot comprehend the abundant powers that nature itself figures forth around him. Nor can he see how Nestor Aamons's own design unites the natural with the human-made, the artful creation out of what is already there. Vonnegut makes this apparent in an outrageous pun that underscores the union between art and life in *Cat's Cradle*. The pun turns on a parody of Stanley's search for the lost explorer Livingstone through the "heart" of darkest Africa. In the novel a plump servant—rare in poverty-ridden San Lorenzo—guides John to his room, a journey "around the heart of the house, down a staircase of *living stone*, a staircase sheltered or exposed by steel-framed rectangles at random. My bed was a foam-rubber slab on a stone shelf, a shelf of *living stone*. The walls of my chamber were canvas. Stanley demonstrated how I might roll them up or down, as I pleased" (my emphases). Led by the servant Stanley, John journeys into the "heart" of Nestor Aamons's house to a bedroom hard by the "living stone" of the mountainside, stone that contains an even more female image of a cave beneath the waterfall, festooned with what resemble ancient prehistoric drawings but which, in contradistinction to Newt's morbid modernistic paintings, are primitive drawings that "treated endlessly the aspects of Mona Aamons Monzano as a little girl." These apparently ancient but actually quite recent playful paintings refute Newt's limited vision and make an indirect comment on his never having been born out of the womb of creation, while the sensual earth mother, Mona, revels in her own fertility / creativity.

Vonnegut offers one final negative verdict on little Newt's vision of art and life through the saintly yet sinister figure of Julian Castle, famous Schweitzer-like doctor at the House of Hope and Mercy. It is Castle whom John originally intended to visit on his journey to San Lorenzo, and it is Castle who gives the final verdict on Newt's jaundiced artistic vision. Castle, who has witnessed and attempted to give comfort to the worst kinds of human misery, including bubonic plague, gazes upon Newt's canvas and says, "It's *black*. What is it—hell?" Receiving no help from Newt, Castle snarls, in his best Edward G. Robinson voice, "Then it's hell." From someone who has seen the hell of human suffering on his god-forsaken island, this seems to ring true. But Castle is a true Bokononist and really means the opposite of what he says. Therefore when he learns from John that the painting is of a cat's cradle, he replies that it is in fact "a picture of the meaninglessness of it all! I couldn't agree more." At this point, after winning Newt's uneasy assent (Newt seems "to suspect momentarily that the case had been a little overstated"), Castle picks up the "blasted land-scape" of a painting and hurls it off the cantilevered terrace, from which it boomerangs and slices into the waterfall.

The painting flows into the maelstrom of the waterfall and down the mountainside, where it "ends" (or seems to) in a "big stone bowl," across which the poor natives have woven out of chicken wire a net (a cat's cradle?) that they use to catch and hold whatever flows down from above. Here is what they find: "Four square feet of gummy canvas, the four milled and mitred sticks of the stretcher, some tacks, too, and a cigar. All in all, a pretty nice *catch* for some poor, poor man" (my emphasis). The proper "use" to which Newt's limited and limiting "artwork" has been put belies its maker's original intention. As we have seen, a "catch" is also a kind of cat's cradle.

This time it is used not only to catch Newt's painting, but figuratively to "catch" Newt himself in an unbokononist lie.

Although "Cat's Cradle" concludes with another of Newt's cynical refrains, this time in criticism of his sister Angela's loveless marriage, Newt once again sees only part of the picture. His gloss on Angela's deluded love for her ruthless husband, "See the cat? See the cradle?," can hardly be gainsaid. But the way in which, out of *her* art, Angela translates her suffering into the Cadenzaed grief and grandeur of her music leads to transcendence of that miserable marriage. This cannot be said of Newt.

At the end of the book, when John searches for a "magnificent symbol" to carry with him to the top of Mount McCabe to give a central meaning to his life (he still is a Christian, and to a Christian such "centers" are important), John can find nothing, least of all a cat's cradle, to take with him. By this time *ice-nine* has nearly destroyed the world, leaving only a small enclave of survivors, among them John and Newt, still alive on San Lorenzo. What could one possibly bring to the top of a supposedly holy mountain, and what use would it be? We already know what Bokonon thinks of such gestures. As Frank Hoenikker tells John, Mount McCabe may have once been "sacred or something," but no more. John then asks, "What is sacred to Bonkononists?" and receives the terse reply, "Man. That's all. Just man!" Nevertheless, John continues to seek the proper symbol to carry to the top of the mountain and, one might argue, to "end" the novel on which he has been working for the past six months. He does not find that symbol by undergoing a conventional quest. Instead, unwittingly, he enacts a Bokononist "solution"—open-ended, inconclusive, ambiguous, and decentered—to his search. He discovers, whether he knows it or not, a cat's cradle.

Driving across San Lorenzo, John proffers his scheme to Newt, who by this time has become somewhat of a Bokononist. "I took my hands from the wheel for an instant to show him how empty of symbols they were. 'But what in hell would the right symbol *be*, Newt? What in hell would it *be?*' I grabbed the wheel again." Then a little later: "'But what, for the love of God, is supposed to be in my hands?'" Holding up his empty hands, as if to pantomime the making of a cat's cradle, John, a writer for whom that cat's cradle functions as a metaphor for writing, can only put them down in defeat. Still, he is beginning to speak the paradoxical language of a Bokononist. His parallel but thematically contrasting phrases, "What in hell" and "what, for the love of God," seem to fit perfectly with the Bokononist counterpointing of those two "separate" forces of good and evil, heaven and hell, which are a part of the Bokononist mythology. In addition, that same phrase, "for the love of God," echoes an earlier exhortation on the part of Julian Castle to his son and John, both writers, not to abandon their craft just because it all seems so hopeless: "for the love of god, both of you, please keep writing!" We remember as well that it is Julian Castle who offers a capsule definition of the very writing style, cat's cradlelike, that Vonnegut invents for his novel. That something "sacred" John hopes to carry to the top of the mountain affiliates writing with responsibility as Julian Castle imagines it, for to write is to create books that entail "a *sacred* obligation to produce beauty and enlightenment and comfort at top speed" (my emphasis).

John also believes that one of his chief purposes in climbing Mount McCabe is to discover the identity of his *karass*. "If you find your life *tangled* up with somebody else's life for no very logical reasons," writes Bokonon, "that person may be a member of your *karass*." John learns that the "tendrils" of his life "began to tangle with those of [the Hoenikker] children" (my emphases). Vital to understanding how a *karass* works is to view it as a creation of God, not man. Thus we can never know for certain who is part of our *karass*, and it is difficult to exclude anyone from it. One thing we do know is that "a 'karass' ignores national, institutional, occupational, familial, and class boundaries." A *karass* is, finally, "as free-form as an amoeba"—or a cat's cradle. It is those words "tangled" and "tangle," associated throughout the novel with cat's cradles (beginning with Felix Hoenikker's waving a "tangled mass of string" before his cowering son, and culminating with Newt's own tangled splotchy paintings of cat's cradles), that imply a connection with the flexible, playful structures called cat's cradles, which we make and unmake, tangle and untangle, never arriving at any final synthesis of their polymorphous possibilities, never knowing what the Platonic essence of a cat's cradle could possibly be. The same is true of our *karass*, for if it is a successful *karass* we never learn who belongs to it and who does not. It is analogous to the Christian notion of grace, of being chosen for eternal salvation out of God's mysterious and ineffable love. It should make us more loving, more "human," for Bokonon worships the human above all other values.

The final chapter of *Cat's Cradle*, entitled "The End," may represent the end of *The Books of Bokonon*, of John's book, and of Vonnegut's book as well (not to mention the end of the world), but it is not a true ending. It can be no more than a cat's cradle, circular, supple, full of possibilities. If each of the many chapters in *Cat's Cradle* is a mini-cat's cradle itself, open to innumerable interpretations, then what is its ending but a beginning? By allowing Bokonon, wise but perdurably mendacious (as in the sense of "foma"), to utter the novel's final words, Vonnegut suggest that those words are suspect. Bokonon in fact duplicates John's own desperate gesture and in so doing gives it the lie. Here is the last "book" in *The Books of Bokonon*:

> If I were a younger man, I would write a history of human stupidity; and I would climb to the top of Mount McCabe and lie down on my back with my history for a pillow; and I would take from the ground some of the blue-white poison that makes statues of men; and I would make a statue of myself, lying on my back, grinning horribly, and thumbing my nose at You Know Who.

Those words are not really addressed so much to the plight of the crazy old Bokonon as to the "young man," John, to whom Bokonon speaks. In the fabulist hyper-fictional world of *Cat's Cradle*, Bokonon, the first half of whose name is an obvious respelling of the word "book," is really the author's creation. We recall that Bokonon's "real" name is Johnson, that Johnson, alias Bokonon, is really "John's son," his author's imagined progeny, and that each of them is Von's son since Johnson became the maker of *The Books of Bokonon* the year he landed on the fictional (but all too real) island of San Lorenzo, which was 1922, the year Kurt Vonnegut was born. Wheels within wheels, and cat's cradles generating newer and more elaborately concatenated cat's cradles in the perpetual process of creation, without beginning and without end.

That is the true meaning of Vonnegut's book, and that is why, despite the imminent demise of the world and of Bokonon himself (now that his creator has become a Bokononist, as he tells us in the novel's first pages, Bokonon's existence is no longer necessary; he has been assimilated into John), suicide is the least Bokononist solution to the desperate situation we witness at the end of *Cat's Cradle*. This, plus the realization that Bokonon is always lying, should prevent us from assuming that John intends to follow Bokonon's advice (an anti-Bokononist response). Indeed, John assumes Bokonon's conditional phrase, "If I were a younger man," into his own writing, takes the last page of *The Books of Bokonon*, and, by changing that conditional "If" to an emphatic "When," incorporates them into the beginning of his own book. John is really satirizing his own pre-Bokononist youth, its failures and its futility, when he writes, "When I was a younger man—two wives ago, 250,000 cigarettes ago, 3,000 quarts of booze ago . . . When I was a much younger man, I began to collect material for a book to be called *The Day the World Ended*." But the world does not quite end in *Cat's Cradle*, and its author, holding in his hands the only cat's cradle he knows, that is his fictional world, can hardly take the advice of Bokonon and thumb his nose at "You Know Who," since he does not in fact know who "You Know Who" is, or whether "He" even exists. Bokononism is referred to as a religion in *Cat's Cradle*, but if it is it is a very different, undogmatic religion, built out of the creative, playful, childlike aspects of human nature, out of our enduring ability to invent meanings in an essentially meaningless world (or a world whose meanings are hidden permanently from us). By *not* following Bokonon's advice, John enacts his own conversion to Bokononism.

Bokononism is a philosophy of flow, resisting entropy and harrowing the fixities that reduce societies to monomaniacal obsessions, to one-sided "truths." Everything it stands for opposes the destructive science of Felix Hoenikker, and for that reason it is fiercely if amusingly unquietistic, refusing to accept that all human action is ultimately futile. Thus it is stridently unlike another Vonnegutian "philosophy" with which it is often paired, the deterministic Tralfamadorianism of *Slaughterhouse-Five*. Because they hold that we are powerless to alter history (in fact "history" has already happened, and the universe has already been destroyed), Vonnegut's Tralfamadorians believe that our only solution is to time-travel, to live in selected "happy moments," to ignore the burden of human misery that drives Bokonon mad but which also forces him to invent a religion of compassion and compensation against our grim human lot. Contrastingly, the Tralfamadorians see humankind in the lowliest terms, as "bugs trapped in amber" for whom they have little sympathy.

Although their reductivist philosophy appeals to such a pathetic and limited person as Billy Pilgrim, the protagonist of *Slaughterhouse-Five*, it is difficult to believe that Vonnegut wants us all to become Tralfamadorians. Bokononism, on the other hand, is Dostoevskian in its riddling contradictions. A true Tralfamadorian would never accept Bokononism's life-lie, its "cruel paradox," which acknowledges "the heartbreaking necessity of lying about reality, and the heartbreaking impossibility of lying about it." For "heartbreaking" read "tragic," a word utterly alien to Tralfamadorian hedonism. So much deeper and more complicated than Tralfamadorianism, Bokononism is at bottom a comic response to a tragic world, yet a response that simultaneously *contains*, in its artful dualism (really a delicate balancing), both the tragic and the comic aspects of human nature. There is no better gloss on Bokononism than the celebrated description of the artistic imagination offered by F. Scott Fitzgerald in *The Crack-Up*. "[L]et me," writes Fitzgerald, "make a general observation—the test of a first-rate intelligence is the ability to hold two opposed ideas in the mind at the same time, and still retain the ability to function." What follows is critical if we are to comprehend Vonnegut's tragicomic Bokononist vision. "One should, for example," Fitzgerald continues, "be able to see that things are hopeless and yet be determined to make them otherwise." Kurt Vonnegut could easily have penned these words. What's more, Vonnegut's own rhetoric follows Fitzgerald's in the latter's summation of his hope-against-hope philosophy: "I must hold in balance the sense of the futility of effort and the sense of the necessity to struggle: the conviction of the inevitability of failure and still the determination to succeed." This is, of course, the language of Vonnegut's "cruel paradox." It is the voice of tragedy, which for Vonnegut, confirmed Bokononist that he is, can only be expressed by its opposite, the author's courageous comedy.

JEROME KLINKOWITZ

From Formula Toward Experiment:
Cat's Cradle *and* God Bless You, Mr. Rosewater

In *Mother Night*, with its historical anxiety and its note of resigned humanism, Vonnegut clearly came close to the mood of the times, when black humor was becoming a dominant feature in American fiction. These were the Kennedy years, when writers seemed to be moving closer to history in order to look at its absurdist disturbances and destruction, yet at the same time were more preoccupied with the nature of fictions—a theme central to Vonnegut's next novel, *Cat's Cradle* (1963). It is a mock-apocalyptic novel, satirizing such doomsday books as *On the Beach* and *Seven Days in May*; it combines Vonnegut's newly perfected form (short units of composition fashioned as three-line jokes) and his emerging ethic (the danger of innocent pretense) to confront the largest possible issue: mankind's threatened self-destruction. In *Mother Night* Howard Campbell so mismanages the business of pretense that the only free act left to him is suicide. Now, in *Cat's Cradle*, Vonnegut flirts with the idea of the death of all creation, though only in order to find a vehicle for exploring the way in which human pretenses and inventions might properly serve us. From *Player Piano* we had seen how a socially derived role is necessary for man's self-esteem; in *The Sirens of Titan* Vonnegut warns us through his Church of God the Utterly Indifferent how dangerous it is to claim divine sanction for any invented role. *Cat's Cradle* takes another step: 'Live by the *foma* that make you brave and kind and

From *Kurt Vonnegut* by Jerome Klinkowitz. © 1982 by Jerome Klinkowitz.

healthy and happy,' reads the epigraph. And what are *foma*? 'Harmless untruths,' advises the footnote just below.

A novel is a harmless untruth as well, as a similar footnote explains on the book's cover. For all the exotic zaniness of the Caribbean religion this book concocts, Vonnegut is careful to show how simple literature does the same for anyone who can keep aware of the playmaking in one's pretense. The narrator, a man named John, is a writer; *Cat's Cradle* begins with his attempt to write one book and ends with his having written another instead; and along the way he is quick to defend the writer's job, which is 'a sacred obligation to produce beauty and enlightenment and comfort at top speed.' His work on the first book, a narrative about the invention and first strategic use of the atomic bomb to be called *The Day the World Ended*, takes him first to the research lab in Ilium, New York, where its inventor worked, and then to the tropical Isle of San Lorenzo, where the scientist's children are involved in a comic plot which will eventually end all life on earth (or at least seem to). Along the way we are introduced to a religion so ridiculous that it resists being taken seriously, but which nevertheless helps the people create happy meaning for their otherwise pitiful lives. And at the same time Vonnegut's narrator converts to this religion and writes the book which survives: *Cat's Cradle*. Of course it's all made up. Just as the Bokononist religion keeps its members aware of the artificial drama they are playing, so too does *Cat's Cradle* draw attention to its own artifice of form. For each to work, Vonnegut believes, there should be no danger of either worshipper or reader mistaking such activity for bedrock-solid truth. When that does happen, we have religious wars, persecutions and deaths; only when Bokononism runs out of control does that happen in San Lorenzo. And, when novels ask to be read as history, their transformative power is sapped. Purpose works best when self-invented. And pretense is evil only when it mistakes itself for something absolute.

And so another book-within-the-novel, *The Books of Bokonon*, will teach:

> In the beginning, God created the earth, and he looked upon it in His cosmic loneliness.
>
> And God said, 'Let Us make living creatures out of mud, so the mud can see what We have done.' And God created every living creature that now moveth, and one was man. Mud as man alone could speak. God leaned close as mud as man sat up, looked around, and spoke. Man blinked. 'What is the *purpose* of all this?' he asked politely.
>
> 'Everything must have a purpose?' asked God.

'Certainly,' said man.

'Then I leave it to you to think of one for all this,' said God. And He went away.

Man must write his own meaning—in religions, in novels. To the complaint that religion is the opiate of the people and that novelists are little different from 'drug salesmen', Vonnegut is quick to have a local historian explain that Bokononism 'did not succeed in raising what is generally thought of as the standard of living. . . . The truth was that life was as short and brutish and mean as ever,' and that everyone on the island knows it. For religion to work, it need not be an opiate—just as the fictional style Vonnegut is here perfecting does not demand the reader's suspension of disbelief. Take joy in the artifice, Vonnegut says, for there—and not in realistic content—is where truth and meaning lie. Bokononism is based on the silliest of sacred texts: Charles Atlas's comic-book advertisements for muscle building through the exercise of 'dynamic tension'. The religion improvises a pantomimic routine of 'the cruel tyrant in the city and the gentle holy man in the jungle', a self-consciously allegorical (rather than symbolic) exercise which gives the people enjoyable roles to play. 'They were all employed full time as actors in a play they understood', the historian explains, 'that any human being anywhere could understand and applaud.'

Here is *Cat's Cradle's* aesthetics of belief: meaning lies not in the content of a novel or the materials of a religion, but rather in the business of dealing with them. Once that process, that act of play, is complete, content should be forgotten. If not, it becomes the stuff of great mischief. The particulars of Bokononism are so patently ridiculous that no one in their right mind would take them seriously: they are simply occasions for the true work of religion, which is self-dignifying play. No Bokononist can claim God's will for his or her peculiar belief; Bokononism does not lead to inquisitions and holy wars. But when the material of either fiction or religion is taken as truth, as a specific endorsement by God himself, it becomes the art that self-destructs, leaving us with content alone, unstructured by form—just more unformed chaos from real life.

As Bokononism displays its own artifice, so does the novel that surrounds it. Psalms are rewritten as 'calypsos' whose rinky-tink beat unsettles their familiar content; parables and admonitions are retranslated in a way that emphasizes the process of *getting to* a provisional belief rather than the belief itself. 'Pay no attention to Caesar,' Bokonon teaches. 'Caesar doesn't have the slightest idea what's *really* going on.' We see the religion constructed by its two inventors just as we watch the novel *Cat's Cradle* being written by the narrator—who except for an editorial veto would have been named 'Vonnegut'. Even within his story, the author keeps disrupting conventional beliefs. Countering expectations that the inventor of the atomic bomb would be a bloodthirsty madman, Vonnegut creates a character—Dr Felix Hoenikker—who is winsomely innocent. A widower, he is cared for by his daughter, as his youngest son explains:

> She used to talk about how she had three children—me, Frank, and Father. She wasn't exaggerating, either. I can remember cold mornings when Frank, Father, and I would be all in a line in the front hall, and Angela would be bundling us up, treating us all exactly the same. Only I was going to kindergarten; Frank was going to junior high; and Father was going to work on the atom bomb.

His invention of the bomb itself is an act of innocent play. His lab is filled with toys and gadgets, passing fancies which spark his interest and which he pursues in the name of pure research. In the midst of his wartime work on the bomb he suddenly becomes interested in dime-store turtles—'When they pull in their heads,' he ponders, 'do their spines buckle or contract?'—and forgets his atomic project completely. 'Some people from the Manhattan Project finally came out to the house to ask Angela what to do,' the son reports:

> She told them to take away Father's turtles. So one night they went into his laboratory and stole the turtles and the aquarium. Father never said another word about the disappearance of the turtles. He just came to work the next day and looked for things to play with and think about, and everything there was to play with and think about had something to do with the bomb.

But just about the time readers are prepared to discard their first impressions, and agree that perhaps Dr Hoenikker is a harmless man after all, we are told of a similar incident of adorable, absentminded foolishness which disrupts our comic response. Driving to work one day, Hoenikker gets stuck in a traffic jam and abandons his car in the street, blithely walking to his lab instead. Another funny story? Not with this ending, which Vonnegut supplies even while we still laugh: his wife is called to retrieve the car, is unused to driving it, has an accident, and suffers a pelvic injury which later kills her in childbirth. Nor, we now realize, is it so funny that Dr Hoenikker's winsome play, ostensibly for no real purpose, produced the horrors of atomic war. Pure form, Vonnegut cautions, is not the answer either; we are what we pretend to be, so that pretense had best be aimed at a moral ideal, even though its realization is not the point of our activity. Performance, not product, is what counts.

And so the bomb is made before our eyes, built of dime-store parts by a childlike genius—just as Bokononism is fashioned out of comic-book ads and as John's book, only metaphorically about 'the day the world ended' at its start, moves frighteningly closer to the realization of that theme. But John's novel is assembled in such a way as to emphasize its making more than its presumed result. John begins his research as a factual reporter but soon disgresses into more idiosyncratic ways of getting his material. Indeed, he is swept up into the whole mad history of the Hoenikker family, which reaches from the bomb's invention in Ilium, New York, to the unleashing of an even more destructive device—*Ice-9*, which freezes all creation—on the Island of San Lorenzo. The train of events is deliberately improbable, and even the titles of the 127 minuscule chapters are challenges to coherent meaning ('Vice-President in Charge of Volcanoes', 'When Automobiles Had Cut-glass Vases', 'A Medical Opinion on the Effects of a Writer's Strike', and so forth). John collects his information from the unlikeliest of sources, and takes delight in the act of collaging it all in: snatches from personal letters, interviews, local histories, memories, gossip, and of course *The Books of Bokonon* themselves. So aware are we of John's own process of making this book that there is only one surprise at the end. By the final page *Ice-9* has been set loose, the earth indeed may be on its way to freezing solid, and John—as one of last men left alive—is pondering what to do. In this final page-long chapter he meets Bokonon, who drafts the final sentence of *The Books of Bokonon* and of *Cat's Cradle* as well:

> If I were a younger man, I would write a history of human stupidity; and I would climb to the top of Mount McCabe and lie down on my back with my history for a pillow; and I would take from the ground some of the blue-white poison that makes statues out of men; and I would make a statue of myself, lying on my back, grinning horribly, and thumbing my nose at You Know Who.

Will such a history ever be written? Within the artifice of plot, it seems that John has done just that, and the result is *Cat's Cradle*. Has life on earth really ended? Of course not, for here we are, all three million of us (the novel's sales to date), quite happily and healthily reading the author's practical joke against the universe.

Cat's Cradle was conceived as another paperback original and delivered to fulfill such a contract. However, the publishers then chose to do a hard-cover edition as part of their arrangement with the Doubleday Book Club, which had ordered 24,000 copies. The switch was important: Vonnegut was now writing again for the serious hardcover trade. And with his fifth novel, *God Bless You, Mr Rosewater* (1965), he clearly had his eye on another market. In the event the book was less successful than its predecessor: *Cat's Cradle* sold much better in paperback than did the similar edition of *Mr Rosewater* which followed a year after the book's hardcover début. Even today *God Bless You, Mr Rosewater* remains one of his least attractive books. A manipulation of the prince-and-the-pauper formula, this story of a rich philanthropist who exiles himself among the poor and unwanted developed a more cynical and darkly comic brand of humor and a seriousness he could not quite control. Indeed, these years, though they contributed to the eventual rise of his success, did not seem Vonnegut's best. His once reliable short-story market had disappeared completely, his novels produced but a meagre income, and his family life was rocky for a time. So, when his work was finished on this book, he was forced by economic necessity to consider another full-time job, his first such commitment away from full-time writing since he had quit GE a decade and a half before. But not completely away from writing: the post would turn out to be a two-year lectureship in creative writing at the University of Iowa, a fresh experience that helped inaugurate a different style in his novels and a new stage in his career. But first there was the rather nasty business of this novel, written when funds were very short, which begins: 'A sum of money is a leading character in this tale about people, just as a sum of honey might properly be a leading character in a tale about bees.'

Just about everything in *God Bless You, Mr Rosewater* is unpleasant. The protagonist, Eliot Rosewater, is a well-meaning but rather oafish, ill-smelling, overweight person whose passing delight is to play with his pubic hair. His antagonist, who will prove him mad as a way of stealing a fat percentage of his millions, is the obnoxious little lawyer, Norman Mushari, the description of whom hardly befits Vonnegut:

> He was the youngest, the shortest, and by all odds the least Anglo-Saxon male employee in the firm [of McAllister, Robjent, Reed and McGee]. He was put to work under the most senile partner, Thurmond McAllister, a sweet old poop who was seventy-six. He would never have been hired if the other partners hadn't felt that McAllister's operations could do with just a touch more viciousness.

When Mushari walks through the office, his associates whistle 'Pop Goes the Weasel'. But Vonnegut hates his own created character so much that even this is not enough. There is one indignity left, which the author savors: 'He had an enormous ass,' we're told, 'which was luminous when bare.'

Lust for money, by despicable people whose only comic attribute is the glee with which their author has created petty indignities for them to suffer, sets the tone for *God Bless You, Mr Rosewater.* Countering this is Eliot Rosewater's hapless attempt to give his fortune away. Money is indeed transformative: Vonnegut had found that out the last time he was so broke, during the Great Depression, and he uses his millionaire philanthropist Eliot Rosewater to teach that lesson now. As in *Cat's Cradle*, writing fiction is an analog— there to religion, here to the transformative power of cash. Taking off from his Foundation's offices on Fifth Avenue, he heads west, stopping to address a science-fiction writers' conference in Milford, Pennsylvania (a real convention, organized by the SF professional, Damon Knight). 'I love you sons of bitches,' Eliot tells these writers. 'You're all I read any more. You're the only ones who'll talk about the *really* terrific changes going on,' he explains, describing the thrust of Kurt Vonnegut's own novels, for these are writers who understand 'what wars do to us, what cities do to us, what big, simple ideas do to us, what tremendous misunderstandings, mistakes, accidents and catastrophes do to us.' Their projective ideas are not empty fantasy, Eliot insists, for science fiction can help reinvent reality, which is itself just an arbitrary convention. To demonstrate, he scribbles a stack of $200 checks and passes them out:

> '*There's* fantasy for you,' he said. 'And you go to the bank tomorrow, and it will all come true. It's insane that I should be able to do such a thing, with money so important. . . . I leave it to you . . . : think about the silly ways money gets passed around now, and then think up better ways.'

Eliot himself then takes off to do just this, on a mad trip through the dead-end small towns of America, to help reinvent the dull and useless lives he finds being lived in such hollow neglect. In typical prince-and-the-pauper fashion, he exchanges his rich clothes for poor, making himself indistinguishable from the people he would serve—indistinguishable, that is, except for the hidden transformative power of his money. But he also knows that money alone is a poor way to transform. 'I'm going to love these discarded Americans,' he tells his wife on the telephone, 'even though they're useless and unattractive. *That* is going to be my work of art.'

The people Eliot embraces, however, are poor makings for a masterpiece. There is nothing sentimental about Vonnegut's treatment of the

Indiana hinterland, a place that challenges the disbelief 'that land anywhere could be so deathly flat, that people anywhere could be so deathly dull.' Nor does Vonnegut idealize poor Eliot: he is alternately kind and rude to these people, and leaves them at the drop of a hat. The proceeds of his charity are just a few threatened suicides bargained back to life at bottom-dollar prices, plus a village oddball or two humored in his or her eccentricity. All this takes place in the devastated, hopeless landscape of strip-mined countryside and automated factories which had originally created the Rosewater fortune. Meanwhile, a distant Rosewater cousin whom Norman Mushari has been using to sue Eliot for the family fortune lives his own life of quiet desperation, his son a fancier of cheap pornography and his wife stewed to the gills on martini-and-chicken-salad lunches. All is either rapaciousness and greed or disappointment and decay. As Eliot himself characterizes the fate of his country, 'Thus the American dream turned belly up, turned green, bobbed to the scummy surface of cupidity unlimited, filled with gas, went *bang* in the noonday sun.'

'You can safely ignore the arts and sciences,' Eliot believes, summing up the wisdom of two generations of Vonneguts, Kurt Senior and Junior: 'They never helped anybody. Be a sincere, attentive friend of the poor.' The progress of *God Bless You, Mr Rosewater* makes it very clear that, at least in this novel, there is to be precious little good done for the poor by throwing money at them. What is needed is a more fundamental rearrangement of the terms of life in America, on a level higher and more inclusive than the simply political. *Rosewater* concludes with some socio-anthropological advice which seems to take us back full circle to the arguments of *Player Piano*, except that in this newer novel the spokesman is not a minister or anthropologist but rather a novelist himself, and the world to which his comments apply is not futuristically dystopian but rather immediately and quite realistically present.

That novelist is Kilgore Trout, the unheeded hack science-fiction writer Rosewater celebrated at Milford, and an image of what Vonnegut once feared he himself might become. 'The problem is this,' Troust announces, when he is summoned to explain both Eliot's insanity and what has prompted it: 'How to love people who have no use?' What does the future, that special domain of the science fictionist's expertise, foretell? Trout explains:

> In time, almost all men and women will become worthless as producers of goods, food, services, and more machines, as sources of practical ideas in the areas of economics, engineering, and probably medicine, too. So—if we can't find reasons and methods for treasuring human beings because they are *human beings*, then we might as well, as has so often been suggested, rub them out.

> Americans have long been taught to hate all people
> who will not or cannot work, to hate even themselves for that.
> We can thank the vanished frontier for that piece of common-
> sense cruelty. The time is coming, if it isn't here now, when it
> will no longer be common sense. It will simply be cruel.

The solution, Trout suggests, has been what Eliot has in fact been practicing: not highpowered philanthropy but rather 'uncritical love'. The practice is as simple as the motto of the rehabilitative hospital now caring for Eliot: 'Pretend to be good always, and even God will be fooled.' A new mythology is needed, however, to replace the outmoded 'American dream' of boundless opportunity for all hard-workers. And this new, workable structure for values must come from writers, just as it was writers who helped create the older, once meaningful myth in the first place.

Kilgore Trout as America's new Crèvecœur? The thought is not as preposterous as it seems, and became even less so as Kurt Vonnegut—for years a shabbily neglected writer much like the character Trout himself—emerged into his first decade of fame. The idiosyncratic novel *Slaughter-house-Five* (1969) was to be Vonnegut's breakthrough, followed at regular intervals by even more personal books. In them, the author would bless America with the same cautionary style Eliot Rosewater used to baptize the children of Rosewater County, Indiana:

> Hello, babies. Welcome to Earth. It's hot in the summer and
> cold in the winter. It's round and wet and crowded. At the
> outside, babies, you've got about a hundred years here.
> There's only one rule that I know of, babies—:
>   'God damn it, you've got to be kind.'

LEONARD MUSTAZZA

Playful Genesis and Dark Revelation in Cat's Cradle

*C*at's *Cradle*, Vonnegut's first end-of-the-world novel, has generated more critical commentary on its theme than any other of his works, save perhaps *Slaughterhouse-Five*. Most of that commentary has centered on what Robert Scholes has called "the old collision between science and religion." "As the scientist finds the truth that kills," Scholes writes elsewhere, "the prophet looks for the saving lie." Likewise, Robert Uphaus argues that "Bokonon, the life-affirming inventor, is matched against the effects of the life-denying inventor, Dr. Felix Hoenikker." Perhaps the most insightful assessment of Vonnegut's intentions in *Cat's Cradle* is Tony Tanner's assertion that "the whole novel is an exploration of the ambiguities of man's disposition to play and invent, and the various forms it may take." Indeed, most of the characters in the novel are, in the bogus prophet Bokonon's words, "busy, busy, busy"—busy making, creating, formulating, conceptualizing, organizing, and reorganizing. Like other characters in Vonnegut's fiction, they are constantly pursuing geneses, beginnings, new ways of looking at life, and like the God of Genesis, they are constantly engaged in coaxing some kind of form and order out of the chaos around them. Unlike God, however, they seem often to have little or no control over the outcomes of their inventions, nor do they seem to take much responsibility for those inventions. The genesis part is easy for them, and by extension for all human beings because they have the

From *Forever Pursuing Genesis: The Myth of Eden in the Novels of Kurt Vonnegut* by Leonard Mustazza. © 1990 by Associated University Presses, Inc.

innate desire to create, but the end is a different matter altogether. Thus, though he alludes to Genesis at various points in this novel, Vonnegut also employs here bitter echoes of the book of Revelation, leaving us with a vivid image of the destroyed Earth, of the Earth where "there was no longer any sea" (Revelation 21:1). Unlike the biblical apocalypse, however, there is in the end no omnipotent creator remaking the world into the New Jerusalem, no one to "make all things new" (Revelation 21:5).

Curiously, though, while Vonnegut uses in *Cat's Cradle*, as he does elsewhere, a variety of resonant biblical allusions, the novel does not "pursue Genesis" in the same way that other novels I am considering here do. Rather than to rely exclusively on mythic invention in this novel, Vonnegut expands the concept of invention considerably to include palpable things as well as intellectual constructs. Hence, in this chapter, I shall examine not so much mythic paradigms as the problematical relationship between human creativity and destructiveness that runs throughout *Cat's Cradle*. To do that, we must begin by considering the world as the novel gives it to us, a world sharply divided into two segments: the modern world, where the dominant form of creation is scientific and technological; and the primitive world of the island republic of San Lorenzo, where invention must take the form of conceptual reinvention. Eventually the two will merge symbolically, and political ambition, irresponsibility, accident, and fatal innocence will conspire to end invention for all time.

Near the beginning of the novel, the narrator, John (or Jonah as he refers to himself) says that he intends in this book "to examine all strong hints as to what on Earth we, collectively, have been up to." The "book" to which he refers is *Cat's Cradle* itself and not the one he set out originally to write, *The Day the World Ended*, a factual account of what important Americans were doing on the day the atomic bomb was dropped on Hiroshima. Ironically, it was his research for the latter book that led to the composition of the former, the writer now being one of the few surviving people left on earth, hence the appropriateness of the other title. John's research begins (and effectively ends) with his inquiry into the life of the late Dr. Felix Hoenikker, "one of the so-called 'Fathers' of the first atomic bomb"; and therefore, one of those directly responsible for the "end of the world" in August of 1945. (As it turns out, he will be solely, albeit indirectly, responsible also for the ruined world from which John narrates *Cat's Cradle*.) Visiting the General Forge and Foundry Company in Ilium, New York, where Dr. Hoenikker did his work, John meets with Dr. Asa Breed, Hoenikker's supervisor at the time of the bomb's development.

On the surface, Asa Breed is very much unlike Hoenikker insofar as he is articulate and shrewd, whereas Hoenikker is described as having been a reticent and distracted man. Unlike Hoenikker, too, Breed is only too willing to serve as a public spokesman for the glories of science, continually denouncing what he regards as superstitions and advocating the "truths" that only science can provide. To him, scientific invention, pure research, ought to be carried out without questions from or accountability to the uninitiated; and its products should be greeted with all the zeal once accorded to religion. Of course, Vonnegut expects us to recognize how self-serving and morally insensitive Breed is; and to show Breed's moral bankruptcy, he employs his usual weapon—satiric comedy. At one point, Breed explains to John that on the site of the research laboratory there once stood an old stockade where public hangings took place. Breed is particularly intrigued by an execution that took place there in 1782, that of a man who had murdered twenty-six people. The man, Breed tells John, sang a song from the scaffold, an indication that he was not sorry for what he had done. "Think of it!" Breed says, "Twenty-six people he had on his conscience," to which the narrator responds, "the mind reels." This bit of sarcasm apparently escapes Breed, but eventually, Breed does recognize that John is passing judgment on the scientists' roles in modern homicide. This awareness occurs when John begins to question him too closely about *ice-nine*, the "seed" that can make water freeze instantly, the invention that Hoenikker once playfully developed at the suggestion of an army general. Breed insists that no such "seed" was ever developed, and that, nevertheless, John does not comprehend the way researchers worked. "Pure research men work on what fascinates them, not on what fascinates other people," he asserts, showing his moral obtuseness to the very end.

What the narrator realizes—what Vonnegut wants us to realize—is that there is really no such thing as "pure research" in the way that Breed intends that phrase, particularly when the results, immediate or eventual, can affect the lives of people. Breed's defense of such invention is tantamount to saying that, since the general public does not understand the technical intricacies of scientific inquiry, it has no right to interfere with such inquiry, a logical confutation if there ever was one. To make his point about the dangers of unquestioned "pure research," Vonnegut uses not direct statement, but indirection, notably in his characterizations. As we have seen, Breed's comment on the conscienceless murderer shows his own incapacity for making sophisticated moral judgments. Vonnegut also includes mention of Breed's son, who had quit his job at the research lab in 1945, claiming that anything scientists work on was likely to end up being used as weaponry and that he wanted no part in such activity. In other words, the younger man was able to extrapolate that which his father could never understand. Although the Hoenikker offspring, whom John will shortly meet, are not quite so

disposed as Breed's son to take a positive moral stand, the effect of their revelations about their father amounts to much the same thing with regard to the
brilliant Dr. Hoenikker's moral vision.

And what sort of man was this creator of such nightmarish
weaponry, this maker of new forms, this father to offspring natural and
contrived? According to his son Newt, he was a man who could assert
genuinely in his Nobel Prize acceptance speech that he was "like an eight-
year-old," a statement that was intended to suggest his continuing capacity
to wonder at the world, but that, to us, ironically suggests his underdevel-
oped moral sensibilities. Despite his claim to a juvenile outlook, moreover,
Hoenikker was a man whom Newt remembers as not very playful. Only once
in his life did he actually play with Newt, making a cat's cradle out of some
string, and that experience made Newt cry. He was also a man not very interested in people, including his own motherless children; a man whose attention was easily distracted, who placed no more importance on, say, the
Manhattan Project than on the question of whether turtles' spines buckled or
contracted when they pulled their heads in. He was a man who, when told at
Alamogordo that science has now known sin, could ask, "what is sin?" (Likewise, Hoenikker once asked a worker at the research lab, "What is God?
What is love?") Finally, he is a man brilliant enough to create *ice-nine* when
someone from the military poses the problem of how to eliminate mud so
that the Marines would not have to walk through or fight in it; but he is also
distracted enough to tell almost no one, including the military, that he has
playfully created a solution to their problem.

What emerges in this description of, in the narrator's words, the
"father of a bomb, father of three children, father of *ice-nine*" is the portrait
of an innocent and naive maker of things that are in themselves either innocent or deadly. Vonnegut's ironic art is seen in the fact that he does not make
Hoenikker the sterotypical diabolical genius or even an Epimethean scientist
like Mary Shelley's Victor Frankenstein, who realizes only afterwards what
damage his irresponsible creativeness has wrought. Hence, I would not agree
with Rebecca Pauly, who maintains that "the demon-scientist figure is well-
portrayed in the character of Dr. Felix Hoenikker." He is not a demon scientist, for a demon is, by definition, a being that is evil and performs evil acts
deliberately. Rather, Hoenikker is unaware of the moral dimensions implicit
in the act of creating anything new, let alone implements that can harm
others. For that, we may loathe him; but Vonnegut really does not go out of
his way to make Hoenikker a despicable character. He is, instead, a pathetic
figure, a product of the preatomic world when science was perhaps as playful
an endeavor as he would have liked it to be. In his address to the American
Physical Society in 1969, Vonnegut told of an incident that may shed some

light on his view of the Hoenikkers in our world. He referred there to the fact that, during a protest at Harvard University against Dow Chemical for its manufacture of napalm during the Vietnam War, the actual inventor of napalm, Dr. Louis Fieser, could circulate through the crowd unmolested. He found that fact, he said, "a moral curiosity"; and it was not until he received a letter from a student explaining what a lovable and "innocent" man Fieser was that he could clarify in his own mind his position on men like Fieser:

> This letter helped me to see that Dr. Fieser and other old-fashioned scientists like him were and are as innocent as Adam and Eve. There was nothing at all sinful in Dr. Fieser's creation of napalm. Scientists will never be so innocent again. Any young scientist, by contrast, when asked by the military to create a terror weapon on the order of napalm, is bound to suspect that he may be committing modern sin. God bless him for that.

Of course, it would be anachronistic to suggest that Vonnegut had Fieser in mind when he created Felix Hoenikker, and yet the description above accords well with his characterization nevertheless. In his way, Hoenikker's inventions are innocent. It is actually his irresponsibility as a father that allows his invention of *ice-nine* to fall into the wrong hands, thus setting in motion the chain of events that would ultimately lead to the end of the world.

Significantly, however, that chain, though it begins in the techno-logically advanced society, ends on a primitive island republic. Its occurrence is, in the strict sense at least, an accident; but an accident which has its roots in Hoenikker's playful creative activity and which has yet another important Hoenikker connection, so to speak—Franklin Hoenikker, the most inventive and destructive of the late physicist's offspring.

Not surprisingly, Vonnegut turns to familiar myth in his portrayal of Franklin Hoenikker: in this case, the prime figures of good and evil in the Judeo-Christian scheme of things. While still in Ilium, the narrator reads in an advertising supplement to the Sunday *New York Times* that Franklin Hoenikker has been appointed the Minister of Science and Progress of San Lorenzo. In that capacity, he has become, the promotional material says, "the architect of the San Lorenzo Master Plan," a program for modernizing the primitive island nation, including building new roads, sewage-disposal plants, hotels, hospitals, and railroads, as well as providing electricity to homes and businesses—in short, "the works." Franklin's expertise and authority for doing all of this seems to derive less from qualifications as from the fact that he is, as the ad copy repeats five times, "the *blood son* of Dr. Felix

Hoenikker," a curious reiteration, which prompts the narrator to extrapolate, correctly enough as it turns out, that Franklin's value lies in his being "a chunk of the old man's magic meat." John now sets off to find the most elusive and bizarre of Hoenikker's offspring, whom he refers to as the "Great God Jehovah and Beelzebub of bugs in Mason jars"—mythic allusions that are quite pregnant with meaning.

We soon discover that Franklin Hoenikker is, for all practical purposes, a god-player, an individual who, as man and boy, has demonstrated an acute interest in the creation and control of "new" worlds. On the other hand, he is also a demonic figure insofar as he reveals, at the very least, hypocritical irresponsibility toward those to whom he commits himself and, at worst, downright malevolence, thus making him, like Beelzebub, a brooding and resentful figure as well. To establish this allusive mythic duality, Vonnegut provides us with what might be regarded as "mirror scenes," in which Franklin is seen as both creator and tormentor of creatures. There are two such scenic pairs, one from each set occurring in Ilium when Franklin was a boy, the other in San Lorenzo, where Franklin is now a government minister.

While conducting his research in Ilium, the narrator first learns of Franklin's impressive creative talent. Visiting the hobby shop where the young Franklin once worked, John gets a chance to see the fruits of the young man's labors, which the owner of the hobby shop, Jack, has left intact these many years:

> And then [Jack] turned on a switch, and the far end of the basement was filled with a blinding light.
>
> We approached the light and found that it was sunshine to a fantastic little country built on plywood, an island as perfectly rectangular as a township in Kansas. Any restless soul, any soul seeking to find what lay beyond its green boundaries, really would fall off the edge of the world.
>
> The details were so exquisitely in scale, so cunningly textured and tinted, that it was unnecessary for me to squint in order to believe that the nation was real—the hills, the lakes, the rivers, the forests, the towns, and all else that good natives everywhere hold so dear.

Franklin, the creator and "Great God Jehovah" of this cunning little world was presumably the only one who could stand outside this world and observe it without the illusion of falling off the edge. One can easily imagine him, as a boy, entering this room many times and turning on that blinding fluorescent sunlight to shed illumination on the world he had made; and had Jack suggested that he had once or twice heard the lad say as he did so, "Let there be light," one would have no trouble believing it.

The mirror image of this small-scale creative activity occurs on San Lorenzo where the adult Franklin, the architect of the new and more progressive island republic, hopes to extend the sphere of his creativity. Just as he did in Jack's basement, Franklin plans to build there a cunningly contrived little world, replete with all the things that science and technology have to offer. Put another way, he hopes to recreate the island in the image of the technologically advanced world; and he will do all of this by virtue not of his skill but of the public relations value of his nominal association with his father, himself a creator, albeit a much less deliberate one. Vonnegut makes the connection between the little world in Jack's basement and the larger one of San Lorenzo inescapable. Employing an echo of his description of the small-scale world as "an island as perfectly rectangular as a township in Kansas," the narrator, looking down on San Lorenzo from an airplane, observes that "the island, seen from the air, was an amazingly regular rectangle." This vivid similarity is, to be sure, hardly coincidental.

Both of these scenes are concerned with Franklin's godlike activities as a creator, but the other mirror pair is intended to show the opposite in Frank—his malevolent influence in worlds large and small, hence the narrator's reference to him as a Beelzebub figure. The narrator has learned in a letter to him from Franklin's younger brother, Newt, a curious and significant detail about the youthful Franklin. It seems that, on the day the atomic bomb was dropped on Hiroshima, Franklin was himself making for some havoc and discord in a world that he could control. Playing in the backyard of their home, he was spooning different kinds of insects into Mason jars, hoping they would fight. "They won't fight," Newt observes, "unless you keep shaking the jar. And that's what Frank was doing, shaking, shaking the jar." The mirror to this description occurs near the end of the novel, after the world as we know it has been destroyed accidentally—an accident made possible by the chunk of *ice-nine* that Franklin had given to the ruler of San Lorenzo, Miguel "Papa" Monzano. After the devastating accident, caused when an earthquake allowed Papa's piece of *ice-nine* to slip into the sea, Franklin occupies his time in much the same way as he did on the day that another product of Dr. Hoenikker's scientific brilliance was unleashed over Japan:

> [Franklin] was up to nothing new. He was watching an ant farm he had constructed. He had dug up a few surviving ants in the three-dimensional world of the ruins of Bolivar,

and he had reduced the dimensions to two by making a dirt and ant sandwich between two sheets of glass. The ants could do nothing without Frank's catching them at it and commenting upon it.

The experiment had solved in short order the mystery of how ants could survive in a waterless world. As far as I know, they were the only insects that did survive, and they did it by forming with their bodies tight balls around grains of *ice nine*. They would generate enough heat at the center to kill half their number and produce one bead of dew. The dew was drinkable. The corpses were edible.

"Eat, drink, and be merry, for tomorrow we die," I said to Frank and his tiny cannibals.

Though Franklin claims to be playing scientist in this little experiment, one doubts it in light of his earlier activity, described by the narrator as his playing "Beelzebub of bugs in Mason jars." What that reference suggests is that Frank is taking on, in these scenes, the function of Beelzebub (Satan) in the fallen world—tempting, stirring up discord, malevolently influencing destinies. In effect, he is the "Adversary" to the insects' Job; and this role runs contrary to his assumed role as creator—though, significantly, not altogether contrary.

Indeed, in both of these roles, Franklin Hoenikker, like his father before him, shows a good deal of irresponsibility and, unlike his father, hypocrisy, duplicity, and even cowardice. For instance, during the time that he was creating the beautifully contrived little world in the hobby shop's basement—the world that earned him the undying admiration of the shop's owner—he was also doing something else under Jack's roof: "I was screwing Jack's wife every day," he tells the narrator. "That's how come I fell asleep all the time in high school. That's how come I never achieved my full potential." Likewise, his hypocrisy and irresponsibility show as scientific minister on San Lorenzo. As noted earlier, his primary claim to fame there is founded both upon his own technical skills and his blood relationship to one of the famed inventors of the atomic bomb. As such, the appeal of this "narrow-shouldered, fox-faced, immature young man" of twenty-six to the military dictator of San Lorenzo is, beyond public relations, much like the appeal that his absent-minded father had to the American military: the ability to provide technical know-how in the national quest for global political dominance.

Indeed, until Franklin's arrival on San Lorenzo, the people of the poor island-nation had maintained their courage and their will to live in the face of overwhelming adversity, by means of a game. This game, a diverting and openly contrived ideological battle that well represents what Vonnegut considers here the saving power of lies, pitted an outlawed religious prophet, Bokonon, against the legitimate and dictatorial powers of the state. In its way, this seeming struggle is subtly in keeping with the activities of the industrialized world insofar as both actively, even playfully, engage in conceptual invention, and pursue geneses of sorts. However, whereas wealthy, scientifically advanced, and politically ambitious America measures its progress in material, technological, and political achievement, poor, backward, and politically inconsequential San Lorenzo sees fit to move backward with regard to the history of human thought, conceptually back to a time when the struggle between religious freedom and repressive government made for a black-and-white world in which the average person lives out his or her poor existence and then dies. In effect, San Lorenzo has found it necessary to move away from knowledge (science) and towards myth in both senses of that term—as lie and as sacred story.

This dual view of myth is well illustrated in the teachings of Bokonon, many of which are concerned with sacred etiology though reflecting his own peculiar—and openly mendacious—view of the Judeo-Christian etiological myth. His announced intent in revising the primal account in Genesis is to give hope to the poor, to allow the world as it is to make better sense to them (myth as causal explanation), and to save them from suicidal despair through the power of lies (myth in the colloquial sense). Bokonon announces these aims in one of his sacred songs, known as *Calypsos:*

> I wanted all things
> To seem to make some sense,
> So we all could be happy, yes,
> Instead of tense.
> And I made up lies
> So that they all fit nice,
> And I made this sad world
> A par-a-dise.

This bit of doggerel neatly sums up Bokonon's chief purposes while openly admitting even to its adherents that what he tells them are lies. Hence, his followers are expected not only to believe the lies but to become participants in their own deception.

One of the chief ways in which this scheme is carried out is through myth, in this case a self-consciously invented story devised to account for why things are as they are in this world. Rather than to invent one in its entirety, though, Bokonon chooses to revise the Genesis myth itself, detailing in this case the initial encounter between God and his best creation, man:

> In the beginning, God created the earth, and He looked upon it in His cosmic loneliness.
>
> And God said, "Let Us make living creatures out of mud, so the mud can see what We have done." And God created every living creature that now moveth, and one was man. Mud as man alone could speak. God leaned close as mud as man sat up, looked around, and spoke. Man blinked. "What is the *purpose* of all this?" he asked politely.
>
> "Everything must have a purpose?" asked God.
>
> "Certainly," said man.
>
> "Then I leave it to you to think of one for all this," said God.
>
> And He went away.

The effect of this humorously revised narrative is to reorder the priorities reflected in the original biblical account. In Genesis (and in full-blown fictional retelling of it, as in *Paradise Lost*), the specific question of human "purpose" need not be addressed, for it is a given. Life there is a "gift," and, along with this generalized gift, human beings are further given sophisticated attributes, such as the ability to speak, to reason, and to choose between right and wrong. Through the misuse of all these intellectual attributes, humankind loses part of the gift (for example, immortality, the carefree Edenic life) and spends the rest of his or her natural life working, fighting for survival in a world that is "fallen" and, therefore, often hostile. To a large extent, Bokonon's revised account makes greater sense, for it does not present the sad and tantalizing prospect of a "golden age" prior to the hard life that now exists. Rather, his narrative shows man as the one who has always been responsible for giving life meaning, lacking inherent meaning as it does, and so the possibility of happiness exists in his world if only we give life the "right" meanings. Inventiveness thus replaces worship as a means of deriving a sense of purpose in this life, and such imagined meaning is what Vonnegut believes even traditional organized religions have to offer to their congregations. As he told the graduating class of Hobart and William Smith Colleges in 1974, religion is a way to allow a person to enter an artificial extended family, and, thus, "it is a way to fight loneliness. Any time I see a person fleeing from reason into religion, I think to myself, There goes a person who simply cannot stand being so goddamned lonely anymore."

Thus, the forms of invention (genesis) to which the people of San Lorenzo subscribe are comparable to those of the civilized world. Whereas the primitive society is concerned with conceptual reinvention, the sophisticated world of America is concerned with technological invention and progress. Both, however, believe that their very survival is dependent upon such designs; and, therefore, both make for optimism in their respective circumstances.

Nevertheless, despite the fact that they have coexisted for years, each subscribing to its own comforting illusion, Vonnegut also shows in *Cat's Cradle* that illusions are good and useful only to the point where no one is harmed by another's inventions. Such has been the case on San Lorenzo, where the contrived struggle between the repressive government and the outlawed religion amounted to a diverting game in which theatrical threats were continually made to keep up the drama, but no one was actually hurt by his or her seemingly contrary allegiances to government and religion. All of that changes when Franklin Hoenikker comes to the island, for he brings with him a seed of *ice-nine*—in effect, he brings with him the dangerous potency of the technologically advanced world. Thus he, and indirectly the military and scientific community that his father served, are responsible for the end of the world as we know it.

The immediate cause of San Lorenzo's demise is conceptual. After Franklin's arrival there, its dictator, "Papa" Monzano, is no longer content to remain a ruler in the traditional sense as director of the diverting game. Rather, he recognizes the potency of science, its political possibilities; and he wants that potency, just as the rulers of the civilized world do. Not only does he want to modernize San Lorenzo through the work of his new minister of science and progress, Franklin, but he also wants to modernize it philosophically. Hence, it comes as no surprise to learn that "Papa" Monzano now wants to kill Bokonon, *really* kill him, for the value of love and the relative meaning of life that Bokonon teaches are contrary to Monzano's political plans. On his death bed, Monzano tells the narrator, whom Franklin has persuaded to become president-designate of the island, that he must continue the pursuit of Bokonon: "He teaches the people lies. . . . Kill him and teach the people truth. . . . You and Hoenikker, you teach them science. . . . Science is magic that *works*." The world view of San Lorenzo is thereby revised; and whether it is prepared to do so or not, it is about to enter for a very brief time the sophisticated and "civilized" sphere of operations, replete with its destructive "truths" to replace its own saving lies.

In planning his rule, the narrator realizes that he cannot change the condition of the people by taking Monzano's advice, and so he decides to leave things as they are. John-Jonah also realizes something else—that

Franklin Hoenikker, who has hastily passed along to a stranger the responsibility of rule, embodies everything that is wrong with the world from which they both come. Franklin Hoenikker—like his father and, by implication, all of their ilk who pursue their own political or professional ends without so much as a thought about the human cost of those ends—is really only interested in receiving "honors and creature comforts while escaping human responsibilities." This is perhaps the only positive moral statement that the narrator makes, and it is an important one. Invention (genesis) at whatever level (social, scientific, religious, artistic), must be carried out with a sense of responsibility if it is to be beneficial; and conversely, when the burden of responsibility is overlooked (as does Felix Hoenikker) or evaded (as does Franklin) or circumvented (as do the military leaders who lust after the products of advanced technology), catastrophes result. In this regard, the destruction of the world, though apparently caused by an accident, is not really an accident at all. Instead, it is caused, in the last analysis, by a way of thinking that places politics above people, material avarice above common decency.

In a chapter of his autobiographical "collage," *Palm Sunday*, entitled "When I Lost My Innocence," Vonnegut speaks of his lifelong "religious" attachment to the products of technology, notably those found in common hardware stores. He claims that he still feels such an attachment, but that his trust in technology is not so strong as it was in his childhood. That trust, he says, was lost on the day the atomic bomb was dropped on Hiroshima, an event that "compelled me to see that a trust in technology, like all the other great religions of the world, has to do with the human soul." He goes on:

> How sick was the soul revealed by the flash at Hiroshima? And
> I deny that it was a specifically American soul. It was the soul
> of every highly industrialized nation on earth, whether at war
> or at peace. How sick was it? It was so sick that it did not want
> to live any more. What other sort of soul would create a new
> physics based on nightmares, would place into the hands of
> mere politicians a planet so "destabilized," to borrow a CIA
> term, that the briefest fit of stupidity could easily guarantee
> the end of the world?

Although he wrote these words in 1980, some seventeen years after the publication of *Cat's Cradle*, they certainly apply to what he is showing in the novel—namely the "sickness" of the modern world.

I think *Cat's Cradle* is one of Vonnegut's most important cautionary tales insofar as it is concerned with nothing less than the fate of the earth itself. Some critics of the novel have argued that Vonnegut's convictions here are not really clear, but I would argue that those convictions could not be clearer. Let us engage in inventions, let us pursue geneses by all means, but let us also do so with concern for the human implications of our activities.

ZOLTÁN ABÁDI-NAGY

Bokononism as a Structure of Ironies

An unmistakable feature of Kurt Vonnegut's creative genius is a refreshing originality in devising new ways in which to examine American culture and society. His originality is exercised in multitudinous new fashions in a highly complex satiric art. Among other things, he invented and fully elaborated two ideologies that are central and all-pervasive in two novels. One is the ironic gospel preached by what he calls "The Church of God the Utterly Indifferent" in *The Sirens of Titan*, and the other is the Bokononism of *Cat's Cradle*. The two ironic religions are constructive and destructive; they mean salvation and damnation to the ironic worlds that choose to be pivoted upon them. Both are satiric syntheses with multiple ironies condensed in them and with multiple satirical functions to perform. This is what the term "ironic religion" is intended to describe in this paper. Parallels with conventional religions are part of the game, but instead of ironically treated historical religions, we are dealing with fictitious religions, whose manifold ironic functions reflect and project the American past, present, and future. They are Vonnegut's original looks at "origins" in diagnostic and prognostic senses. The former is the retrospective look tracing the origins of the social and cultural present in the past; the latter is the prophetic warning pointing to some aspects of the present that can be origins of an apocalyptic future.

Originally published in *The Vonnegut Chronicles: Interviews and Essays*, Reed & Leeds, eds. © 1996 by Peter J. Reed and Marc Leeds. Reprinted with permission of Greenwood Publishing Group, Inc., Westport, CT. All rights reserved.

73

Bokonon's is the more elaborate ironic religion of the two with a comic cosmogony and admirably systematic ironic teachings related to man, society, and transcendence. Vonnegut markets the whole thing with the bargain gift of his original terminology. The cult founder's secret pact with the dictator of San Lorenzo, the Caribbean locale of the novel, makes Bokononism an outlawed religion, reckoning that anything outlawed and persecuted attracts more followers. It is a tragicomic social game made much more intricate by Bokonon's gospel. A tough nut to crack, his new religion is rendered even tougher for the critic to interpret when the founder himself seems to crush that nut by the deceptively self-discrediting statement on the title page of *The First Book of Bokonon:* "Don't be a fool! Close this book at once! It is nothing but *Foma!*" "*Foma*, of course, are lies," the narrator explains. According to a more accurate definition, *foma* are "harmless untruths." For those to whom this doubly ironic negation is still beautifully simple—some aspects of reality negated in Bokononism, then Bokononism negated by its founder—there is Vonnegut's own ironic disclaimer at the head of the novel turning it into a book of triply ironic negation: "Nothing in this book is true." And this time not just the religion of lies is meant, but Vonnegut's whole novel with the implication that Bokonon's warning about his religious truths being untruths is itself an untruth.

Cat's Cradle's Bokononism unfolds parallel with the plot so the obvious way to interpret it is to confront it with the plot. After all, it is on the one hand a reaction against San Lorenzan social conditions, but on the other hand its social relevance undergoes the crucial test of the apocalyptic annihilation of the same society. When correlated with San Lorenzan social developments, Bokononism appears to be a subtle interpenetration of five ironic layers each representing a cardinal constituent of Vonnegut's satire:

1. the ironic layer of belied truths;
2. the ironic layer of true lies;
3. the layer of ironic fatalism;
4. the ironic layer burlesquing conventional religions;
5. the ironic layer of self-invalidating Bokononist contradictions.

The first layer is the bedrock of Vonnegut's innermost historically and sorely tried but basically unshaken belief in the sanctity of man. Inviolable convictions violated by history, time-honored truths slighted in our time. San Lorenzan history *is* an insult to humanitarian principles, something that causes Vonnegut to introduce them in bitter irony as *foma*. Bokononist beliefs in the sanctity of man are not allowed to shape San Lorenzan history which slights and belies these truths thus indirectly requalifying them as untruths. So let them be untruths—*foma*—Vonnegut suggests ironically. Central to the layer of belied truths is the Bokononist conviction that only man is sacred, "not even God." And as man is sacred, the *sin-wat* "who wants all of somebody's love" is a wicked person since "Bokonon tells us it is very wrong not to love everyone exactly the same." The true Bokononist vision is "of the unity in every second of all time and all wandering mankind, all wandering womankind, all wandering children." In other words, we are urged to think in terms of all time and all mankind. The comic Bokononist foot ceremony, *boko-maru*, is an exercise in this; it is a ritual of "the mingling of awarenesses." Besides being based on the sanctity of man, Bokononism is also tailored to less imposing realities of human existence. Disappointment and pain are taken into consideration as part and parcel of human life, as are "the shortness of life and the longness of eternity." The founder of Bokononism reports his "avocation" as "being alive" and his "principal occupation" as "being dead."

The ironic layer of true lies differs from that of belied truths in the function it performs in the ironic structure called Bokononism. In a sense, when the novel is viewed from outside (when viewed as authorial messages), both types of "untruths" are truths, of course. The layer of what we called belied truths—some of Bokonon's *foma*—are Vonnegut's set of human norms applied to a dehumanized world and found to be violated, dead, and absent. On another level, Vonnegut is exploring the very essence of that dehumanized reality, providing the reader with a sarcastic anatomy of what *is* present in that world. So some of Bokonon's *foma* are Vonnegut's diagnoses concerning the negativity of San Lorenzo. While in the realm of belied truths Vonnegut's irony aims at absent positivity, in the true "lies" of Bokononism prevailing negativity is rebuked. The very existence of Bokononism is a scornful judgment passed on a bloodsucking, ridiculously corrupt dictatorship. "Well, when it became evident that no governmental or economic reform was going to make the people much less miserable, religion became the one real instrument of hope. Truth was the enemy of the people, because the truth was so terrible, so Bokonon made it his business to provide the people with better and better lies."

But some of those lies are too good to be lies. Some of them *are harmful* if not subversive social *truths* ironically masked as harmless untruths. We must put it out of our mind that Bokonon deceptively calls them "lies" since it is easy to see them as sheer, sober social criticism. That is why this layer of irony is called that of "true 'lies.'" Bokonon's strategy in presenting appalling social truths is the old ironic one that says, "Don't listen to me! I'm a liar." By using this simple device, by disguising truths as untruths, he can be as outspoken as he wants to. Some examples: "Pay no attention to Caesar. Caesar doesn't have the slightest idea what's *really* going on"; "good societies could be built only by pitting good against evil." This makes it possible for Vonnegut to rage at twentieth-century madnesses of all kinds. Here is Bokonon's utopia: "Let us start our Republic with a chain of drug stores, a chain of grocery stores, a chain of gas chambers, and a national game. After that, we can write our Constitution."

The third layer of irony is that of ironic fatalism. A recurring idea in *Cat's Cradle* is that there was no other course for events to take. "Bokononists believe that humanity is organized into teams, teams that do God's will without ever discovering what they are doing. Such a team is called a *karass*." A *karass* has nothing to do with national, institutional, occupational, familial, and class communities. In a karass, lives are "tangled up" with each other "for no very logical reasons." The pivot of a *karass* is a *wampeter:* "Whatever it is, the members of its *karass* revolve about it in the majestic chaos of a spiral nebula." The orbits are "spiritual orbits, naturally." The *wampeter* of the novel's *karass*, the novel's hub about which the characters revolve, is *ice-nine*. Actually, there is a term in Bokononist vocabulary, *Zah-mah-ki-bo*, meaning "fate—inevitable destiny."

As for the whys of Bokonon's fatalism, Vonnegut interspersed the novel with answers. The most comprehensive one is expressed in Bokonon's closing remark implying that the history of San Lorenzo is that of "human stupidity." Vonnegut's Bokononist fatalism is an ironic pose condemnatory of man who instead of drawing a lesson from history, is stupid enough to repeat the same dreadful mistakes that invite devastation. This hopelessness is to a great extent occasioned by science. *Cat's Cradle* lashes out at human stupidity and brazen dictatorships, but the irresponsibility of science is also one of the main targets. What San Lorenzo rates from progress is the electric guitar and world-freezing *ice-nine*.

The fourth fold of Bokonon's fivefold ironic religion is itself twofold: a direct satirical attack launched against Christian dogma and an indirect parody of the origin of religions in general. The former is the philosophical; the latter is the social side to the same coin. The Bokononism of *Cat's Cradle* is, in a way, a descendant of the Church of God the Utterly Indifferent, Vonnegut's other ironic religion in *The Sirens of Titan,* in that he allows for the existence of a God almighty only to cast God's indifference, even cynicism into God's teeth. When the apocalypse comes and "the moist green earth" is frozen into a "blue white pearl" in no time, Bokonon paints this on the arch of the palace gate, "the only man-made form untouched":

And if, on that sad day, you want to scold our God,
Why Go right ahead and scold Him.
He'll just smile and nod.

It is exactly this sentiment that solidifies in the most fundamental doctrine enunciated by Bokonon,

. . . a really good religion
Is a form of treason.

Since Bokononism is declared to be an "untruth" by its own inventor, it is no exaggeration to infer that the novel extends the doctrine symbolically to all religions. And this *is* the Bokononist idea, no mistake. As one of the followers, Dr. von Koenigswald puts it, "all religions, including Bokononism, are nothing but lies." But we propose that the new religion itself is more than a lie, it is treason, too.

The irony afforded by Bokononism as a parody of the rise of religions is indirect but richer and more refined than in *The Sirens of Titan* and enhances Vonnegut's social satire. Religions are generally considered to have originated as primitive man's attempt to codify his dependence on transcendental powers believed to be determinative of his fate and also as an attempt to influence those powers. Opposed to all this is Bokonon's attitude that transcendental forces are disinterested in man; there is no way to communicate with them and no way to influence them. A predominant feature of religions is that they use *fantasy* to minister to needs unappeasable in the world of reality. Bokononism also rests on the recognition that certain needs are not answered but these are needs that traditional religions do expect social reality to appease and where Bokonon has no answers—fantastic or otherwise.

The narrator of the novel has a clear vision of what really good news would be for the island in contrast to all the political and religious histrionics: "There would have to be plenty of good things for all to eat . . . nice places for all to live, and good schools and good health and good times for all, and work for all who wanted it." These, he adds helplessly, were things "Bokonon and I were in no position to provide." So Bokonon's ironic religion glosses the truth rather than reveals it, but the emphasis on the necessity of untruths to gloss over truths implies a highly revealing irony burlesquing the function that traditional religions performed in human history when state and religion became entwined. Bokononism is an opiate, its persecution is a secret arrangement between its inventor and the dictator of the island to divert San Lorenzans' attention from a sordid reality.

Bokononism is invalidated not only by its founder who defined it as *foma* and warns that "he would never take his own advice, because he knew it was worthless," but also by those contradictions that Vonnegut builds into the new faith. It is built-in vulnerability, the fifth fold of the fivefold irony, something that undermines Bokononism. When all is said and done, or to put it more appropriately, when all Bokononist teachings are said and the apocalyptic deed with *ice-nine* is done, and the earth is frozen up into an iceball, Bokonon's "harmless untruths" prove to be not so harmless after all. The intentional and refined deception of San Lorenzans has been devised and executed too well: the religious game has distracted the people's attention from the most essential social developments too well. The general social teaching, "pay no attention to Caesar," is subversive and socially activizing on one level, but it is vague and worse, it is ambiguous in that it can be read as an encouragement to turn away from social problems and not pay attention to what is going on; it may be just another Bokononist distraction. Besides human stupidity and irresponsible science, the social passivity of depoliticized San Lorenzans is one of the factors culminating in global catastrophe. By depoliticizing San Lorenzo, Bokonon commits treason. He is a traitor to San Lorenzans because he delivers them as helpless prey to uncontrolled irresponsibility. Bokononist fatalism is not only justified but also undercut by events since Vonnegut's counterpointing plot demonstrates that nothing happened because it *had to*. The tragic conclusion to the island's history was shaped under the San Lorenzans' nose by irresponsible people, who could just as easily have done the very opposite of what they did. The gospel of Bokononist "harmless untruths" is inclusive of noble ideas and sane social criticism, but their ironic Messiah discredits himself with his method of distraction, thereby becoming a *wrang-wrang*, a person "who steers people away from a line of speculation by reducing that line, with the example of the *wrang-wrang*'s own life, to an absurdity." Bokonon steers San Lorenzo away from a grim social reality by reducing it, with the example of his own life, to an absurdity. While he believed this act to be harmless, he inflicted irreparable harm, a cataclysm that reduces Bokononism to an absurdity on this level of the fivefold irony. Bokononism cancels itself.

The self-discrediting fivefold irony of Vonnegut's Bokononism illustrates the structure of his ironies: "the cruel paradox of Bokononist thought, the heartbreaking necessity of lying about reality, and the heartbreaking impossibility of lying about it."

JEROME KLINKOWITZ

Mother Night, Cat's Cradle,
and the Crimes of Our Time

Kurt Vonnegut, Jr., through six novels and more than forty stories, has crafted for his readers an exceedingly mad world. He holds his own with the black humorists, matching Yossarians with Howard Campbells, Guy Grands with Eliot Rosewaters, and Sebastian Dangerfields with Malachi Constants. But unlike Joseph Heller, Vonnegut is prolific, tracing his vision through many different human contexts. He surpasses Terry Southern by striking all limits from human absurdity: destruction by nuclear fission is for Vonnegut the most passé of apocalypses. Moreover, he teases us with a Mod Yoknapatawpha County; "Frank Wirtanen" and "Bernard B. O'Hare" (originally characters in his third novel, *Mother Night*) and others appear again and again, always (as befits the modern county) in a maddening metamorphosis of roles. Favorite cities such as "Rosewater, Indiana" and "Ilium, New York" are storehouses for the paraphernalia of middle-class life which so delight Vonnegut, whose religion is one of cultural value rather than geographical place. But unlike Southern and Bruce Jay Friedman, who mock such culture in the sociosatiric mode of Evelyn Waugh (Southern scripted *The Loved One* for the movies), Vonnegut uses his roots more like John Barth uses Maryland: interest lies beneath the surface, and the surface itself is constantly changing. Vonnegut, in short, demands independent investigation. One finds at the end of Vonnegut's vision a "fine madness" indeed, but a madness at the

From *Critical Essays on Kurt Vonnegut* edited by Robert Merrill. © 1990 by Robert Merrill.

same time more clinical and more cosmic than found in conventional black humor—or, indeed, nearly anywhere else.

Perhaps a reason for the long critical neglect of Kurt Vonnegut is that his vision is superficially akin to that of Orwell, Huxley, and others who have written dolefully of the mechanical millennium to come. His first novel, *Player Piano*, warns of the familiar *Brave New World* future, while the much-praised title story of *Welcome to the Monkey House*, with its Ethical Suicide Parlors and waning sentimental romanticism, recalls Evelyn Waugh's alternatives of "Love Among the Ruins" and *Scott-King's Modern Europe*. Karen and Charles Wood have shown how Vonnegut's material moves beyond the bounds of science fiction, the label used so long to restrain his recognition. But to justify a reputation for Vonnegut, one must also recognize the essential elements in his technique which surpass the efforts of a black humorist like Terry Southern, and understand the complexity of his vision.

Both technique and theme are well represented by two novels published well into his career: *Mother Night* and *Cat's Cradle*. In *Mother Night*, Vonnegut's panorama of the Nazi world is a black humorist's dream: all the stuff of middle-class life is present, but the people in the picture are not G. E. flaks or Indiana brewers but rather honest-to-goodness "criminals against humanity." Rudolph Hoess, Heinrich Himmler, and Adolf Eichmann himself (the book was published in 1962 when Eichmann was in the news) are presented to the reader, who gasps and giggles like a tourist on a Beverly Hills sightseeing bus. And Vonnegut exploits our fascination by giving us these men in their utter banality. This, of course, is orthodox black-humor technique, and signals Vonnegut's departure from the standard humanistic approach to the subject of the rise and fall of the Third Reich: in all of William L. Shirer's heavily documented book there is not a single Ping-Pong tournament, which is one of the things Vonnegut gives us. But the absurdity of this world yields more than an affectatious glimpse behind the scenes, as Terry Southern offers in *Dr. Strangelove*. Life in Vonnegut's Nazi realm is more properly absurd: the hero, Howard W. Campbell, Jr., acts out an Ionesco drama as he broadcasts vital secrets to the Allies in coded gestures he cannot understand. Vonnegut toys with ironic *déjà-vu* as the documents of 1960's "White Christian Minutemen" are recognized as crafted a generation earlier by Howard Campbell when in the service of the Nazis. The morbid dance of life reaches its black-humor climax when no less than the neo-Nazi journalist Rev. Doctor Lionel Jason David Jones, D.D.S., D.D., the unfrocked Paulist Father Patrick Keeley, Robert Sterling Wilson (the "Black Fuehrer of Harlem"), Russian agent Iona Potapov, Legion Post Americanism Chairman, Lt. Bernard B. O'Hare, O.S.S. spy-maker Col. Frank Wirtanen, and various

FBI agents and sundry nineteen-year-old Minutemen from New Jersey battle over the body and soul of Vonnegut's hero.

Neither does Vonnegut's absurd humor stop here. Terry Southern's *The Magic Christian* is equal in single absurdities; Vonnegut surpasses him by working in triplets. Campbell's wartime buddy Heinz Schildknecht is not merely comically robbed of his dearer-than-life motorcycle; on the second turn Heinz shows up as a gardener for a rich expatriate Nazi in Ireland, courting fame as an authority on the death of Hilter ("Hello out there, Heinz. . . . what were you doing in Hitler's bunker—looking for your motorcycle and your best friend?"), and on the third is revealed to have been a secret Israeli agent all the time, gathering evidence for Campbell's prosecution. Vonnegut's is a spiraling, madly rebounding absurdity. A hangman's noose suggestively placed in Campbell's apartment by the American Legion is not merely laughed at and discarded. Instead, "Resi put the noose in the ash can, where it was found the next morning by a garbageman named Lazlo Szombathy. Szombathy actually hanged himself with it—but that is another story." Double turn: Szombathy is despondent because as a refugee he is barred from practicing his profession of veterinary science. Triple turn: Szombathy is particularly despondent because he has a cure for cancer, and is ignored. Absurdity to the third power rules the entire world: not only is Campbell's dramatic work pirated and plagiarized by a looting Soviet soldier, but the best of the loot turns out to be Campbell's secret and sensitive love memoirs, which at once become the *Fanny Hill* of postwar Russia. Third turn: the soldier is caught and punished, but not for plagiarism: "'Bodovskov had begun to replenish the trunk with magic of his own,' said Wirtanen. 'The police found a two-thousand-page satire on the Red Army, written in a style distinctly un-Bodovskovian. For that un-Bodovskovian behavior, Bodovskov was shot.'" Other examples abound: Arndt Klopfer, official Reich chancellery portrait photographer, turns up in Mexico City as the country's greatest brewer. But not for long; he's really a Russian spy. We are teased with the knowledge that one of the world's greatest admirers of Lincoln's *Gettysburg Address* is Paul Joseph Goebbels. But the greatest admirer, literally brought to tears by the document, is Adolf Hitler. Triple turn: the most gleeful fan of Campbell's anti-Semitic broadcasts is Franklin Delano Roosevelt.

The triplet madness, besides being an ingenious technique, serves to introduce Vonnegut's more serious theme. George Kraft, alias Iona Potapov, becomes at one and the same time Howard Campbell's most sincere friend plus the agent who is working most seriously to engineer his exploitation, torture, and death in Moscow. Moreover (triplets again), Kraft is widely acknowledged as the best of modern artists ("surely the first man to understand the whole of modern art," according to a *Herald Tribune* review supplied by the Haifa Institute). Others besides Kraft-Potapov lead double lives. One of Campbell's Israeli prison guards is Arpad Kovacs, who spent the war as a Jewish spy among the S.S. in Germany. He boasts to Campbell:

> "I was such a pure and terrifying Aryan that they even put me in a special detachment. Its mission was to find out how the Jews always knew what the S.S. was going to do next. There was a leak somewhere, and we were out to stop it." He looked bitter and affronted, remembering it, even though he had been that leak.

Campbell himself, of course, had lived a double life for the years of World War II. He was, at the same time, *the best* Nazi radio propagandist and *the best* spy in the service of the Allies. He understands this apparently contradictory situation, even finding the clinical name for it: "'I've always known what I did. I've always been able to live with what I did. How? Through that simple and widespread boon to modern mankind—schizophrenia.'" Schizophrenia indeed seems the proper name for the madness devouring Vonnegut's world. When federal agents raid the basement quarters of the White Christian Minutemen, an incredulous G-man wonders how the professedly anti-Catholic and anti-Negro Reverend Jones can have as his two most loyal cohorts Father Patrick Keeley and Robert Sterling Wilson, the black Fuehrer of Harlem, the latter who announces plans for killing all whites. Campbell's explanation is worth seeing at length:

> I have never seen a more sublime demonstration of the totalitarian mind, a mind which might be likened unto a system of gears whose teeth have been filed off at random. Such a snaggle-toothed thought machine, driven by a standard or even a substandard libido, whirls with the jerky, noisy, gaudy pointlessness of a cuckoo clock in Hell.
>
> The boss G-man concluded wrongly that there were no teeth on the gears in the mind of Jones. "You're completely crazy," he said.
>
> Jones wasn't completely crazy. The dismaying thing about the classic totalitarian mind is that any given gear, though mutilated, will have at its circumference unbroken sequences of teeth that are immaculately maintained, that are exquisitely machined.
>
> Hence the cuckoo clock in Hell—keeping perfect

time for eight minutes and thirty-three seconds, jumping ahead fourteen minutes, keeping perfect time for six seconds, jumping ahead two seconds, keeping perfect time for two hours and one second, then jumping ahead a year.

The missing teeth, of course, are simple, obvious truths, truths available and comprehensible even to ten-year-olds, in most cases.

The willful filing off of gear teeth, the willful doing without certain obvious pieces of information—

That was how a household as contradictory as one composed of Jones, Father Keeley, Vice-Bundesfuehrer Krapptauer, and the Black Fuehrer could exist in relative harmony—

That was how my father-in-law could contain in one mind an indifference toward slave women and love for a blue vase—

That was how Rudolf Hoess, Commandant of Auschwitz, could alternate over the loudspeakers of Auschwitz great music and calls for corpse-carriers—

That was how Nazi Germany could sense no important differences between civilization and hydrophobia—

That is the closest I can come to explaining the legions, the nations of lunatics I've seen in my time. And for me to attempt such a mechanical explanation is perhaps a reflection of the father whose son I was. Am. When I pause to think about it, which is rarely, I am, after all, the son of an engineer.

The key to Vonnegut's vision, however, is not merely this clinical diagnosis of the illness of an age. The traditional desire to maintain the integrity of self in the face of a too chaotic world has always been a schizophrenia of sorts. Faced with the pressures of Nazi Germany, Campbell takes a solace not unusual in Western culture: he retreats first to art, and then to love. Crucial to this solace is that man have a self to flee to, a self which cannot be reached and abused by others. Like any fictive artist of the ages, Campbell offers "lies told for the sake of artistic effect." His self knows that on their deepest level his fictions are "the most beguiling forms of truth," but the surface is all art. Hence in the thirties, when Hilter's war machine is building, Campbell is the apparent escapist, scripting "medieval romances about as political as chocolate *éclairs*." When forced as a spy into the service of the Nazis, he finds refuge in parody and satire. "I had hoped, as a broadcaster, to be merely ludicrous." Campbell's second traditional refuge is that of love, where the escapist and even schizoid tendencies are more marked. From the terrors of daily social existence Vonnegut's hero flees to *Das Reich der Zwei*. "It was going to show how a pair of lovers in a world gone mad could survive by being loyal only to a nation composed of themselves—a nation of two." Its geography, he admits, "didn't go much beyond the bounds of our great double bed." In both artistic and emotional form, Campbell's theme becomes "Reflections on Not Participating in Current Events," and he honestly states that "My narcotic was what had got me through the war; it was an ability to let my emotions be stirred by only one thing—my love for Helga." Art and love are two traditional ways of coping with the chaos of the outside world. Come what may, the self should be inviolate, and it is here that Campbell places his hope.

Vonnegut's point, however, is that in this modern world the self can indeed be violated, and is so at every turn. Campbell's love is the first casualty. Helga is captured on the Russian front, but this alone is no more than a challenge to Campbell's romantic imagination. He will nurture his grief and celebrate his melancholy. Modern espionage, however, not only mocks his grief, but uses him to do the mocking.

> This news, that I had broadcast the coded announcement of my Helga's disappearance, broadcast it without even knowing what I was doing, somehow upset me more than anything in the whole adventure. It upsets me even now. Why, I don't know.
>
> It represented, I suppose, a wider separation of my several selves than even I can bear to think about.
>
> At that climactic moment in my life, when I had to suppose that my Helga was dead, I would have liked to mourn as an agonized soul, indivisible. But no. One part of me told the world of the tragedy in code. The rest of me did not even know that the announcement was being made.

Neither will history let his love rest. The intimate diary of his life with Helga is plagiarized and made into pornography, complete with fourteen plates in lifelike color. "That's how I feel right now," Campbell admits, "like a pig that's been taken apart, who's had experts find a use for every part. By God—I think they even found a use for my squeal."

Art is no safer a refuge. Campbell had hoped, as a propagandist, to be satirically ludicrous—on the one hand, it would cover his self-respect, while on the other it might indeed, by *reductio ad absurdum*, bring down the

Nazi regime in gales of laughter. "But this is a hard world to be ludicrous in," Campbell learns, "with so many human beings so reluctant to laugh, so incapable of thought, so eager to believe and snarl and hate. So many people wanted to believe me!" At the end of the war Campbell is confronted with the awful possibility that his intended satire may have in fact prolonged the war. His high-ranking father-in-law confides, "'I realized that almost all the ideas that I hold now, that make me unashamed of anything I may have felt or done as a Nazi, came not from Hilter, not from Goebbels, not from Himmler—but from you.' He took my hand. 'You alone kept me from concluding that Germany had gone insane.'" Campbell reflects on the fate of his several selves: "The part of me that wanted to tell the truth got turned into an expert liar! The lover in me got turned into a pornographer! The artist in me got turned into an ugliness such as the world has rarely seen before." Throughout the book Campbell has been priding himself on his integrity. He has devoted a full chapter to the lunatic Reverend Doctor Jones "in order to contrast with myself a race-baiter who is ignorant and insane. I am neither ignorant nor insane." Unlike the trite and banal Eichmann, Campbell knew right from wrong, "the only advantage" being "that I can sometimes laugh when the Eichmanns can see nothing funny." But the self, Campbell finally learns, offers no refuge. Art and love are impossibilities, themselves easily manipulated into cruel absurdities. The self is not inviolate; there is no place to hide.

To this point Vonnegut is on firm if traditional ground. Howard Campbell has in these terms learned no more than Winston Smith did in *1984*, and Vonnegut's vision seems one with Wylie Sypher's: the loss of the self in modern art and literature (and love) is exactly what has happened to our hero. Vonnegut, however, has more to say. His vision extends backward as well as to the fore. How has the modern world come to be such a chamber of horrors? Where lies the cause for the loss of the self? Vonnegut answers that the very cause may be found in the traditional notion of the inviolate self. Because men have abandoned all else and have selfishly fled to their selves as the romantic center of the universe, when the self collapses, everything, quite literally, is lost. This is what Vonnegut's character finally recognizes. Campbell, after all, does not follow through on his offer to surrender to the Israelis and accept punishment for his crimes against humanity. At the last moment, on the eve of his trial, when in fact conclusive evidence for his innocence has come with the day's mail, he makes his decision: "I think that tonight is the night *I* will hang Howard W. Campbell, Jr., for crimes against *himself* [italics added]. In spite of all humanistic arguments to the contrary, Campbell sees the absurd use that he has made of his self, and the evil which has come of it. Vonnegut's indictment, in his own signed head-note to the story, is no less severe: "This book is rededicated to Howard W. Campbell, Jr., a man who served evil too openly and good too secretly, the crime of his times."

Mother Night remains, to date, Vonnegut's only book with an explicitly stated moral: "We are what we pretend to be, so we must be careful about what we pretend to be." The author has been clear in his condemnations: art and love are selfish, false escapes. But if one is "careful," can there be a valid pretense? *Cat's Cradle*, Vonnegut's next novel, presents a tempting program. Its opening disclaimer is also an imperative: "Nothing in this book is true. / Live by the *foma* that make you brave and kind and healthy and happy." "Foma" are the magic elements, correcting the rampant cowardices, cruelties, sicknesses, and sadnesses of *Mother Night*. A comparison to the "soma" of *Brave New World* is alarming but intentionally immediate: sounding similar, working similar, Vonnegut dares to confront us with something too good to believe: a pain pill for the ills of the world.

Mother Night presents the destructive pretenses that make modern life a nightmare; *Cat's Cradle*, however, offers *foma* as "*harmless* untruths" [italics added]. They are the key elements in the book's religion, Bokononism. Why is religion a valid pretense, whereas love and art are not? The answer lies with the peculiar state of modern man, and with his need for a unique religion. Other modern novelists, particularly Saul Bellow, have written of the "romantic over-valuation of the Self" which most terrifyingly makes "each of us . . . responsible for his own salvation." But Vonnegut's Bokononism is a religion after alienation, for it seeks a way for man to be comfortable in a world he no longer wishes to admit is his own. The "lies" of this particular religion are purgative, restoring man's happiness, balance, and comfort. Bokononism reorders our notion of the finite world so that we may accept it, rather than simply rebel against it in fruitless anger. It is the first step toward accommodating oneself to the schizophrenic reality given full treatment in *Slaughterhouse-Five*.

The danger that Vonnegut actively courts in *Cat's Cradle* is religion's becoming an opiate. His writer-narrator is told that "When a man becomes a writer . . . he takes on a sacred obligation to produce beauty and enlightenment and comfort at top speed." The writer accepts the methodology of religion by seeking the ultimate meaning of things. Bokononism cooperates by teaching that "humanity is organized into teams, teams that do God's Will without ever discovering what they are doing. Such a team is called a *karass*." Therefore the writer tries to include in his book "as many members of my *karass* as possible," and "to examine strong hints as to what on Earth we, collectively, have been up to." If one sought the reason for the madly twisted life of Howard W. Campbell, Jr., the answer might be found in *Cat's Cradle*: "'If you find your life tangled with somebody else's life for no very logical

reason,' writes Bokonon, 'that person may be a member of your *karass*.'"
Hence the writer studies the affairs of Dr. Felix Hoenikker, for, as his memo-
rial states, "THE IMPORTANCE OF THIS ONE MAN IN THE HISTORY OF
MANKIND IS INCALCULABLE."

Bokononism follows tradition in its eschatological imperative; it
departs, however, when at the same time it calls any such search absurd:

> "In the beginning, God created the earth, and he looked
> upon it in His cosmic loneliness.
>
> "And God said, 'Let Us make living creatures out of mud, so
> the mud can see what We have done.' And God created every
> living creature that now moveth, and one was man. Mud as man
> alone could speak. God leaned close as man sat up, looked
> around, and spoke. Man blinked. 'What is the *purpose* of all this?'
> he asked politely.
>
> "'Everything must have a purpose?' asked God.
>
> "'Certainly,' said man.
>
> "'Then I leave it to you to think of one for all this,' said God.
> And He went away."

The first axiom of this religion, then, is that if there is to be an ultimate
meaning for things, it is up to man's art to find it. But as we know from
Mother Night, his art can be selfish and escapist. Vonnegut's writer is at one
point mistaken for a drug salesman, and is then encouraged to write a book
for "people who are dying or in terrible pain." The writer suggests an improvisation on the Twenty-Third Psalm, and is told "Bokonon tried to overhaul
it" but "found out that he couldn't change a word."

Whether religion is an opiate, and whether the "consolations of
literature" are little more than the wares of drug salesmen, must be decided
by comparison with men's other eschatological artifices. For consolation
Felix Hoenikker played games: one resulted in the chance invention of the
atom bomb, another in the creation of *ice-nine*. His daughter Angela's "one
escape" is playing weirdly authentic blues clarinet, but "such music from
such a woman could only be a case of schizophrenia or demonic possession,"
and from the lessons of *Mother Night* must be dismissed. Little Newt paints,
but his works appear "sticky nets of human futility hung up on a moonless
night to dry." Art lies, we are told again. Recalling the game of cat's cradle
his father played with him, Newt comments:

> "No wonder kids grow up crazy. A cat's cradle is nothing but
> a bunch of X's between somebody's hands, and little kids look and

look at all those X's . . ."
    "And?"
    "No damn cat, and no damn cradle."

Newt is objecting that the cat's cradle has excluded the real, or the finite. The necessary artifice is one which will handle the finite on its own terms, without recourse to "lies." Finite existence in San Lorenzo is depressingly futile, and so "the religion became the one instrument of hope." McCabe and Bokonon, founders of the Republic, "did not succeed in raising what is generally thought of as the standard of living," the writer is told. "The truth was that life was as short and brutish and mean as ever." But Vonnegut's world cannot remain Hobbesian; Bokononism provides a system whereby "people didn't have to pay as much attention to the awful truth. As the living legend of the cruel tyrant in the city and the gentle holy man in the jungle grew, so, too, did the happiness of the people grow. They were all employed full time as actors in a play they understood, that any human being anywhere could understand and applaud." The writer learns that "for the joy of the people, Bokonon was always to be chased, was never to be caught." Vonnegut speaks elsewhere in *Cat's Cradle* of "the brainless ecstasy of a volunteer fireman," anticipating the role Eliot Rosewater will find most comfortable in *God Bless You, Mr. Rosewater*. Here the idealized, sustained game is part of a "dynamic tension" which argues that "good societies could be built only by pitting good against evil, and by keeping the tension between the two high at all times." Not surprisingly, we learn that as a student in Episcopal schools Bokonon was "more interested in ritual than most."

Vonnegut's religion is a type unto itself: heretical, in fact, but to a particular purpose. Within the situation of San Lorenzo one finds both tragic and comic possibilities; it is the daily life which is tragic, however, while its religion is comic. Nathan Scott, in relating the comic to the religious, has remarked that only comedy can tell us "the whole truth." When the whole truth is not told, when a salient element of reality is denied concrete existence, we have the heresy of Gnosticism, which posits "a God unknowable by nature . . . and utterly incommensurable with the created order." Vonnegut's impetus is in the opposite direction. The finite is granted a real existence, rather than being an imperfect shadow of some higher ideal. Pushed far enough, such doctrine would constitute the heresy of Manicheanism. The value of Bokononism, however, is that it makes possible what Scott terms the "cosmic *katharsis*," which involves "such a restoration of our confidence in the realm of finitude as enables us to see the daily occasions of our earth-bound career as being not irrelevant inconveniences but as possible roads into what is ultimately significant in life." A

Gnostic approach to the evils of San Lorenzo would indeed encourage a flight from "meaningless" finitude. But such flight would be hopeless, as Vonnegut demonstrated in *Mother Night*. Modern man, romantically placed at the center of the universe and responsible for his own salvation, cannot flee from evil, even into himself; for in himself he will find only evil's deepest source. Vonnegut's alternative in Bokononism is a recognition of the finite for what it is: an external repository of certain elements, some of which may be evil but none of which are egocentrically identified with Man. Wylie Sypher, whose discussion of the loss of the self coincides with the theme of *Mother Night*, makes a plea for a new fiction which is answered in *Cat's Cradle*. Sypher speaks of "our need for unheroic heroism" or "anonymous humanism" which will relieve man of his untenable position as center of the universe, a position which the terrible amounts of evil wrought in the twentieth century have caused man to become alienated from his very self. Bokononism is a religion after alienation because it carefully removes evil from the self and deposits it in a finitude granted real existence, not a finitude vaguely (and Platonically) reflective of Ideal Man.

Bokononism is not an opiate, nor is it irresponsible. It is not a turning away at all, but rather an acceptance of the finite for what it is, as part of the whole truth. The single identified saint in *Cat's Cradle* is Julian Castle, who "forestalled all references to his possible saintliness by talking out of the corner of his mouth like a movie gangster." Castle heroically saves countless lives, but can also appreciate the grotesqueness of his situation; as Robert Scholes agrees, "an excess of the horrible is faced and defeated by the only friend reason can rely on in such cases: laughter." If evil is securely located in a coexisting finitude, there is no compulsive need "to concentrate on [Castle's] saintly deeds and ignore entirely the satanic things he thought and said." Bokononism is one religion which accommodates the finite. In a whimsical manner, a psalmlike "Calypso" reminds us that "We do, doodley do . . . What we must, muddily must . . . Until we bust, bodily bust." And the last rites of this curious Church simply affirm, "I loved everything I saw."

The theme of *Cat's Cradle* is repeated in Vonnegut's later work, where, perhaps because of his growing prominence, he writes more directly and even personally. To a new edition of *Mother Night* in 1966 Vonnegut added an introduction, speaking not as "editor" of the "American edition of the confessions of Howard W. Campbell, Jr.," but as an individual who has had "personal experience with Nazi monkey business." In *Slaughterhouse-Five* Vonnegut includes a great deal of autobiography and comment as the first chapter of his otherwise fictional work. Here he contrasts his anthropology courses at the University of Chicago, where he was taught that man is a benign creature, with his after-school work as a police reporter. The deliberately retrospective preface to *Welcome to the Monkey House* features the same duality; recalling his brother's adventures with a newborn son and his sister's dignified death from cancer, Vonnegut states: "And I realize now that the two main themes of my novels were stated by my siblings: 'Here I am cleaning the shit off of practically everything' and 'No pain'." When in *Slaughterhouse-Five* Vonnegut's father accuses him that "you never wrote a story with a villain in it," we need not fear that Vonnegut has been an irresponsible jokester or even a blithe optimist. Indeed, Vonnegut's public pronouncement has been that he is "a total pessimist," and has been since the experiences of Dresden, Hiroshima, and Dachau. Writing on the fall of Biafra, he admits that "joking was my response to misery that I can't do anything about," but he has also reminded us that "to weep is to make less the depth of grief." The joking in Bokononism is not a palliative: instead it is a fundamental reordering of man's values, solving the problem which has made man uncomfortable as the center of the universe. Wylie Sypher decries egocentric romanticism, and charges that it has alienated man from himself; Vonnegut begs that we still trust "the most ridiculous superstition of all: that humanity is at the center of the universe," proving that to sustain such a position "all that is required is that we become less selfish than we are." That selfishness, however, is strong enough to have spawned a heresy and determined man's expression in art. Shaping a new religion is no small achievement.

Despite their rogues' galleries of unpleasant incidents, both *Mother Night* and *Cat's Cradle* are finally optimistic works. Howard W. Campbell, Jr., commits not so many "crimes against humanity" as "crimes against himself," the latter which, once recognized, can be successfully and personally purged. *Cat's Cradle* goes a step farther by relieving man of his unbearable egocentric responsibility for the conditions of existence. Granted that the world can become absurd, and that any good life may be unliveable: at this point Vonnegut's man can responsibly bow out, having "the good manners to die," and with great composure and respectability "turn the humor back on the joker." Modern life, for all its errors, has a great clarifying power in helping man find his proper place in the universe. Rightly positioned, the Vonnegut hero can honestly say of his life, "Everything was beautiful, and nothing hurt."

PETER FREESE

Vonnegut's Invented Religions as Sense-Making Systems

The strong Puritan heritage of early American literature is still very much in evidence today. The initial religious impetus of American writing has survived the onslaught of Darwinism and psychoanalysis, the political eschatology of Marxism, and assorted philosophies of existential anguish. In diverse stages of secularization, the central plots, motifs, and images of biblical history have turned into shared elements of American fiction, and even those authors who passionately reject fundamental Christian doctrines often do so in the language of the Authorized Version. In the modern American novel, Biblical references proliferate from Ernest Hemingway's *The Sun Also Rises* to William Faulkner's *Absalom, Absalom!* and Nathaniel West's *The Day of the Locust* to James Baldwin's *Go Tell It on the Mountain* and Toni Morrison's *Song of Solomon*. Spiritual brothers of Nathaniel Hawthorne's hapless Arthur Dimmesdale play central roles in countless novels from Harold Frederick's *The Damnation of Theron Ware* and Sinclair Lewis' *Elmer Gantry* to Flannery O'Connor's *The Violent Bear It Away* and Joyce Carol Oates' *Son of the Morning*. Literary transfigurations of Jesus Christ abound from Jim Conklin, the lanky soldier with a wound in his side in Stephen Crane's *The Red Badge of Courage*, and Jim Casey, the migrant preacher killed by vigilantes in John Steinbeck's *The Grapes of Wrath*, to Joe Christmas, the sacrificial victim in William Faulkner's *Light in August*, and James Castle, the prep-school saint in J. D. Salinger's *The Catcher in the Rye*. And the Christian imagery of the apocalypse is endlessly varied from Bernard Malamud's *God's Grace* to Don DeLillo's *White Noise*.

In short, then, in a world in which, for the first time in human history, mankind can annihilate itself by means of its technological inventions, American literature is as concerned as it was in its earlier phases with probing questions about the meaning of existence, the purpose of human life, and the workings of a divine providence. But the erstwhile certainty of belief has given way to the anguish of doubt, the analogies between fictional events and their biblical models have lost their typological significance, the frequent apocalyptic visions no longer imply the promise of a new beginning to come after the end, and the literary transfigurations of Christ are more often than not used in a comical or farcical mood. More and more authors treat traditional Christianity in critical fashion, and, while some have moved toward atheism and nihilism and some have sought solace in religious systems other than Christianity, a growing number of novelists, especially in the field of science fiction, have begun to invent their own religions.

One of the most successful among these is Kurt Vonnegut, who grew up in Indianapolis, Indiana, as the son of a prominent German family. His "first American ancestor, atheistic merchant from Munster," came to the Midwest as one of the German "Forty-Eighters" and brought with him a long family tradition of *Freidenkertum*, defined by Vonnegut as "the most corrosive sort of agnosticism—or worse." Thus, Vonnegut grew up in a climate of profound scepticism, and when the *Playboy* interviewer asked him about his religious background, he answered:

> My ancestors, who came to the United States a little before the Civil war, were atheists. So I'm not rebelling against organized religion. I never had any. I learned my outrageous opinions at my mother's knee. My family had always had these.

When the young Vonnegut went to Cornell University in 1940 to study biochemistry and help advance the progress of science, when he survived the atrocious firebombing of Dresden in a subterranean meatlocker in 1945, and when, after his release from a German prison-camp, he went to Chicago to study anthropology, he found his religious skepticism reinforced by all of these experiences. There is ample evidence that his rejection of organized religion became ever more pronounced. About his study of anthropology, for example, he said in his *Paris Review* interview: "It confirmed my atheism, which was the faith of my fathers anyway. Religions were exhibited and studied as the Rube Goldberg inventions I'd always thought they were."

Vonnegut, then, is a confirmed atheist who scathingly comments on almost every organized religion from traditional Catholicism to the more recent Born-Againism. But it is this very impassioned agnostic who in novel after novel devises new religious systems and who emphatically argues in his autobiography that "we need a new religion," substantiating such a surprising claim by saying:

> An effective religion allows people to imagine from moment to moment what is going on and how they should behave. Christianity used to be like that. Our country is now jammed with human beings who say out loud that life is chaos to them, and that it doesn't seem to matter what anybody does next.

How, the puzzled reader is bound to ask, can a cynical atheist who calls the "White House prayer breakfasts . . . about as nourishing to the human spirit as potassium cyanide" devote his creative fantasy to the invention of ever new religions? And how can he, as he did in a sermon he preached in St. Clement's Episcopal Church in New York, call himself "a Christ worshiping agnostic"? The obvious conjecture that Vonnegut accepts the Christian doctrine but rejects its institutionalization is far too simple, and only a detailed investigation of his novels will lead to a more appropriate answer.

In all of his eleven novels to date, Vonnegut portrays a world on the brink of a homemade apocalypse, and in most of them he employs what he calls "science fiction of an obviously kidding sort" to put human affairs in a wider perspective, to illustrate his conviction that "there are lots of alternatives to our own society" and to provide some comic relief from the unbearable state of affairs in a world hovering on the verge of destruction. His protagonists are lonely and desperate men faced with the arbitrary atrocities of war and the heartless competition of a money-orientated capitalistic society, with the pathetic uselessness of human beings as they are replaced by ever more efficient machines, with the crumbling of human communities and the ensuing loneliness and despair, with man's ruthless destruction of the planet's ecological balance and the loss of human decency, respect, and consideration.

On the sociopolitical level, then, Vonnegut's oeuvre is a scathing indictment of America as a country that has turned the dreams of its founding fathers into the nightmares of their contemporary descendants. But on a deeper, existential level life in America turns out to be just a paradigm of human existence in general, and at the heart of the protagonists' despair is their inability to understand the cruel workings of a contingent universe that is revealed as a "nightmare of meaninglessness without end" and their resulting incapacity to detect a meaning and a purpose for their existence.

In a 1974 graduation speech Vonnegut observed that graduation speakers are usually hired "to answer the question: what is life all about." It is this very question that pervades his novels in countless variations and that he answers with his inimitable mixture of cynical pessimism, black humor, and bourgeois sentimentality, creating a contradictory crackerbarrel philosophy of life that thrives on the irritating strategy of the "unconfirmed thesis" and denies his flustered readers any satisfactory answer to the frightening riddles of existence.

In his first novel, the conventional Huxleyan dystopia *Player Piano* (1952), Vonnegut sketches a society in which "machines were doing America's work far better than Americans had ever done it." Consequently, men have become utterly superfluous and robbed of their purpose, their "feeling of being needed on earth," and their sense of human dignity. What motivates the privileged but discontented manager Paul Proteus (who not accidentally bears the name of the Greek god of change) to stage a revolution against the computer-controlled system is his need to understand "Why did it have to happen?"—an outcry defined by the narrator as "the question humanity had been asking for millenniums, the question men were seemingly born to ask." The motley revolutionary band that sets out to fight the omnipotent technocracy is indoctrinated by an unemployed reverend cum anthropologist who predicts that "things . . . are ripe for a phony Messiah." For Paul, who is willing to be that "new Messiah" and who yearns "to deal, not with society, but only with Earth as God had given it to man," the "big trouble, really" consists of "finding something to believe in," that is, of complementing his entirely rational approach to life with some emotionally satisfying belief.

Predictably, the poorly prepared revolution, which intends "that the world should be restored to the people," fails miserably. The latter-day Luddites, who have just smashed the hateful machines, immediately begin to rebuild them in the tradition of "the American tinker," and "the intemperate faith in lawless technological progress—namely, that man is on earth to create more durable and efficient images of himself, and, hence, to eliminate every justification at all for his own continued existence"—remains unchecked. It becomes painfully evident that the insurgents were just out to replace one kind of "human engineering" with another and that there is no hope that mankind will ever overcome its *Zauberlehrling* syndrome. But when the captured rebels are led to prison, one of them says: "This isn't the end, you know. . . . Nothing ever is, nothing ever will be—not even Judgment Day." It is left to the reader to grasp this concluding statement as a ray of hope against a bleak horizon of despair or to dismiss it as a cynical reference to the endlessly recurring pattern of man's self-destructive hubris.

Vonnegut's first novel shows that he not only uses apocalyptic imagery to infuse secular events with deeper meaning but also concentrates on two essentially religious questions:

1) why do things happen the way they do, and who directs life's seemingly arbitrary course; and
2) what is the purpose of human existence, and what are the values that can make it meaningful?

These questions, which ask for a sense-making structure that can explain the world and man's place in it, have remained at the core of Vonnegut's work from *Player Piano* to *Galápagos*.

In his second novel, the hilariously inventive space opera *The Sirens of Titan* (1959), the jaded playboy Malachi Constant, a latter-day Jonah, has to go through an arduous intergalactic journey of initiation before he can finally realize the value of a simple, self-sufficient existence and of disinterested love and decency. He turns out to be the plaything of Winston Niles Rumfoord, an East Coast aristocrat and fictional rendition of Franklin Delano Roosevelt, who attempts to bring about his 'New Deal' by founding a new religion and who uses Malachi as his unwilling and unknowing Messiah. Here, then, Paul Proteus' sketchily realized Ghost Shirt Society becomes the first full-fledged religious creed in Vonnegut's fictional cosmos, namely, the Church of God the Utterly Indifferent.

The many characters in this "true story from the Nightmare Ages" are all haunted by the question "who was actually in charge of all creation, and what all creation was all about," and they pine for "some kind of signal that would tell [them] what it was all about." The disillusioned tycoon Noel Constant, whose Horatio Alger career is a biting satire on the connections between Calvinism and capitalism as investigated by Max Weber, can find as little meaning in the world as his intellectual manager Ransom K. Fern, who tries to imitate Aristotle, but attempts in vain to detect some "pattern in what he knew" and searches unsuccessfully for "the vaguest light on what life might be about." Noel's son Malachi, who whiles away his inherited riches with women and drugs and personifies the most thoughtless carpe diem mentality, desperately waits for "just one thing—a single message," and Beatrice Rumfoord, the touch-me-not aristocratic lady, who refuses to become soiled by life, suffers from the despair bred by uselessness and lack of purpose. Thus the ethics of Calvinism, philosophical humanism, hedonism, and isolationism are all shown to be equally inappropriate for a meaningful human existence because they all postulate a transcendental agency to which they ascribe the responsibility for the otherwise inexplicable events of life.

Their attempts at explanation reach from the simple concept of luck—
Noel is thought to have just been lucky with his speculations—and the
intellectual presumption of some hidden order—Fern searches for a
'pattern'—to the assumption of a divine providence—Malachi thinks that
"somebody up there likes me." And it is this very concept of a transcendental agency of whichever kind that is rejected by Rumfoord, and
Vonnegut, as the crucial aberration of human thinking and in which both
see the ultimate reason for all human sorrow.

Rumfoord decrees that there is "nothing more cruel, more
dangerous, more blasphemous than a man can do than to believe that—that
luck, good or bad, is the hand of God!", and he argues that the postulation
of some God is nothing but an abdication of human responsibility, that
throughout history men have killed and tortured each other in the name of
their gods and that mankind has suffered endlessly *ad maiorem dei gloriam.*
Since the concept of a higher agency intervening in human affairs through
punishments and rewards is only an alibi for man's greed and lust for
power, Rumfoord creates the Church of God the Utterly Indifferent,
which follows the motto "Take Care of the People, and God Almighty Will
Take Care of Himself."

Rumfoord's new religion, which Vonnegut unfolds in some detail,
might be understood as a variation upon the notion of a *deus absconditus* or as
a fictional translation of "God is Dead" theology, but Vonnegut goes a deci-
sive step further when he unmasks the founder of this new creed as a
scheming and power-hungry manipulator. Rumfoord, who once drove his
private spaceship into a chronosynclastic infundibulum, a hilarious science
fiction equivalent of the astrophysicians' black hole, exists as a wave phenomenon pulsing as a distorted spiral between the Sun and Betelgeuse. As a
consequence, he knows about the past and the future and can use his
prophetic gifts to establish his credentials: During his first revelation he
predicts "fifty future events in great detail" and admonishes his spellbound
audience to think about "the Spanish Inquisition." Thus, of course, he
becomes guilty of the very manipulation his religion proposes to overcome.

But Rumfoord, who cynically stages a war between Mars and the
Earth to make mankind ripe for his teachings and create the necessary
martyrs, turns out to be a trickster tricked. The whole history of mankind is
revealed as part of a complicated communication system between robots
from the extragalactic planet Tralfamadore, with the great buildings from
Stonehenge to the Palace of the League of Nations being telecontrolled
hieroglyphics that the Tralfamadorians made unknowing earthlings erect to
convey coded messages to their fellow robot Salo stranded on Titan. The
hilarious unmasking of mankind's greatest achievements as links in an other-

directed intergalactic communication system engendered by an immeasurably more advanced civilization of machines, then, is not only the most drastic debunking of man's claim to greatness and importance, but it also provides Vonnegut with a perspective from which to evaluate human follies and aspirations. Rumfoord, who uses Malachi as his telecontrolled Messiah, is himself only a pawn of the Tralfamadorians: man has no free will whatsoever. And Malachi's message, when he comes down to earth in a scene based on the Christian epiphany—"I was a victim of a series of accidents, as are we all"—is reinforced on an all-encompassing universal scale.

The *prima causa* at the center of Vonnegut's complex spiraling plot is not a supreme godhead but a society of robots that are the creations of a manlike species that exterminated itself through its development of ever more advanced technology. And the ultimate message of the novel is that first, scientific attempts at understanding and mastering the universe inadvertently lead to disaster and self-extermination; and second, religious creeds are mendacious but nevertheless necessary inventions that cannot explain the meaning of a world which has no meaning, but that are necessary to provide man with the sense of purpose and direction without which he cannot live. Consequently, man must give up all attempts at understanding the unfathomable workings of an arbitrary universe and must realize, instead, that the meaning of life can only be found in its unconditional acceptance. "A purpose of human life, no matter who is controlling it, is to love whoever is around to be loved" is the sum of Malachi's experience; and Beatrice, who writes a book about *The True Purpose of Life in the Solar System*, comes to a similar conclusion.

It is in his fourth novel, *Cat's Cradle* (1963), that Vonnegut presents his most detailed religious system. Most of the action of this highly accomplished tale, which is both a postmodern exercise in storifying and a fictional treatise on the limits of epistemology, takes place on the poverty-stricken island of San Lorenzo. There two strangers, the American Marine deserter McCabe and the Black globetrotter Lionel Boyd Johnson alias Bokonon from Tobago, are shipwrecked, and they decide to turn it into a "Utopia." "To this end, McCabe overhauled the economy and the law, Johnson designed a new religion." It soon becomes obvious, however, that the economy of the godforsaken Carribean island cannot be improved, and thus the new religion becomes "the only real instrument of hope." Consequently, Bokonon works on the assumption that "truth was the enemy of the people, because the truth was so terrible," and he makes "it his business to provide the people with better and better lies."

Like Rumfoord in *The Sirens of Titan*, Bokonon never pretends to receive divine inspirations. On the contrary, he offers his new creed and his continually growing body of holy writ as a system of man made inventions which he calls *foma*, defined as "harmless untruths, intended to comfort simple souls" and recognized by the well-read reader as the spiritual equivalent of Huxley's *soma* in *Brave New World*. Bokonon, whose initials LBJ pun on President Lyndon B. Johnson and his "War on Poverty" and whose complicated life history is charged with analogies to Christ, Jonah, and St. Augustine, bases his religion on the principle of "Dynamic Tension" taken over from Charles Atlas' body-building courses and redefined as "a priceless equilibrium between good and evil." From this principle he deduces the axiom "that good societies could be built only by pitting good against evil, and by keeping the tension between the two high at all times." Therefore, he arranges with McCabe that he become outlawed and that his adherents be threatened with capital punishment to give his religion the lure of the forbidden, and together they create "the living legend of the cruel tyrant in the city and the gentle holy man in the jungle."

The Manichean dualism of good and evil, God and Satan, holy man and evil tyrant thus becomes linked with traditional opposition between country and city, corrupt civilization and pastoral nature, and the exercise of Bokononism turns into an exciting role play full of risk and promise. Since all the inhabitants of the island, including the evil tyrant, are Bokononists, life on San Lorenzo becomes "a work of art," and Vonnegut's warning from the preface to his third novel *Mother Night* (1961), "We are what we pretend to be, so we must be careful about what we pretend to be," fulfills itself. The new religion serves as "opium for the people" by keeping them busily engaged in rituals which make them forget their unbearable reality. Bokononism, then, with its doctrines of the *karass*, the *vin-dit*, the *duprass*, the *wampeter*, the *granfalloon*, and the *zah-mah-ki-bo* and with its central sacrament of *boko-maru*, the mingling of awareness through the rubbing of the soles of the feet (which is, of course, a facile pun on the mingling of souls), is an openly admitted system of "bittersweet lies," an extended spiritual therapy, as it were, that consists of helpful illusions and that works on the assumption that the meaning and purpose without which man cannot live must be invented since they cannot be discovered.

The world is arbitrary, indifferent, and utterly meaningless, and therefore Bokonon invents purposes to explain and make bearable its contingency. Like Walter Starbuck, the hapless protagonist of the later novel *Jailbird* (1979), he knows that we are here for no purpose, unless we can invent one," and thus he teaches his followers that instead of "it happened" they are to say "it was *meant* to happen" or "it was *supposed* to happen," that they have to proceed on the premise that "each of us has to be what he or she is," and that the concept of free will must be abandoned as totally "irrelevant."

Of course, any invented sense-making system is continuously disproved by man's immediate experience of the world, and the arbitrariness of events perpetually defeats any system of alleged causalities. Therefore, Bokonon cautions man against "the folly of pretending to discover, to understand," and he expresses this folly in an ingenious variation of the biblical story of creation:

> In the beginning, God created the earth, and He looked upon it in His cosmic loneliness.
>
> And God said, "Let Us make living creatures out of mud, so the mud can see what We have done." And God created every living creature that now moveth, and one was man. Mud as man alone could speak. God leaned close as mud as man sat up, looked around, and spoke. Man blinked. "What is the *purpose* of all this?" he asked politely.
>
> "Everything must have a purpose?" asked God.
>
> "Certainly," said man.
>
> "Then I leave it to you to think of one for all this," said God. And He went away.

Man, however, a species defined in *Player Piano* as seemingly born to ask "Why?", cannot think of convincing purposes, although he needs them in order to survive and to not end in self-extermination as did the desperate Tralfamadorians in *The Sirens of Titan*. Therefore, he must pretend to understand, and Bokonon sums up this insoluble conundrum in the most famous of his calypsos, which he offers as Carribean versions of biblical psalms:

> Tiger got to hunt,
> Bird got to fly;
> Man got to sit and wonder, "Why, why, why?"
> Tiger got to sleep,
> Bird got to land;
> Man got to tell himself he understand.

The ineradicable contradiction, then, between man's need to understand and his inability to understand is mirrored by the fact that on an empirical level Bokononism considers man nothing but "sitting-up mud," but that on a spiritual level man forms the center of the universe: The only thing that is holy to a Bokononist is "Man, . . . that's all. Just man." Ultimately, therefore, Bokononism is a desperate answer to "the cruel paradox" of human existence, namely, "the heartbreaking necessity of lying about reality, and the heartbreaking impossibility of lying about it." And it is small wonder that against such a backdrop the Bokononist jungle doctor Julian Castle, with the initials of Jesus Christ, defines *maturity* as "a bitter disappointment for which no remedy exists, unless laughter can be said to remedy anything."

Although Bokononism is a self-avowed system of helpful lies, it proves much more beneficial than its opponent in the novel, namely, natural science. It is this allegedly enlightened science, as practiced by amoral and inhumane experimenters smirking at such superstitions as "God" or "sin," that brings about the end of the world by freezing the earth into a ball of solid ice. And when the illiterate tyrant of San Lorenzo praises science as "magic that *works*," he unknowingly reveals that a belief in technological progress is just another, and terribly dangerous, religion.

Cat's Cradle, which is narrated by one of the few survivors of the apocalypse, uses as its title a children's game. It is this simple and ubiquitous game, that provides the central symbol of man's essential task: The universe he finds himself in is an arbitrary and ever-changing system of meaningless strings, which man, through an act of his creative imagination, has to define as meaningful. If he cannot do that, that is, if he proves unable to invent a meaning that cannot be discovered, he will succumb to the despair of nihilism like the character in the novel who repeatedly observes that there is "*no damn cat, no damn cradle*." But if he bases his imaginative creation of meaning on the helpful lies of religion, he will be much better off than if he grounds his understanding of self and world in the inhumane truths of science. This message, then, which made *Cat's Cradle* a cult book of the youthful counterculture of the sixties with its revolt against technocratic rationality, takes up and unfolds the concerns of Vonnegut's previous novels, and Bokononism can be understood as a combination of Paul Proteus' need to "find something to believe in" and the insistence of the narrator of *The Sirens of Titan* that the universe is "a nightmare of meaninglessness without end" and that everybody has "to find the meaning of life within himself."

Such a reading is corroborated by what Vonnegut said in his famous "Address to Graduating Class at Bennington College, 1970," in which he stated:

> A great swindle of our time is the assumption that science has made religion obsolete. All science has damaged is the story of Adam and Eve and the story of Jonah and the Whale. Everything else holds up pretty well, particularly the lessons about fairness and gentleness.

And he implored his young listeners:

I beg you to believe in the most ridiculous superstition of all: that humanity is at the center of the universe, the fulfiller or the frustrator of the grandest dreams of God Almighty.

If you can believe that, and make others believe it, then there might be hope for us. Human beings might stop treating each other like garbage, might begin to treasure and protect each other instead. Then it might be all right to have babies again.

To Vonnegut, then, all religions—and Bokononism is only the most obvious example so far—are manmade myths or lies, but they provide the sense-making structures necessary for man's survival. And they are more necessary today than ever before because they serve as the essential antidote against the most dangerous "religion" of all, the belief in unbridled technological progress with its alleged objectivity, which is nothing but amorality, and its built-in tendency toward ultimate self-destruction.

This conviction, which might be defined for the time being as agnostic humanism, can also be seen in Vonnegut's next novel, *God Bless You, Mr. Rosewater* (1965), in which the author's alter ego, the unsuccessful and eccentric science-fiction writer Kilgore Trout, who looks "like a frightened, aging Jesus," makes his first appearance. In one of Trout's countless stories, which are summed up in *God Bless You, Mr. Rosewater*, and which will from now on be an essential ingredient of Vonnegut's novels, a man about to commit suicide states that he wants to ask God a single question, namely, "What in hell are people for?" This turns out to be a repetition of a character's request in *Player Piano*, who begs the technician in charge of the central computer, "Would you ask EPICAC what people are for?"

In the America of *God Bless You, Mr. Rosewater*, the Sermon on the Mount has been replaced by the hunger for "money as dehydrated Utopia," and a perverted Calvinism is used to justify the distinction between haves and have-nots and to make poor men ashamed of themselves. It is Kilgore Trout who saves the crazy protagonist from being committed to an asylum by the lawyers waiting for "his lunacy . . . to make the great leap into religion" when he defines the essential moral problem of technologically advanced societies as "how to love people who have no use" and when he thus upgrades Eliot's drunken bouts of helpfulness into an advanced philanthropic experiment.

Organized religion, the message of *God Bless You, Mr. Rosewater*, might be summed up, has turned into an instrument of class warfare, and it needs a new Jonah figure like Eliot Rosewater, who is compared several times to the Old Testament prophet, and a new "Jesus figure" in the guise of an eccentric science fiction writer dreaming up "fantasies of an impossibly hospitable world" to redeem a stupid mankind on the brink of self-destruction and to teach humans that it is not progress and success that will save them, but mutual care, love, and common decency.

It is in *God Bless You, Mr. Rosewater* that Vonnegut makes his first oblique attempt to come to terms with one of the traumatic experiences of his life when he makes Eliot read Hans Rumpf's book *The Bombing of Dresden* and has him undergo a hallucinatory vision of Indianapolis "being consumed by a fire-storm." But it is only in his next novel, his generally acclaimed masterpiece *Slaughterhouse-Five* (1969), that Vonnegut squarely faces the holocaust of Dresden and finally manages to exorcise his haunting memories in one of the most accomplished tales of postwar American literature. Here he brilliantly recombines his attack on the hubris of technological progress from *Player Piano*, his playful contrast between a faulty human and an advanced robot civilization from *The Sirens of Titan*, his depiction of the atrocities of World War II from *Mother Night*, his vision of a scientifically induced apocalypse and the innovative narrative stance of *Cat's Cradle*, and the figures of Eliot Rosewater and Kilgore Trout from *God Bless You, Mr. Rosewater*.

One of the artfully intertwined narrative strands of *Slaughterhouse-Five* deals with the passive antihero Billy Pilgrim, an optometrist from Ilium, New York, who acts out his Bunyanesque pilgrim's progress as a contemporary Everyman confronted with and overwhelmed by the cruelties of war and the atrocity of the firebombing that he survives, like Vonnegut himself, in a subterranean meatlocker of the Dresden slaughterhouse. Billy "has come unstuck in time," and the erratic and disjointed narrative follows his uncontrollable time travels, thus providing Vonnegut with a chance to escape the limits of chronology. One of the main destinies of Billy's journeys is the extragalactic planet Tralfamadore, where he learns that it is useless to worry about the future and to cast around for explanations of the incomprehensible events of existence. Appointing himself a missionary, bringing the philosophy of Tralfamadorian fatalism to troubled humans and thereby "prescribing corrective lenses for Earthling souls," Billy attempts to teach his fellow humans that their repeated question "Why?" is useless and inappropriate because "*everything* is all right, and everybody has to do exactly what he does" and that they should "concentrate on the happy moments of . . . life, and ignore the unhappy ones." People therefore should give up being "the great explainers" and abandon their silly concept of "free will."

The Tralfamadorian philosophy with its aesthetics of simultaneity, its rejection of time as succession and its consequent denial of the finality of death, its ridiculing of any attempt at causal explanation—"There is no why"—and its stance of fatalistic acceptance of whatever might happen and the ensuing ethics of momentary enjoyment has frequently been misunderstood as an expression of Vonnegut's escapist nihilism. This, however, is a grave misunderstanding caused by the unwarranted identification of Vonnegut, the narrator, with Billy, his hero. Admittedly, Vonnegut is a cynical pessimist, and his black humor shows a streak of deep despair, but as in *The Sirens of Titan*, where the terrible revelation of man's uselessness and folly is counterbalanced by an emphatic plea for courtesy and kindness, and as in *Cat's Cradle*, where the desperate self-betrayal of Bokononism is undertaken in the name of decency and love, in *Slaughterhouse-Five* the facile fatalism of Billy is contrasted with the narrator's defiant altruism.

Through a series of complex narrative strategies, Vonnegut leaves open whether *Slaughterhouse-Five* is a science fiction novel or a novel with a schizophrenic hero haunted by science fiction fantasies. He carefully avoids taking sides and creates numerous unresolved contradictions. He simultaneously makes Billy a latter-day Christ crucified by a world of cruelty and lovelessness and a postlapsarian Adam pining for a return to paradise. These and other strategies deny the reader a quasi-pragmatic reception and force Billy to realize that "there is nothing intelligent to say about a massacre," that appearance and reality indistinguishably intertwine, and that an innovative narrative presented "in the telegraphic schizophrenic manner of the planet Tralfamadore" does not offer a clearcut message but needs to be coauthored, as it were, by every individual reader against the background of his own experience. This is why the misreading of the novel as an expression of Vonnegut's resigned advocacy of the inevitable can be understood, but a careful analysis of the text leads to a different conclusion.

In the novel's final passage, it is "springtime" and the trees are "leafing out," and Billy drives in a horse-drawn wagon, which is "green and coffin-shaped," through the moonlike landscape of burnt-out Dresden. Like John in *Cat's Cradle*, who opens his tale with "Call me Jonah" and thus invites comparison with Ishmael in *Moby-Dick*, who drifts ashore in a coffin to bear witness to the shipwreck of the *Pequod*, Vonnegut offers *Slaughterhouse-Five* as his testimony to one of the greatest atrocities of modern history. And when he conjures up the annual rebirth of nature and contrasts it with the all-encompassing inferno of human history, he pits the hope for cyclical renewal against the despair bred by linear "progress." While Billy with his resigned fatalism becomes guilty of complicity and self-abandonment and thus inadvertently encourages the repetition of Dresden—his son fights as a Green Beret in Vietnam—Vonnegut tells us that he instructed his sons that they "are not under any circumstances to take part in massacres" and adopts the defiant stance of Lot's wife who, despite God's warning, turned around to look at the destruction of Sodom and Gomorrah: "she *did* look back, and I love her for that, because it was so human."

In *Slaughterhouse-Five*, then, the impassioned pacifist and acknowledged atheist presents no testament of fatalistic acceptance but a passionate plea for resistance against the self-destruction of a mankind that all too often tries to justify its greed and cruelty by references to divine providence. "Earthlings who have felt that the Creator clearly wanted this or that," Vonnegut says in his essay on the American space program, "have almost always been pigheaded and cruel"; and Dresden and Vietnam, the Children's Crusade of the Middle Ages, and the race riots of the American sixties are evoked in *Slaughterhouse-Five* as convincing examples of the inhumanity perpetrated in the name of God.

As in Vonnegut's previous novels, the characters in *Slaughterhouse* desperately attempt to find some purpose and meaning for their existence. Billy's disoriented mother, who cannot make up her mind about which church to join, for example, buys a crucifix in a souvenir store, and the narrator caustically comments: "Like so many Americans, she was trying to construct a life that made sense from the things she found in gift shops." When Billy commits himself, after a mental breakdown, to a ward for nonviolent mental patients, he makes the acquaintance of another inmate, Eliot Rosewater, who introduces him to the science fiction of Kilgore Trout. Both Billy and Eliot have "found life meaningless, partly because of what they had seen in the war," and now they use Trout's extrapolations of better worlds to get their bearings again, "trying," as the narrator says, "to re-invent themselves and their universe," a process in which "science fiction [is] a big help."

One of the books of "this cracked messiah" Trout, which Billy reads in the hospital, is *The Gospel from Outer Space* in which a visitor comes to earth and makes "a serious study of Christianity to learn, if he could, why Christians found it so easy to be cruel." He comes to the conclusion that this is due to "slipshod storytelling in the New Testament" because, instead of teaching us to be merciful to the lowliest person, the gospel, by making Jesus the son of God, teaches that "*before you kill somebody, make absolutely sure he isn't well connected*" and thus makes Christians assume that poor and unimportant people can be lynched with impunity. Another Trout novel deals with a time traveler who journeys back to see Jesus and who encounters him as a twelve-year-old boy learning the carpentry trade in his father's shop. Jesus and his father are busy building a cross for a rabble-rouser and "glad to have the work."

These and other direct references to Christianity and its failure to make people behave decently drive home a point that Vonnegut also makes in his expository writings. In his *Playboy* interview, for example, he says: "I admire Christianity more than anything—Christianity as symbolized by gentle people sharing a common bowl." But in his commemoration speech for William Ellery Channing, he states: "I have had even more trouble with the Trinity than I had with college algebra" and rejects the notion of Jesus as the son of God as an invention of the Council of Nicea.

Vonnegut, then, is "enchanted with the Sermon on the Mount" because "being merciful, it seems to me, is the only good idea we have received so far," but he rejects the idea of the divinity of Jesus and of an omnipotent God being his father. He accepts Christianity, that is, as a "*heartfelt moral code*" and as an ethics of morally responsible behavior, but he rejects the claim that this code is divine law. This explains why neither Rumfoord, the founder of the Church of God the Utterly Indifferent in *The Sirens of Titan*, nor Bokonon, the inventor of Bokononism in *Cat's Cradle*, ever claim to have been inspired by divine revelations, but why they offer their creeds as manmade ways toward a better and more human life.

Critics generally agree that after *Slaughterhouse-Five* Vonnegut's novels lose their erstwhile power. Their religious implications, however, remain as central as ever. In *Breakfast of Champions* (1973), which attacks the environmental pollution that has brought our "damaged planet" to the brink of uninhabitability, the central idea is the thesis advanced by Trout that "human beings are robots, are machines" powered by chemical reactions. Again we meet desperate people casting around for an understanding of what happens to them: "*Why me?*" for example, is a "common question," and the frustrated protagonist asks in vain "what life is all about."

Although Vonnegut paints a bleak picture of "a planet which [is] dying fast" and of a society that suffers from loneliness, despair, and insanity, he also suggests a means of redemption again. The minimalist painter Rabo Karabekian, who is accused that his nonrepresentational picture of the Temptation of St. Anthony is a fraud, explains that the unwavering band of light on his canvas shows "the immaterial core of every animal," namely, its awareness, and that the picture expresses his conviction that "our awareness is all that is alive and may be sacred in any of us. Everything else about us is dead machinery." This important correction of Trout's thesis about humans as mere robots is just another way of asserting that man has a soul. And Vonnegut, who figures as a desperate and suicidal character in his own novel and is present at this revelation, defines Karabekian's statement as the "spiritual climax of this book" and confesses that by listening to the painter's statement of faith he is "being reborn."

Admittedly, this scene smacks of what Vonnegut himself calls the "almost intolerable sentimentality beneath everything I write," but apart from its questionable artistic value it provides another instance of a self-avowed atheist's search for the spiritual consolation of a belief in some transcendental link. *Breakfast of Champions*, we know from Vonnegut's biography, is its author's rather desperate attempt at artistic autotherapy in the face of a deep life crisis, and while this fact may account for the novel's aesthetic weakness, it makes Karabekian's assertion and the fictional "Vonnegut's" reaction to it all the more significant.

In *Slapstick or Lonesome No More!* (1976), which is certainly Vonnegut's weakest novel, the creed to become "the most popular American religion of all time" in a country ravaged by changing gravity is "The Church of Jesus Christ the Kidnapped." More important than this grotesque invention is the fact that the novel portrays the growing despair of men and women for whom the American Dream has become a "form of Idiot's Delight," who are "outraged by the human condition in the Universe," and who can find no answer to their question "What does it all mean?" They even have no hope for improvement after death since a scientific experiment has revealed that "the life that awaits us after death is infinitely more tiresome than this one" and should rightly be called "The Turkey Farm" instead of "Heaven" or any other euphemism.

Here, then, where Vonnegut's savage despair and disgust are expressed in a tone reminiscent of Mark Twain's *The Mysterious Stranger,* the meaning of life is reduced to a mere day-by-day survival fight, and Laurel and Hardy are praised as embodiments of the pathetic human task of "bargaining in good faith with destiny." "The low comedy of living" is thus grimly reduced to a mere series of slapstick situations.

In *Jailbird* (1979), a realistic comment on the Watergate affair, the hero-narrator Walter F. Starbuck bemusedly recounts his eventful life unfolding between moral idealism and shameless opportunism. He bears the name of the first mate on Melville's *Pequod,* and his narrative is colored by a curious mixture of Tralfamadorian fatalism with regard to the universe and the history of mankind and a stubborn faith with regard to individual man's daily existence. Finding himself on a "planet, where money matters more than anything," and being surrounded by people who do not give "a damn any more about what's really going on," he chooses to live for his convictions and to hold up courtesy and decency as the only means that make a purposeless life bearable. Patterning his answer before a congressional committee on one given by the labour organizer Powers Hapgood, he defends his actions with a reference to "the Sermon on the Mount," thus providing an answer to the ubiquitous "Why?" that is a testimony of faith. In spite of the overwhelming proof for his wife's conviction that "human beings were evil by nature," Starbuck asserts, like other Vonnegut heroes before him, that man can learn to be kind and to care for others. If mankind in general may be doomed, individual man is given the chance to live his own life, and as Melville's Starbuck pitted his faith against the monomania of Captain Ahab, so Vonnegut's Starbuck sets his moral convictions against the cynical opportunism of a Richard Nixon.

Deadeye Dick (1982) is another sweeping indictment of "man's festive inhumanity to man" in "an era of pharmaceutical buffoonery" where there are "pills for everything." At the age of twelve, its nondescript protagonist-narrator shoots a pregnant woman. His accidental crime, bred by the foolish irresponsibility of his gun-collecting father, is repeated on a grand scale by the American government when it accidentally drops a neutron bomb on Midland City, Ohio. Individual murder and mass destruction signal the end of the American Dream, and the openly raised suspicion that the dropping of the bomb was no accident but that "Midland City had been neutron-bombed on purpose" because the government needed to test the new weapon, signals the feeling of a bewildered population that they are the victims of some unfathomable conspiracy.

In this novel, again, people ask "that wonderful question . . . 'why, why, why?',," and the apocalyptic motif of the dropping of a neutron bomb, which kills 100,000 people but leaves everything else intact, turns out to be a perfect symbol of a materialistic world. The narrator's resigned question, "Since all the property is undamaged, has the world lost anything it loved?" leads him to the concluding statement, "We are still in the Dark Ages. The Dark Ages—they haven't ended yet."

In *Galápagos* (1985), Vonnegut's latest novel to date, he returns to his outrageous brand of science fiction and employs the son of Kilgore Trout, Leon Trotsky Trout, as his narrator. Leon is a deserter from the Vietnam War, in which he learned that "life was a meaningless nightmare, with nobody watching or caring what was going on." Having been decapitated in an industrial accident in Sweden, he roams the earth as an incorporeal ghost trying to satisfy his "curiosity as to what life is all about," and from a vantage point of a million years hence he tells us what has become the species of *homo sapiens.*

Through a series of wars and famines brought about by the species' ability to think and thus "to make a mess of everything," and through a mysterious bacterium that makes all women infertile, mankind has dwindled in size and finally become extinct. As the result of hilariously funny and cruel accidents, however, a group of ten freakish outsiders, who have been shipwrecked on the desolate Galápagos island of Santa Rosalia, survive and continue procreating. Since most of them are genetically deficient and as their surroundings call for certain abilities and make others superfluous, genetic mutations and environmental influences lead to the "evolution of modern humankind," that is, to seal-like fish-eating beings with flippers instead of hands and with greatly reduced brain powers. These beings are a link in the planet's food chain—they can no longer wield tools, and sharks see to it that there is no overpopulation—and thus Darwin's theory of evolution comes true with a vengeance: "the Law of Natural Selection did the repair job" and sees to it that the faulty "evolution of something as distracting and irrelevant and disruptive as those great big brains of a million years ago" is corrected.

Here Vonnegut's earlier interest in the theory of evolution comes to outrageous fictional fruition. In *Slaughterhouse-Five*, for example, the Tralfamadorians had considered Darwinism much more interesting than the teachings of Christ; and in a 1972 essay Vonnegut had observed that "the two real political parties in America are the *Winners* and the *Losers*" and that "losers have thousands of religions, often of the *bleeding heart* variety," whereas "the single religion of the Winners is a harsh interpretation of Darwinism, which argues that it is the will of the universe that only the fittest should survive." In *Galápagos* he solves what he had earlier referred to as the "compromise between the need to believe in a traditional paternal God and the contemporary pressures to accept the pronouncements of science" by ingeniously compounding the myth of Noah's ark and the alleged facts of evolution theory. Thereby he turns into its opposite the traditional science fiction motif of man's evolution into an ever more perfect species: On the very islands on which Darwin once conceived of his theory, mankind's fate is decided through evolutionary regression, an obvious mistake in the development of the species is corrected, and man is relieved of his destructive brain.

With this outrageous extrapolation of mankind's future history, the climax of despair and pessimism seems to have been reached, but again there is a ray of hope in the sea of desperation. Of the "twenty-thousand quotations from literature" stored by the portable computer Mandarax—a miraculous achievement of human inventiveness that proves to be totally useless on Santa Rosalia—Leon chooses the following statement by Anne Frank as the epigraph for his tale: "In spite of everything, I still believe people are really good at heart." Like John in *Cat's Cradle*, he writes his book although he knows full well that there is nobody left to read it. Thus he asserts his belief in human goodness and his stubborn faith in the importance of art. This faith is obliquely corroborated by a character who dies of a brain tumor and who says to his wife on his deathbed: "I'll tell you what the human soul is. . . . Animals don't have one. It's the part of you that knows when your brain isn't working right." Like Rabo Karabekian in *Breakfast of Champions*, he asserts that man has a soul and thus need not be the helpless victim of his brain, the "only real villain" of human history.

Were men to listen to the advice of their souls instead of following the scheming propositions of their oversized brains—one could interpret the unresolved contradictions of *Galápagos*—the aberrations of "science and progress" could be avoided and Leon's belief that "human beings are good animals" could be confirmed in spite of the overwhelming evidence to the contrary.

The preceding survey shows that Vonnegut does not offer an exclusively pessimistic or even nihilistic view of man. Bosworth's charge that he constantly defeats himself because, "although he abhors our mechanized culture, he believes the world view on which it is based" and thus cannot offer anything but "pessimism, cynicism, resignation, despair" is disproved by a careful reading of his novels. The opposing view, however, is equally inappropriate. Tunnel's assertion that Vonnegut makes "an important contribution to a contemporary understanding of Christian redemption" is certainly unwarranted. The fact that such contradictory readings are at all possible shows that Vonnegut's oeuvre is full of unresolved conflicts and offers anything but a sustained and easily summarized worldview. But there are certain recurring convictions, and with regard to the role of religion in his novels, the following conclusions can be drawn.

A God conceived of as a *prima causa* or a supreme mover of the universe does not exist, or if he does, man is constitutionally unable to discover or understand him. "No one really understands nature or God," and anybody who pretends to be in possession of some final truth is a charlatan. This, Vonnegut repeatedly shows in his novels, has been amply proved by history because, whenever people have claimed to act in the name of a divine providence, they have used such claims as an alibi for their greed, cruelty, and lust for power. Consequently, religions can never be divine laws, and any creed that claims to have been established by divinely inspired prophets is a fake. The crucial question, therefore, is not whether a religion is true or false but whether it is useful or not, whether it provides its adherents with a protective sense of community and with helpful *foma*, that is, harmless untruths that make their lives more bearable and their behavior toward each other more decent and more humane.

The most dangerous of all "religions" is the unconditional belief in science and technology because that belief pretends to be based on verifiable premises, facts, and proofs. As is amply demonstrated in each of Vonnegut's novels, science is inherently destructive, has time and again led to "the construction of . . . doomsday machine[s]," has made our planet almost uninhabitable, and has led mankind to the brink of self-annihilation. It has replaced ever more humans by machines and has divided mankind into a great mass of useless people robbed of their purpose and their dignity and a small elite of engineers playing at God and hell-bent on their way to ultimate self-destruction.

It is this very belief in the infallibility of science and the unending progress of technology that makes more humane religions necessary. As the parable of the Tralfamadorians' self-destruction in *The Sirens of Titan* most emphatically demonstrates, the blind trust in science must be counterbalanced by a belief in a human-centered and humanistic set of values. Therefore, humans, who should "pray to be rescued from [their] inventiveness," need a sense-making system as a means of coping with the meaninglessness of their world. Such a system, however, can only be built on an anthropological fundament, that is, on the fact that a part of man, be it called his awareness by the Bokononists of *Cat's Cradle* or Rabo Karabekian in *Breakfast of Champions* or his soul by the dying man in *Galápagos*, is sacred. Therefore, a religion in Vonnegut's sense is essentially a "*heartfelt moral code.*" It must not endeavor to explain the inexplicable workings of a contingent universe, but concentrate on the provision of rules for human behavior. Any attempt at a theodicy, then, is bound to fail—and from the Ghost Shirt Society and the Church of God the Utterly Indifferent to Bokononism and the Church of Jesus Christ the Kidnapped, Vonnegut's fictional characters must invent their own purposes, must establish themselves, in true existentialist fashion, as the only available reference points for their world pictures.

The continuously recurring question "What are people for?" which expresses man's search for meaning, purpose, and design, cannot be answered with reference to some transcendental providence. Man, Vonnegut argues, is cursed with a "cruel paradox," that is, with his need to ask for meaning and purpose and his inability to find them. Consequently, he must attempt to discover meaning in himself, and instead of looking for some higher purpose, which does not exist, he must accept the conditions of his life and attempt to fulfill his obligations to himself and his fellow beings. Like Malachi after his strenuous initiation in *The Sirens of Titan* or the Bokononists in *Cat's Cradle*, man must love who is around to be loved, or like Starbuck in *Jailbird*, he must show courtesy and decency to make his purposeless existence bearable.

The danger bred by such a position and the concomitant plea for a stoical acceptance of the unavoidable is the relapse into a resigned fatalism. This position, which Billy Pilgrim in *Slaughterhouse-Five* becomes guilty of, must by all means be avoided. The nonexistence of any external meaning does not allow man to give up and passively drift with the unpredictable flow of events because such an attitude would lead to despair and self-abandonment. On the contrary, it is the very contingency of the universe that makes every individual responsible for his own fate and puts him under an obligation to construct his existence in a meaningful way.

Vonnegut, who can rightly say of himself that "my books are probably more widely used in schools than those of any other living American author," is thus certainly an apostate when judged from a dogmatic Christian viewpoint. But instead of being the pernicious blasphemer so many self-appointed censors try to ban, he is a humanist who desperately pleads for love and decency in a world of cruelty and injustice; a novelist who denies the paternal Christian god but proclaims the very message of the Sermon on the Mount; an atheist who holds up Jesus as a person to revere and emulate; and a "Christ-worshiping agnostic" who time and again evokes the imminent end of mankind only to alert his readers to the necessity of preventing it through their conversion to a more human "religion."

WENDY B. FARIS

Icy Solitude: Magic and Violence in Macondo and San Lorenzo

In the well-known opening sentence of García Marquez' *One Hundred Years of Solitude* the town of Macondo flocks to see the marvel of ice. At the end of Vonnegut's *Cat's Cradle* the island of San Lorenzo is frozen by means of a dreadful and miraculous invention called *ice-nine*. The forms of ice, like the novels that contain them, differ in many respects, but in both cases the ices may serve as metaphors for the temporal spaces the fictions occupy. And the idea of an insular domain may serve as an image of solitude, a solitude which contributes to man's final eclipse at the end of both texts.

The referent for *ice-nine* is of course much clearer than for the ice in *One Hundred Years of Solitude*. In *Cat's Cradle* the cold war literally ends up freezing the world; the scientists develop a weapon that backfires. In *One Hundred Years of Solitude* we need to move outwards from the initial ice— presented as a harmless enough wonder, in order to establish a meaningful comparison. In an article on «The Future Perfect of Macondo,» Marta Gallo has analyzed the linguistic action of the first sentence of *One Hundred Years of Solitude* and shown how its future perfect tense provides a paradigm for the entire novel. She associates the idea of ice with the final «talking mirror» of the parchments, and maintains that they both represent a kind of permanent frozen future—the future perfect—where all actions are possible and yet move inevitably towards death. The fiction partakes of the same «immor-

From *Latin American Literary Review* 13, no. 25 (January–June, 1985). © 1985 *Latin American Literary Review*.

tality for a fixed period» as Coronel Aureliano, for whom «the certainty that his day was assigned gave him a mysterious immunity». This closed temporal space resembles the chalk circle Colonel Aureliano has drawn around himself so that «no human being, not even Ursula, could come closer to him than ten feet». In both *Cat's Cradle* and *One Hundred Years of Solitude*, the magical coldness of ice is a sign of solitude. We might say that solitude plus, or even productive of, violence, leads to existence in a frozen future.

Ice-nine is distinct of course from the ice at the start of *One Hundred Years of Solitude* because it is literally «magic»; we know of no such substance (*yet*—one of Vonnegut's points). And *ice-nine* is a man-made miracle, whereas regular ice is natural. Horror at an invention of man contrasts with wonder at the inventiveness of nature. In Macondo, however, ice is not part of the natural environment and so for the inhabitants it is finally very similar to the telephone or the magic carpet. And at one point José Arcadio believes he understands a dream he has had, which leads him to want to use the ice in some way, to invent it.

> He thought that in the near future they would be able to manufacture blocks of ice on a large scale from such a common material as water and with them build the new houses of the village. Macondo would no longer be a burning place, where the hinges and the door-knockers twisted with the heat, but would be changed into a wintry city. If he did not persevere in his attempts to build an ice factory, it was because at that time he was absolutely enthusiastic over the education of his sons.

Luckily, more human concerns intervene, and foil this «scientific» experiment. In *One Hundred Years of Solitude* we see only the potential danger of man's use of a principle like ice (which in any case would have been a failure); in *Cat's Cradle* we see the actual danger of man's misuse of experimentation with atomic structures. (*Ice-nine* results from a recombination of atoms.)

The quotient of horror is much larger in *Cat's Cradle* than in *One Hundred Years of Solitude* because it is a more relentlessly satirical discourse, a more sustained criticism of a particular society. The satirical impulse towards social criticism is only a minor component of *One Hundred Years of Solitude* and *Cat's Cradle* is perhaps dwarfed by the comparison. Even so, this comparison is a particular example of the general sense that a new variety of non-realistic fiction exists and is being used, as often in the past, as a vehicle for social satire. This «pan-American» mode suggests the inadequacy of realistic fiction to expose the marvels and the horrors of the new world, of modern war. Violent actions are paralleled by violation of literary realism.

These two novels create imaginary worlds that constitute allegories of our own in many ways. In such allegories, the framing devices take on particular importance. In particular terms, the beginning and the end of a novel are the points at which the reader enters and leaves its fictional world. Both of these novels form a kind of circle—a serpent that bites its tail perhaps—for their endings explain, or contain, their beginnings. They are both «apocalyptic» in the sense that they narrate the end of the world they describe—and, by implication, the end of the world, period. In both cases our assumptions about «point of view» undergo a shift; we thought we were listening to one person, and «actually» we have been listening to someone else. This is clearer in the case of *One Hundred Years of Solitude* than that of *Cat's Cradle*. At the end of the former we find out we have been reading not the account of an omniscient narrator, but the manuscripts of Melquíades, who has appeared earlier on as a character in the novel.

At the start of *Cat's Cradle* the narrator says that the book he never finished was «to be called *The Day the World Ended.*» At the end, as we watch the world being destroyed by *ice-nine*, he reads from a piece of paper given him by Bokonon—the high-priest-like leader of «Bokonism»—which says: «If I were a younger man, I would write a history of human stupidity; and I would climb to the top of Mt. McCabe . . . » On the preceding page he has «blurted out my dream of climbing Mount McCabe . . . », and at the start of the book he writes that «when I was a younger man, I began to collect material for a book to be called *The Day the World Ended*,» and which he never finished. It is just possible that John the narrator may also «be» Bokonon, and that the two books alluded to are the same one—the one we are reading. In each instance we are also suddenly presented with the idea that perhaps we have been reading the prophetic book of the world which is about to be destroyed, and that it's now therefore too late to avert the disaster that rushes toward us.

The similarity between the two endings extends also to the question of why the world is consumed. The idea that «races condemned to one hundred years of solitude did not have a second opportunity on earth» might also serve to end *Cat's Cradle*. For isolation and alienation have brought on the catastrophe. Again, the connection is clearer in *Cat's Cradle* than in *One Hundred Years of Solitude*. It is not clear just why the Buendías have been condemned to a hundred years of solitude, whether we should blame «character» or «fate.» In *Cat's Cradle* the selfish thoughtlessness and isolation that engenders *ice-nine*, or its companion, the atomic bomb, is latent in the extreme alienation of their inventor from his children. On the day the bomb went off, the narrator's father

all of a sudden came out of his study and did something he'd
never done before. He tried to play with me. Not only had
he never played with me before; he had hardly ever even
spoken to me. . . . My sister Angela has told me many times
that I really hurt my father that day when I wouldn't admire
the cat's cradle . . . but I don't think I could have hurt him
much. He was one of the best-protected human beings who
ever lived. People couldn't get at him because he just wasn't
interested in people.

Compare Colonel Aureliano's isolated fanaticism in war, or in his room
manufacturing little gold fishes. Again, *One Hundred Years of Solitude* seems
much less grim. Aureliano temporarily loses all feeling from extended partic-
ipation in the war:

Then he made one last effort to search in his heart for the
place where his affection had rotted away and he could not
find it. . . . all of that had been wiped out by the war.

But Dr. Hoenikker never seems to have had any feelings at all. Aureliano
grows cold from an excess of passion, Hoenikker from a lack of it.

A glance at the beginnings of *One Hundred Years of Solitude* and *Cat's
Cradle* reveals a similarity of style related to the idea of a «frozen future»—
fictional action bounded by death. The future perfect mode, the «was to,»
which Marta Gallo shows to recur throughout *One Hundred Years of Solitude*,
figures prominently on the first page of *Cat's Cradle:*

The book *was to be* factual.
The book *was to be* an account of . . .
It *was to be* a Christian book . . . [it] *was* the book I never finished,
the book *to be* called *The Day the World Ended.*
(my emphasis)

As in *One Hundred Years of Solitude*, the mode establishes the end-stopped
freedom of action appropriate to García Marquez' magical realism and
Vonnegut's fantasy. Vonnegut specifies the sense of fatality that looms over
its use: «somebody or something has compelled me to be certain places at
certain times». Marquez leaves the tenses and the ending to accomplish
this sense.

Apocalyptic endings and fantastic events both point up man's
apparent lack of control over his environment and his destiny. But rather

than lamenting this fact, these works suggest that we might be better off controlling less rather than more. *One Hundred Years of Solitude* illustrates this idea both positively and negatively, *Cat's Cradle* principally negatively. There are no real equivalents in *Cat's Cradle* to the magical moments in *One Hundred Years of Solitude* when Remedios la bella ascends amidst the sheets or when the yellow butterflies enter with Mauricio Babilonia and remain with him until his death. Vonnegut's novel builds with the aid of comedy but without the relief of joyous magic towards the disastrous result of man's desire to invent and to control. But both societies have in a sense gone beyond the point where control seems desirable. Perhaps they manifest a kind of late romanticism, a post-frontier mentality. «Civilization» is winning too easily over the natural world and it turns out to be equal in many respects to «barbarism.»

Both texts respond to this situation in a similar way, though Vonnegut's of course more single-mindedly. They both attack the maniacal tendency to carry things—war and «progress,» in particular—too far. In this process, the means take over the ends. *Ice-nine*, designed as a weapon to protect one region, ends up destroying it, as, we are meant to conclude, our highly valued atomic bomb may do. A smaller example of the tendency of inventions to overpower their inventors occurs when the inhabitants of an elegant mansion in San Lorenzo are «awakened by a series of bangs and a flood of light.» These turn out to come «from a radio, from an electric dish-washer, from a pump—all restored to noisy life by the return of electric power,» but not before giving all of the people involved a good scare.

Aureliano, who begins a war to establish certain principles, is taken over by his own greed for power, originally a means to an end:

> The intoxication of power began to break apart under waves of discomfort . . . His orders were being carried out even before they were given, even before he thought of them, and they always went much beyond what he would have dared have them do. Lost in the solitude of his immense power, he began to lose direction.

Interestingly enough, the technological invention of the telegraph contributes to the dehumanization of the war effort for Colonel Gerineldo Marquez. Early on, Colonel Aureliano

> many times . . . would prolong the talks [with Colonel Gerineldo] beyond the expected limit and let them drift into comments of a domestic nature. Little by little,

however, and as the war became more intense and widespread, [Aureliano's] image was fading away into a universe
of unreality . . . [Gerineldo] finally lost all contact with the
war . . . it became a remote point of reference for him: an
emptiness.

Cat's Cradle is a more obvious reaction to the 20th century's worship
of science. It mocks people who believe they can understand, can control
everything, and survive the world's mysteries. H. Lowe Crosby asks «how
can anybody in his right mind be against science?» and his wife Hazel adds,
«I'd be dead now if it wasn't for penicillin». In the next chapter, called «Pain
Killer,» Papa Monzano becomes «the first man in history to die of *ice-nine*».
Similarly, it is the banana company gringos who modify the climate and the
rivers and who are then washed away by the rains they have tried to control.
And after these foreigners have imported an exaggerated number of love
potions into Macondo, one of them appears to die from a kind of living love
potion that emanates from Remedios la bella. The presence of Bokonon's
writings, which, in a less clear way, but perhaps like Melquíades' manuscripts,
constitute the text we are reading, gets one up on people who believe they
can control the future. For Bokonon, like Melquíades, will always have been
there before them, and suggests that fate, not they, may rule the world.

In addition to these similarities, several other minor points of
comparison suggest that *One Hundred Years of Solitude* and *Cat's Cradle* belong
to the same trend. The concept of insularity—of cosmic solitude—is empha-
sized by the isolated locations of Macondo and San Lorenzo, the first a kind
of island in the jungle, the second a literal island in the sea. The coincidental
location of Vonnegut's island in what seems to be the Caribbean provides an
interesting contrast with *One Hundred Years of Solitude*, for he shows us an
outsider's view of a typical Latin American country with all the cliches—a
dictator and his progeny, a one-crop economy, a one-city nation, and a rich
American's view of «the people of San Lorenzo,» who «are interested in only
three things: fishing, fornication, and Bokonism». Macondo is also a carefully illustrated example of a typical Latin American town, with its recapitu-
lation of the historical events of exploration, conquest, and more, but it is
shown from the inside with a wealth of detail. The dictator and the one-crop
economy are only phases here, and though the natives are quite interested in
fornication they have many other activities as well.

Both texts use the device—frequent in satire—of an isolated realm
where magical events take place without problematical contact with «real»
places. This kind of setting permits the use of what we might term the «man-
from-Mars» technique. A «real life» situation is seen as if with fresh eyes,

and our world is called into question. Typically, in *Cat's Cradle*, the process constitutes social criticism:

> Bokonon had been there, too, had written a whole book about Utopias . . . which he called «Bokonon's Republic.» . . . Let us start our Republic with a chain of drug stores, a chain of grocery stores, a chain of gas chambers, and a national game. After that, we can write our Constitution.

In *One Hundred Years of Solitude* it projects a sense of wonder; a magnet makes it seem as if «things have a life of their own» and a telescope as if «science has eliminated distance». Though, even here, the sense of wonder is not always unabated. While we enjoy seeing the new train's entry into Macondo through the eyes of its inhabitants, we worry about what it will bring—«the innocent yellow train that was to bring so many ambiguities and certainties, so many pleasant and unpleasant moments, so many changes, calamities, and feelings of nostalgia to Macondo.» And there are threatening moments: like the scientists with their *ice-nine*, José Arcadio, «whose unbridled imagination always went beyond the genius of nature and even beyond miracles and magic,» tends to go too far. When he tries endlessly—«with the abnegation of a scientist»—to turn a magnifying glass into an instrument of war, it turns on him and burns him, nearly setting the house on fire.

Another variation on the idea of «insularity» in these two novels, is the «family romance.» Incest is central and literal in *One Hundred Years of Solitude*, which ends with the disastrous result of an incestuous coupling. In *Cat's Cradle* the subject is there, but only hinted at in passing, and no sexual act takes place. The narrator simply mentions that «I don't blame Angela for slapping me. Father was all she had. She didn't have any boy friends. She didn't have any friends at all».

A final specific parallel that points up a more profound difference between Vonnegut's satirical fantasy and García Marquez' magical realism is the similarity between the sense of playful artifice represented by a cat's cradle and by an endless series of little golden fishes. Both are the monomaniacal play of a potentially powerful man. And they represent in different ways, as do many other phenomena in each novel, *mises-en-abyme*—images of the texts that contain them. The «little fishes» that Aureliano melts down and remakes resemble the cyclical and repetitive yet richly decorative and endlessly inventive narrative of *One Hundred Years of Solitude* that works continuously on the same town. They are like the «recycled» time that Ursula keeps reminding us of: «I know all of this by heart . . . It's as if time had turned around and we were back at the beginning.»

The cat's cradle is a tour-de-force, the construction of a artifice over a void; for the version that the narrator's father tries to amuse him with on the day the bomb went off is made from a piece of string that was originally tied around a book sent to Hoenikker by a prisoner, a book about the destruction of the world by a bomb, and which Hoenikker has never read. The volume we are reading is also a game in its way. It is very funny, even playful, but it is strung over the horror of nuclear war. It needs to be funny, in order to be suitable reading for «people who are dying or in terrible pain». Children show us the difference between the fishes and the cat's cradle, for young José Arcadio Segundo is attracted to Aureliano's workroom, while Hoenikker's child is terrified of his father and his construction, as if he glimpses the horror of the nuclear toy behind the string one. The «play» here is more obviously irresponsible, and leads more clearly to disaster than in *One Hundred Years of Solitude*. When Dr. Hoenikker «got so interested in turtles that he stopped working on the bomb,» the directors of the project took away the turtles:

> Father never said a word about the disappearance of the turtles. He just came to work the next day and looked for things to play with and think about, and everything there was to play with and think about had something to do with the bomb.

The bomb and *ice-nine* are not cat's cradles, but Dr. Hoenikker can't see the difference. Near the end of the novel, the narrator thinks to himself:

> What hope can there be for mankind, . . . when there are such men as Felix Hoenikker to give such playthings as *ice-nine* to such short-sighted children as almost all men and women are?

Even though, as I've already mentioned, Aureliano's single-minded devotion to his little fishes stems from the same characteristic tenacity that made him a fanatic and often brutal soldier, his activities are less harmful than Hoenikker's, and in the end he takes responsibility for his actions. At one point in the war, for example,

> the certainty that he was finally fighting for his own liberation, and not for abstract ideals, for slogans that politicians could twist left and right according to the circumstances, filled him with an ardent enthusiasm.

Each of these novels draws on several literary traditions that span centuries. García Marquez recognizes the romances of Amadis of Gaul, Don

Quixote, and (Woolf's) Orlando, the works of Faulkner and Borges, among others, as literary ancestors of *One Hundred Years of Solitude*. The whole tradition of magical realism in Latin American fiction, controversial, perhaps, as to definition, but not as to diffusion, grows out of earlier writers of fantasy— Poe, Quiroga, European surrealism, and tales of explorers who, in their turn, drew on earlier romance traditions. In the case of *Cat's Cradle*, one thinks immediately of Swift, for Gulliver looms large over any satirical voyage; and next of the well established tradition of American science fiction, of the humorists, black or not.

Yet each text brings these traditions to bear on a particular historical situation. This historical context, as I've noted repeatedly, is much more important in *Cat's Cradle* than in *One Hundred Years of Solitude*, but to miss the contemporary political overtones—primarily the anti-imperialist sentiments—in *One Hundreds Years of Solitude* is to miss part of its message. These novels constitute a recent renewal of the tradition that couples fantasy with political and social satire. Earlier American magicians like Poe, Quiroga, Borges, are more consistently a-temporal. The magic and the violence in their works generally come from the heart. *Cat's Cradle*, and to a lesser extent, *One Hundred Years of Solitude*, tacitly acknowledge that one source of violence may be exterior; political and social reality engender violence of language and action, and may lead towards universal destruction. This specific historical context lessens the risk of the kind of programmatic fantasy that Carpentier complained of years ago with reference to European surrealism.

In the United States, this linking of fantasy and history is often recognized in the works of Barthelme, Pyncheon, Coover, and Vonnegut. In Latin America it has long been discussed chez Carpentier, Lezama Lima, and Fuentes, to name only a few. But critical comparisons of the two continents are still relatively rare, except, perhaps in the case of Borges. Though Borges is an acknowledged precursor of magical realism in Latin America, one would hesitate to suggest that he had any direct influence on *Cat's Cradle*, since most of Borges' works became popular in this country during the sixties. But his presence is increasingly felt in recent American literature. Vonnegut's most striking similarity to Borges is his repeated refusal to leave any system of thought, any statement, without looking behind it, to see its opposite number. In *Cat's Cradle*, for example, he sees, like Borges, «the heartbreaking necessity of lying about reality, and the heartbreaking impossibility of lying about it».

Though *Cat's Cradle* was published in 1963 and *One Hundred Years of Solitude* in 1967, they are approximate contemporaries, for Marquez took many years to write his novel. Though they share many similar techniques and concerns, (as well as this chronological identity), *Cat's Cradle* and *One Hundred Years of Solitude* belong to two very different points in the history of the novel in their respective cultures. Morris Dickstein argues that the sixties «the dream of the Great American Novel» disintegrated, «but that original novels continued to be written.» At this very time—or slightly before—the dream of the Great Latin American Novel was coming true. It is as if the impulse migrated southward, and produced *One Hundred Years of Solitude*. The important differences between *Cat's Cradle* and *One Hundred Years of Solitude* that I've felt compelled to note throughout this comparative study well illustrates this apparent décalage of literary ambitions.

DAVID H. GOLDSMITH

Vonnegut's Cosmos

The universe of Kurt Vonnegut's novels is a hostile and ridiculous one, in which a sense of humor and an eye for the absurd are necessary. The humanist in Vonnegut is often defeated by the pessimist in a continuous teleological tug-of-war. The tussle is to decide whether or not there is any meaning in Stonehenge beyond its ironic and essentially useless message to the Tralfamadorian messenger, whether the destruction of the earth by fire or ice would subtract from a universal total, or merely exchange some frozen popsicles or charred hunks of steak for a figure that already adds up to zero. The hero of *Cat's Cradle* puts it this way:

> I blurted out my dream of climbing Mount McCabe with some magnificent symbol and planting it there. I took my hands from the wheel for an instant to show him how empty of symbols they were. "But what in hell would it *be*?" I grabbed the wheel again. "Here it is, the end of the world; and here I am, almost the very last man; and there it is, the highest mountain in sight. I know now what my *karass* has been up to, Newt. It's been working night and day for maybe half a million years to get me up that mountain." I wagged my head and nearly wept. "But what, for the love of God, is supposed to be in my hands?"

From *Kurt Vonnegut: Fantasist of Fire and Ice* by David H. Goldsmith. © 1972 by the Bowling Green University Popular Press.

Except for the brilliant *Sirens of Titan* and its implication of nothingness, each of Vonnegut's novels indicates a belief in a meaningful universe,
and each of his heroes (again with the exception of *Sirens*)—Proteus, Howard
W. Campbell, Jr., Jonah, Rosewater, and Billy—is a modern pilgrim engaged
in an uncertain quest along an unmapped route. Although the pilgrim often
must go it alone, Vonnegut provides an unusually large number of messiahs,
real and phony, major and minor, to aid in the quest. Nor surprisingly, the
first one, Winston Niles Rumfoord, is as deluded as those he seeks to lead,
yet his messianic intentions, if a bit cynical, are nonetheless sincere. He is out
to prove to the inhabitants of Earth that their old religions are useless and
myopic, while his at least has the benefit of being headed by someone who
can see into the future. His elaborately engineered invasion of the planet,
while based on an advanced degree of Machiavellian callousness toward the
individual, accomplishes its purpose of uniting the peoples of the Earth
under one banner. His use of Malachi Constant as an unwilling junior
partner in the reformation is for a valid metaphysical purpose:

> "We are *disgusted* by Malachi Constant," said
> Winston Niles Rumfoord up in his treetops, "because he
> used the fantastic fruits of his fantastic good luck to finance
> an unending demonstration that man is a pig. He wallowed
> in sycophants. He wallowed in worthless women. He
> wallowed in lascivious entertainments and alcohol and drugs.
> He wallowed in every known form of voluptuous turpitude.
>
> "At the height of his good luck, Malachi Constant
> was worth more than the states of Utah and North Dakota
> combined. Yet, I daresay, his moral worth was not that of
> the most corrupt little fieldmouse in either state.
>
> "We are *angered* by Malachi Constant," said
> Rumfoord up in his treetop, "because he did nothing to
> deserve his billions, and because he did nothing unselfish or
> imaginative with his billions. He was as benevolent as Marie
> Antoinette, as creative as a professor of cosmetology in an
> embalming college.
>
> "We *hate* Malachi Constant," said Rumfoord up in
> his treetop, "because he accepted the fantastic fruits of his
> fantastic good luck without a qualm, as though luck were
> the hand of God. To us of the Church of God the Utterly
> Indifferent, there is nothing more cruel, more dangerous,
> more blasphemous that a man can do than to believe that—
> that luck, good or bad, is the hand of God!"

Rumfoord's religion is, finally, spurious; the three people most intimately involved with its inception, Malachi, his wife Beatrice and son Chrono, are not believers. Beatrice spends her last days on Titan writing "a book called *The True Purpose of Life in the Solar System*," refuting Rumfoord's claims, and Chrono flits about the satellite making miniature Stonehenges in true primitive fashion. Malachi, manipulated as he was by Rumfoord, least of all believes the tenets of the Church of God the Utterly Indifferent. More important than all this, of course, is the fact that Rumfoord discovers he is an unwitting agent of Tralfamadore, making any success he might have had meaningless in the larger scheme of things. All that he has actually accomplished is the death of thousands of people. Rumfoord bears an embarrassing resemblance to Yahweh in this respect. Essentially a tribal god, Rumfoord fails to see the larger pattern into which his chosen people fit, and thus causes more harm than good, the "good" being the exhortation to love other people, which is the only ethic the novel suggests.

The next major messiah to appear is, of course, Lionel Boyd Johnson, alias Bokonon. His contributions seem more substantial, because they are based on love and compassion for others, but they are basically as cynical and turn out to be as illusory as Rumfoord's. And like his predecessor, Bokonon becomes disillusioned with his own teachings, when the world is destroyed by the freak accident of ice-nine. He had been forced into believing them by the nature of his role, which in itself is a trenchant comment on all messiahs or would-be messiahs:

> "But people didn't have to pay as much attention to the awful truth. As the living legend of the cruel tyrant in the city and the gentle holy man in the jungle grew, so, too, did the happiness of the people grow. They were all employed full time as actors in a play they understood, that any human being anywhere could understand and applaud."
>
> "So life became a work of art," I marveled.
>
> "Yes. There was only one trouble with it."
>
> "Oh?"
>
> "The drama was very tough on the souls of the two main actors, McCabe and Bokonon. As young men, they had been pretty much alike, had both been half-angel, half-pirate.
>
> "But the drama demanded that the pirate half of Bokonon and the angel half of McCabe wither away. And McCabe and Bokonon paid a terrible price in agony for the happiness of the people—McCabe knowing the agony of

the tyrant and Bokonon knowing the agony of the saint.
They both became, for all practical purposes, insane."

Vonnegut's aims in this respect seem clear. He is attempting to show, in *Sirens* and *Cat's Cradle*, the futility of, first, metaphysics, and then organized religion, while conceding the comforting qualities of each. And each time he is employing the satirist's weapon of dystopian divorcement to remove his targets from the battle-ground of uncomfortable reality. The character and role of Kilgore Trout, the next messiah, seems somewhat less clear. When he first appears in *Rosewater* it seems apparent that if he is not actually the reincarnation of Jesus Christ, representing the ineffectuality of the Christian ethic today, he is at least a Christ figure. The fact that the eccentric Eliot Rosewater is the only one who can appreciate him is appropriate, because Christ-Kilgore's teachings are no more palatable to the other characters than Prince Myshkin's or Faulkner's corporal's would be. If one interprets Eliot's recovery from his nervous breakdown and subsequent acknowledgement of all the bastards of Rosewater County, Indiana, as a triumph, then Trout must be given at least part of the credit for it, which would make him the most effective messiah in the novels. This is the impression one gets from *Rosewater*. However, in the next novel, Vonnegut goes to some length to vitiate this impression by showing his "cracked messiah" at Billy Pilgrim's eighteenth wedding anniversary party, "gobbling canapes, . . . talking with a mouthful of Philadelphia cream cheese and salmon roe to an optometrist's wife," and in general playing the litterateur among the peasantry. Instead of working in a TV stamp redemption store here, he is in charge of newsboys (an irritating habit of Vonnegut's, by the way; in his Lewisian use of characters in several novels and stories he is not consistent in their names, occupations, *etc.*) and exhibits very little compassion for them, exhorting them as he does to "get their daily customers to subscribe to the fucking Sunday edition too." Yet Trout is the only character in the novel to believe Billy's contention that he travels in time; indeed, he suspects it. Perhaps Vonnegut is attempting to show that even such a sincere and perceptive thinker as Trout is forced by the ethically hostile climate of the modern world into the role of jester, or it could be that he is simply not willing to commit himself to a totally favorable picture of any character; certainly none exists anywhere in his work. In the basically absurd world of Vonnegut's writing, it would be asking too much of any person to make perfect sense.

In addition to these acknowledged messiahs in the novels, other characters fulfill a similar function on a lesser plane. Malachi Constant, already mentioned in this connection, is the putative messiah of *The Sirens of Titan*, Eliot plays a crackpot Christ in Rosewater County, Indiana; and in

Mother Night there are several charismatic leaders of an even less respectable sort, notably the Reverend Doctor Lionel Jason David Jones, D.D.S., D.D. With the exception of *Player Piano*, which contains a political messiah, Paul Proteus, each of Vonnegut's novels has at least one figure who is concerned with the theological well-being of the race, even if, like Rumfoord, he is a Machiavel, or like Bokonon, a fraud, or, as Billy Pilgrim says of Trout in a moment of candor, "his prose [is] frightful."

One hesitates to draw more implications from this extensive use of the messiah other than the obvious one that Vonnegut, like Hesse, is a writer who is interested in theological problems and thus by including characters who represent various forms of the Promised One is able to comment on His illusory nature, yet indicate a yearning for Him nonetheless. It is perhaps significant that Kilgore Trout plays only a minor part in the sixth novel, the author's most resigned and hopeful to date. The next published work will help answer the question of whether the messiah belongs to the early, searching Vonnegut and will have no place in his later novels.

There is indeed a definite tendency away from nihilism and toward some sort of tentative affirmation in the six novels published to date. Placing the first book in the category of "preparation," it is possible to make the following analysis of the thematic progress of his work:

> *The Sirens of Titan*—Early disillusionment
> *Mother Night*—Preoccupation with guilt
> *Cat's Cradle*—Folly of collective answers such as religion
> *God Bless You, Mr. Rosewater*—Possibility of individual
>   answers
> *Slaughterhouse-Five*—Mature acceptance of man's condi-
> tion

In each of the last four books Vonnegut becomes increasingly less pessimistic. The meaninglessness of *Sirens* is replaced in *Cat's Cradle* with a nose-thumbing gesture at "You Know Who," but at least there *is* a You Know Who. *God Bless You, Mr. Rosewater* strikes the same wary but hopefully teleological note. Eliot, besieged by greedy relatives, deserted by his wife, fighting for what remains of his sanity, is still trying on the novel's last page to put his money to work for the common good. He is still trying to "love the unlovables," to play beneficent god to them in the hope that there really is a beneficent god, or at least an alert one. At the end of the novel he tells his flock to "be fruitful and to multiply." And, one might add, while multiplying, to take time out for work. Vonnegut comes back again and again in his writing to the Voltairean work ethic, which is frequently the last refuge for the failed metaphysician. In *Player Piano* only those people who still have manual labor to perform are happy; in *Rosewater*, the fishermen-turned-soupmakers engage in an idyllic work scene, which although not illustrative of Vonnegut's best prose, indicates that if he ever writes a sentimental novel with a conventional happy ending, the hero almost certainly will wear a blue collar.

It is difficult to understand why Vonnegut was dismissed for so long with the disreputable title of science-fiction writer, since from the very beginning he has been dealing with metaphysical, ethical, and epistemological questions in his work. One must conclude that his imagination and talent for eccentric detail actually worked against him with the critics, who rarely looked beneath the surface gloss to the rugged terrain underneath. On first reading, the intricate plot and fascinating detail of *The Sirens of Titan* can indeed obscure the serious intent and probing, if not traditionally scholarly examination of the cosmological question. Vonnegut, after all, is a novelist, not an academician or a philosopher, and he deals with theme in the manner of a creative writer—with all the stylistic devices at his command. Certainly he is fond of space ships, time travel, and other gimmickry, but these phenomena, after all, represent the latter half of the twentieth century far better than would the riverboat journeys of Twain, the small town life of Sherwood Anderson, or the physical encounters with death of Ernest Hemingway. At any rate, neither Vonnegut's motives nor techniques need be defended in a discussion of his themes, which are without doubt as respectable a collection as could be found anywhere in the modern American novel.

Player Piano (1952) is an interesting starting point, because it shows Vonnegut first rather dimly perceiving how he feels about man's place in the cosmos. This first novel is a work of science fiction in that it is set in the future and uses mechanical gadgetry to some extent. Its thematic concerns, however, are economic and political, its tone polemic. Of previous novels it most closely resembles *1984* and *Brave New World*.

The setting is Ilium, New York, sometime in the future, when war has been abolished, and the scientific revolution has extended the fruits of its technology to all citizens. Ilium is a microcosm of society, "divided into three parts. In the northwest are the managers and engineers and civil servants and a few professional people; in the northeast are the machines; and in the south, across the Iroquois River, is the area known locally as Homestead, where almost all of the people live."

During World War II, business and industry discovered that they could function more efficiently without inefficient people; the result is that society has become almost fully automated, with the exception of such skills as barbering and bartending, deemed necessary when attempts to automate them failed.

They'd set up the experimental unit . . . with coin machines and endless belts to do the serving, with full light, with continuous soft music from a tape recorder, with seats scientifically designed by an anthropologist to give the average man the absolute maximum in comfort.

The first day had been a sensation, with a waiting line extending blocks. Within a week of the opening, curiosity has been satisfied, and it was a boom day when five customers stopped in. Then this place had opened up almost next door, with a dust-and-germ trap of a Victorian bar, bad light, poor ventilation, and an unsanitary, inefficient, and probably dishonest bartender. It was an immediate and unflagging success.

Nearly everything else has been automated, however, with the natural result that millions of people have nothing to do. Upon graduation from secondary school, each person has an "Achievement and Aptitude Profile" keypunched for him, reducing him to an IBM card. Any man or woman whose IQ is insufficient to qualify him for college work leading to the Ph.D. and thence into a supervisory position, is forced into either the Army or the Reconstruction and Reclamation Corps, the "Reeks and Wrecks," who are, simply, road repairmen. The only cash they receive for this work is spending money, since regular deductions are made from their pay for car and furniture payments, rent, and the myriad insurances that make their lives secure. The women, blessed with fully automated homes, likewise have nothing to do.

Pride in accomplishment exists only on the managerial level, and it is a bogus pride kept alive by a lodge-brother atmosphere and yearly retreats to "The Meadows," where careers are made or broken amidst "an orgy of morale building—through team athletics, group sings, bonfires and skyrockets, bawdy entertainment, free whisky and cigars; and through plays, . . . which pleasantly but unmistakably made clear the nature of good deportment within the system . . ." This elite class of engineers and managers, all with Ph.D.'s, keeps the machinery running smoothly, although they too actually have little to do and are occasionally put out of work by a machine of their own invention. They form also a sort of religious hierarchy, constantly concerned with rationalizing its own existence and proclaiming the superiority of the system. The hero of the novel, Paul Proteus, is of this class, and the conflict in the story is played out through his gradual awareness that the system strips the masses of their dignity, and his unsuccessful attempts to reform it.

Proteus' credentials are impeccable; he is the son of the nation's "first National Industrial, Commercial, Communications, Foodstuffs and Resources Director, a position approached in importance only by the President of the United States." He is happily married to a rather unintelligent but faithful girl whom he rescued from false pregnancy, and who would rather die than admit that she is in the elite only through marriage. Director of the Ilium works, Proteus is soon to be tapped for a more important, regional position. He betrays, however, some typical weaknesses. He is fond of the inefficient Building # 58 for its historical interest (it is Edison's old machineshop, built in 1886; Vonnegut might have charged Edison with the crime of initiating automation, but he does not, neither here nor in the rest of his writings), he drives an old car with a broken headlight, and he occasionally slips off to Homestead to drink in the Victorian saloon there. Through his best friend, Finnerty, who is thoroughly disillusioned with Utopia, Proteus meets the underground resistance in the area and eventually, inadvertently aided by his wife, leads the insurrection against the government, which ends in an orgy of destruction and the defeat of the rebels.

Annoyed at the trend toward automation and the submergence of the individual in a collective state, Vonnegut alternately pokes fun at the situation and rather pessimistically describes the attempts of a few right thinkers to do something about it. What begins as a diatribe against his real life enemies—General Electric, academe, and the United States government—gradually takes on more impressive proportions with the introduction of two foreign observers, who force both the author and the reader to examine the questions raised in a brighter, more objective light. What starts as a sort of technological *Bildungsroman* focussed on Paul Proteus as hero adds layers of meaning as Proteus' importance diminishes. He is on stage more often than any other character, but Vonnegut manipulates him more as the novel progresses; the satiric attack, while still individualized, begins to deal with its targets in a more universalized fashion. Proteus' conspirators in the insurrection are finally unmasked as unworthy, exposed as, in their own ways, just as corrupt as the society they sought to overthrow, because none of them had any real concern for the people they were ostensibly trying to save.

> The bottle went around the group.
> "The record," said Finnerty, and he seemed satisfied
> with the toast. He had got what he wanted from the revo-
> lution, Paul supposed—a chance to give a savage blow to a
> close little society that made no comfortable place for him.
> "To the record," said von Neumann. He, too, seemed

> at peace. To him, the revolution had been a fascinating experiment, Paul realized. He had been less interested in achieving a premeditated end than in seeing what would happen with given beginnings.
>
> Paul took the bottle and studied Lasher for a moment over its fragrant mouth. Lasher, the chief instigator of it all, was contented. A lifelong trafficker in symbols, he had created the revolution as a symbol, and was now welcoming the opportunity to die as one.

Only Paul is "pure," and he is pure because he alone has been an idealist, has believed that individual man was worth salvaging, while the others, by their presuppositions, indicate nothing but contempt for the masses. The point to all this is that Vonnegut is examining the question of man's worth first through the eyes of man—his insurrectionists—and he is illustrating *man's* historically negative answer, which has produced centuries of war, oppression, poverty, and the final debasement of the individual in modern society.

It was seven years later, in 1959, before Vonnegut got a second novel published, and in paperback form. This book, *The Sirens of Titan*, despite its humble origins and its science fiction trappings, is a serious and highly original metaphysical treatise which, although totally different in style, is in the tradition of *Siddhartha*, *Der Zauberberg*, and *L'Etranger*. Beneath the surface interest and amusement generated by space ships, an invasion of Earth by Mars, a sojourn in the caves of Mercury, and an exile on one of the moons of Saturn, Vonnegut is wrestling with nothing less than the cosmological question.

The novel's plot is fascinating. In the days of the "Nightmare Age," "between the Second World War and the Third Great Depression," Winston Niles Rumfoord, wealthy Newport socialite, has accidentally flown his space ship into a "chrono-synclastic infundibulum," a curved time funnel, which has resulted in the disintegration of Rumfoord and his dog and their subsequent reappearance as "wave phenomena—apparently pulsing in a distorted spiral with its origin in the Sun and its terminal in Betelgeuse." Rumfoord, who, because of his accident, can read minds and see into the future, summons to his estate Malachi Constant, the richest and luckiest man in America, to inform him that he will be bred like a farm animal on Mars—with Rumfoord's wife, Beatrice—and will be exiled to Mercury and Titan before returning to Earth.

Constant, whose first name means "faithful messenger," Vonnegut points out, tries to forestall this prophecy by selling *his* space ship, going on a fifty-two day debauch, and sending Mrs. Rumfoord insulting letters: "Hello from sunny California, Space Baby! Gee, I am sure looking forward to jazzing a high-class dame like you under the twin moons of Mars. You're the only kind of dame I never had, and I'll bet your kind is the greatest. Love and kisses for a starter. Mal." Beatrice, for her part, is prepared to take cyanide rather than to prove her husband right.

The next third of the novel describes the invasion of Earth by Martians (who are transplanted Earthlings), the defeat and slaughter of the invaders, and the subsequent revelation that the entire campaign, encompassing as it did the kidnapping of thousands of people, the establishment of an entire society on Mars, and the invasion itself, made possible by a new power source called the "Universal Will to Become," had all been engineered by Winston Niles Rumfoord for the purpose of inaugurating a new religion on Earth—the Church of God the Utterly Indifferent. Rumfoord, whose vantage point in the galaxy enables him to see how ridiculous is the idea of a personal deity, is playing the role of a Nietzschean Superman. He brings out the Winston Niles Rumfoord Authorized Revised Bible, for his three billion converts, provides them with martyred saints (the Martians), sickens them on war (the invasion, because the Martians have nothing but outdated weapons and attack in forces no more than battalion size, is a massacre that even Earthlings cannot enjoy), and gives them for the first time a sound, empirical basis for a religion. "'Why should you believe in this religion, rather than any other?' said Rumfoord. 'You should believe in it because I, as head of this religion, can work miracles, and the head of no other religion can. What miracles can I work? I can work the miracle of predicting, with absolute accuracy, the things that the future will bring.'" The religion's motto is: "Take Care of the People, and God Almighty Will Take Care of Himself."

Beneath all this fantastic detail, of course, Vonnegut is seriously grappling with a deadly serious theological problem. Rumfoord's Martians are Vonnegut's Job, as this excerpt from an Utterly Indifferent sermon shows:

"O Lord Most High, Creator of the Cosmos, Spinner of Galaxies, Soul of Electromagnetic Waves, Inhaler and Exhaler of Inconceivable Volumes of Vacuum, Spitter of Fire and Rock, Trifler with Millennia—what could we do for Thee that Thou couldst not do for Thyself one octillion times better? Nothing. What could we do or say that could possibly interest Thee? Nothing. Oh, Mankind, rejoice in the apathy of our Creator, for it makes us free and truthful and dignified at last. No longer can a fool like Malachi Constant point to a ridiculous accident of good luck and say, 'Somebody up there likes me.' And no longer can a tyrant say, 'God wants this or that to happen, and anybody who doesn't help this or that to happen is against God.' O Lord Most High, what a glorious weapon is Thy Apathy, for we have unsheathed it, have thrust and slashed mightily with it, and the claptrap that has so often enslaved us or driven us into the madhouse lies slain!"

—The Reverend C. Horner Redwine

Malachi, meanwhile, is performing another function of Rumfoord's plan. He is in exile in the caves of Mercury, awaiting return to Earth as the Messiah, who will prove this time not that there is a beneficent God, but exactly the opposite. He is, in his apotheosis as Space Wanderer and his real identity of Malachi Constant, both Christ and Satan. When, upon his arrival in Newport, he utters the prophecy-fulfilling words, "I was a victim of a series of accidents as are we all," and Rumfoord exposes him as the hated Constant, he becomes an object-lesson for all mankind, and, because he is to be further exiled to Titan, "a dignified sacrifice to remember and ponder through all time."

At this point in the novel, it would seem that Vonnegut is expounding, through his agent Rumfoord, a cynical brand of Deism, simply manipulating his characters by means of Rumfoord's fantastic scheme, to prove his contentions. While this is true, if the allegory stopped there, it would not have the impact the author obviously intends. What makes this novel unique is that in the final chapters Vonnegut shows us that Rumfoord himself is but a dupe of a higher power—a messenger from another galaxy—and that the chain of unknowing does not stop even there, because the force that is pulling Rumfoord's strings is being guided by an equally meaningless power from above!

The messenger is Salo, a tangerine-colored robot from Tralfamadore (all of whose inhabitants are robots), whose duty it is to carry a "sealed message from 'One Rim of the Universe to the Other.'" We are led to believe that it is of great importance; indeed, after Salo is forced down on Titan by the mechanical failure of his Universal-Will-to-Become-powered space ship, the Tralfamadorians go to great lengths to get him a replacement part. As a matter of fact, as Rumfoord discovers just before his death, everything that has happened on Earth for the past 203,117 years has been guided by Tralfamadore, for the single purpose of getting the part to Salo. What were considered some of our greatest achievements in Art, Science, Religion, Politics, and Architecture, prove to be nothing more than giant letters in the sand:

It was through this viewer [on his space ship] that he got his first reply from Tralfamadore. The reply was written on Earth in huge stones on a plain in what is now England. The ruins of the reply still stand, and are known as Stonehenge. The meaning of Stonehenge in Tralfamadorian, when viewed from above is: *"Replacement part being rushed with all possible speed."*

Stonehenge wasn't the only message old Salo had received.

There had been four others, all of them written on Earth.

The Great Wall of China means in Tralfamadorian, when viewed from above: *"Be patient. We haven't forgotten about you."*

The Golden House of the Roman Emperor Nero meant: *"We are doing the best we can."*

The meaning of the Moscow Kremlin when it was first walled was: *"You will be on your way before you know it."*

The meaning of the Palace of the League of Nations in Geneva, Switzerland, is: *"Pack up your things and be ready to leave on short notice."*

Thus, Malachi and Beatrice, instead of being Rumfoord's puppets, turn out to be working for Salo. Their Martian son, Chrono, delivers the vital piece of metal, "about the size of an Earthling beer-can opener," which has been his good luck charm. Rumfoord, of course, has the same master. His new religion of the Utterly Indifferent, although more than ever appropriate, turns out to be just another agent for making the right things happen at the right time.

And what is this momentous message that is so important two hundred centuries of Earthly life have gone into the spreading of it?

He [Salo] held out the square of aluminum in a cupped foot.

"A dot," he said.

"A single dot," he said.

"The meaning of a dot in Tralfamadorian," said Old Salo, "is—"

"Greetings."

The novel ends with Malachi, who has decided that "a purpose of human life, no matter who is controlling it, is to love whoever is around to be loved," returning to die in Indianapolis, Indiana, because it was the first place in the United States where a white man was hanged for murdering an Indian. "The kind of people who'll hang a white man for murdering an Indian—" said Constant, "that's the kind of people for me." Beatrice and

Rumfoord are already dead, Constant's son Chrono is living with birds on Titan, and Salo, finding nothing better to do, decides to continue on his fool's errand.

In this novel Vonnegut has raised his eyes to the heavens, and further universalized the problem. *The Sirens of Titan* picks up where *Player Piano* left off, and, although he disguises it by making the reader think that the conflict in the novel is between Winston Niles Rumfoord and humanity represented by Malachi Constant, later to be known as "Unk," the opponent here is actually none other than God himself. Does anybody up there really like us? Is there really anybody up there at all? Are those who are manipulating us here on earth being in turn manipulated by a higher power? Vonnegut's answer to all these questions is a firm, but not nihilistic no. Although the book is deeply pessimistic in its philosophical conclusions, showing an earth that is nothing more than a semaphore for the signal needs of another planet equally engaged in a meaningless pursuit, the story is told with a good deal of detachment, and there are some indications of meaning, e.g., the fact that Malachi writes a history and Beatrice a poem. Vonnegut has never in his writing seemed willing to settle for Carl Becker's conclusion that man has supplied his own meaning to the universe, but he seems to approach it here and in other places, most notably in the saintly Eliot's attempts to love everybody. Yet *The Sirens of Titan*, taken on its face value, presents a world in which the earth and the other planets in the solar systems are no better off than the citizens of Ilium who are being mechanically directed by computers and forced to perform according to the facts and figures punched on their IBM cards. The novel represents a cul-de-sac for the cosmological question, one which Vonnegut was not to get out of until he had progressed to *God Bless You, Mr. Rosewater.*

Rosewater and *Mother Night*, neither of which is actually a metaphysical novel, deal with opposite sides of another, related question, but one which has implications strictly on the terrestrial level—guilt. They form a sort of tandem of polarity on the problem.

Mother Night (1961) purports to be the reminiscences of Howard W. Campbell, who has been a sort of "Nazi Edgar Guest," although the comparison to Pound is more accurate. A playwright, married to a German girl and living in Germany in the thirties, Campbell is approached by an American intelligence agent, Frank Wirtanen, and asked to become a spy while posing as loyal to the Nazis. We are not told this until chapter eight, however, while Vonnegut gives us a chance to observe Campbell in his prison in Israel, to which he has been abducted by Israeli agents he could easily have avoided. In the prison also is Adolf Eichmann, who asks Campbell if he should get a literary agent. "For book clubs and movie sales in the United States of

America, absolutely," Campbell tells him. His guard is an Estonian Jew who spent two years in Auschwitz, in which he was a volunteer corpse carrier. From him Campbell learns of the daily, grisly announcement, "*Leichentrager zu Wache*," which was always "crooned, like a nursery rhyme," and which meant "Corpse-carriers to the guard-house." It is with the corpse-carriers as well as corpse-makers that Vonnegut deals in this novel.

The plot of *Mother Night* is a relatively simple one, but because Vonnegut configures it like a murder mystery (which, in an ironic sense, it is) the reader is kept guessing until the final page. Briefly, and chronologically, this is what happens: Campbell, released after the war by his intelligence contact, buries himself in Greenwich Village to mourn his dead wife, the beautiful actress Helga Noth (in *Slaughterhouse-Five* she is called North), and live out quietly the remaining years of his life listening to one of his twenty-six recordings of Bing Crosby's *White Christmas* and playing chess with a neighbor, George Kraft. This self-entombment, however, is interrupted by the appearance of an article, titled "American Tragedy!" which appears in *The White Christian Minuteman*, a right-wing hatesheet written by the Reverend Doctor Lionel Jason David Jones, D.D.S., D.D., who considers Campbell an unsung hero. Jones also produces Helga, still beautiful if white-haired, back from slave labor in Russia. Helga's reappearance leads to several chapters of flashback, during which we see Campbell in Germany at the time of the fall of Berlin. The reunion idyll is broken up by the beating of Campbell by a veteran and the disclosure that Helga is really her little sister, Resi, who is working for Kraft, who in turn is really Iona Potapov, a Russian spy. The two of them plan to spirit Campbell off to Mexico and then to Russia under the pretext that they are protecting him from further beatings and abduction by the Israelis. During a meeting of Jones' Iron Guardsmen of the White Sons of the American Constitution, however, they are arrested by American agents (Campbell is soon released), Resi commits suicide, and Kraft goes to Leavenworth. Campbell then returns to his flat to confront his conscience, Bernard B. O'Hare, who has come to kill him in the name of humanity, but who instead gets a lecture and a broken arm from Campbell. The "traitor" then turns himself in to the Jewish couple living in the building and hears again the phrase, *Leichentrager zu Wache*, which the old woman croons to him as they wait for Israeli agents. In the final chapter, although he receives a letter from Wirtanen exonerating him, the hero decides to commit suicide.

Between the two-part ethical discussion of hate and love in the third and fifth novels, Vonnegut returned to the themes introduced in *Player Piano*. The fourth novel, *Cat's Cradle* (1963), is simply an update of the themes first introduced there, done with greater novelistic skill and brevity. Although the plot of *Cat's Cradle*, ending as it does in the destruction of life on earth, is as potentially pessimistic as any other he has used, the author's reaction to this tragic turn of events is to thumb his nose at the One responsible. The satire is there, but it is Horatian. The denouement is catastrophic, but this time there is an added element to make it less horrible. Without being facetious, it is possible to assert that *Cat's Cradle* is Vonnegut's "Ash Wednesday."

Bokononism—the gentle religion practiced only on a small Caribbean island and unknown in the powerful United States of America—which tells its adherents to "Live by the harmless untruths that make you brave and kind and healthy and happy," is the real hero of this novel. It is palpably a hoax, believed in neither by its originator and prophet, Bokonon, the former Lionel Boyd Johnson, Negro, ex-infantryman, sailor, gardener, carpenter, and alumnus of Charles Atlas' body-building school, nor by its sworn enemy, "Papa" Monzano, dictator of San Lorenzo, who has made adherence to the religion punishable by death (although he is a secret adherent himself). But to its followers, the underprivileged inhabitants of the island, it provides the most important element in their drab lives—hope. As Bokonon says in one of his calypsos, which are the equivalent of the Judaeo-Christian psalms:

> I wanted all things
> To seem to make some sense,
> So we all could be happy, yes,
> Instead of tense.
> And I made up lies
> So that they all fit nice,
> And I made this sad world
> A par-a-dise.

Bokononism has, in fact, been manufactured by two marooned soldiers, Johnson and Earl McCabe, one of whom becomes the outlawed prophet, the other the political ruler. "When it became evident that no governmental or economic reform was going to make the people much less miserable, the religion became the one real instrument of hope. Truth was the enemy of the people, because the truth was so terrible, so Bokonon made it his business to provide the people with better and better lies."

The putative hero of the novel is a writer and a Melville admirer. He begins his book with the admonition, "Call me Jonah. My parents did, or nearly did. They called me John." Jonah, or John, working on a non-fiction book titled *The Day the World Ended*, is searching for information about the late Dr. Felix Hoenikker, father of the atomic bomb. His quest takes him to Ilium, New York, to discover more about Hoenikker's three children, Newt, a midget, Frank, who is wanted by the police, and Angela, a six-foot, "horse-faced platinum blonde" clarinet player, and then to San Lorenzo, where Frank has become "Minister of Science and Progress" to Papa Monzano. Not so coincidentally, according to Bokonon, Newt and Angela are on the same flight as Jonah—the reason it is not coincidence is that they are part of the same *karass*, a religious cell organized by God without the knowledge of its members for a purpose equally beyond their understanding. The *wampeter*, or pivot, of their *karass* is a nasty little invention of Dr. Hoenikker's, called ice-nine, which he has fabricated in his spare time, and is more dangerous than all the atomic weaponry of the major powers. It is a form of ice which, because its melting point is 114.4 degrees Fahrenheit, has the capacity to freeze instantly any water with which it comes into contact. Dr. Hoenikker, the apotheosis of the disinterested scientist, has casually given his three children a chip of the material (which they dutifully divided) upon his death on Christmas Eve—a combination Nativity-Thanatos present.

The remainder of the novel chronicles the hero's increasing under-standing of Bokononism, his elevation to the presidency of San Lorenzo and betrothal to the beautiful Mona Aamons Monzano, who goes with the office, the death of Papa Monzano by ice-nine, and the subsequent accident in which Papa's body slides into the Caribbean, thus freezing the earth's water and ending life on the planet. Jonah, Mona, and a handful of others survive on the island, but because of the ever-present danger of imbibing ice-nine, their survival will be only temporary. It is during six months of living on frozen animals and canned goods that Jonah writes his account. At the very end he meets a disgusted Bokonon, "his feet . . . frosty with ice-nine," who tells him that he has written the last sentence of his bible:

> If I were a younger man, I would write a history of human stupidity; and I would climb to the top of Mount McCabe and lie down on my back with my history for a pillow; and I would take from the ground some of the blue-white poison that makes statues of men; and I would make a statue of myself, lying on my back, grinning horribly, and thumbing my nose at You Know Who.

This is also the last sentence of the novel.

Cat's Cradle is Vonnegut's first full-fledged satire. Although witty ridicule was a vital element in all of the first three novels, it did not dominate the proceedings as it does in the fourth. Religion, politics, business, science, and a gaggle of minor geese are all gleefully plucked here. Bokononism, of course, is a satire on primitive Christianity, with its ex-carpenter founder, its Caesar (McCabe), its outlawed status, its parabolic teachings. Mr. Johnson's religion, however, takes itself much less seriously, and is more overt about the canonical nature of its pronouncements. As the first sentence of The Books of Bokonon says, "All of the true things I am about to tell you are lies." And the author-protagonist also warns us, "Anyone unable to understand how a useful religion can be founded on lies will not understand this book either." The religion, incidentally, is also founded on a variation of Charles Atlas' principle of dynamic tension, the building of muscles by exercising them against each other. In Bokononism, Papa Monzano is the opposing muscle, the Yang to Bokonon's Yin.

The religious satire in *Cat's Cradle* is gentle, however, because Bokononism performs a necessary function—and its essential untruth does no one harm. It has no priesthood to be corrupted and no property to be coveted. Its ritual consists simply of *boko-maru*, the act of taking one's shoes off and sitting sole-to-sole [sic] with another person, for "the mingling of awarenesses." Bokononism began as a rather cynical response to the island's poverty and oppression:

> "When Bokonon and McCabe took over this miserable country years ago," said Julian Castle, "they threw out the priests. And then Bokonon, cynically and playfully, invented a new religion."
>
> "I know," I said.
>
> "Well, when it became evident that no governmental or economic reform was going to make the people much less miserable, the religion became the one real instrument of hope. Truth was the enemy of the people, because the truth was so terrible, so Bokonon made it his business to provide the people with better and better lies."

The better and better lies, of course, being Bokononism. Eliot Rosewater applies the same principle when he answers the telephone in his Foundation offices; he tells lies to Diana Moon Glampers and the other unlovables. He tells them, in effect, that they are worth something—otherwise, why would a man of his importance give his time, money, and consideration to them?

God Bless You, Mr. Rosewater (1965) is unquestionably Vonnegut's best novel to date. Instead of focussing on the abstract, philosophical aspects of the human condition, as he had done previously, this time he sought a practical answer, one that could be of more tangible use than the nihilistic whining of Howard W. Campbell or the hero of *Cat's Cradle*. This time he asked an answerable question, *viz.*, "how to love people who have no use." Although the angst is still evident, and the major villains of his novels—business, fire, and automation—are just as virulently active, they do not triumph this time. Eliot Rosewater triumphs.

The book's subtitle is *Pearls Before Swine*, but it could easily be *Mr. Deeds Goes to Town and Becomes an Alcoholic Who Chases Fires*. Eliot, who is a Christ-figure, a Hamlet, a Lear, a Miss Lonelyhearts with a Million, has ensconced himself in a dingy attic in Rosewater, Indiana, with two telephones, one red (for fire calls) and one black (with the Rosewater Foundation's number), over which he acts the part of financial and social ombudsman to the suffering souls of Rosewater County. Eliot hopes that by daily dispensing his fortune of three and a half million dollars a year interest to the victims of the American economic system (of which he is one of the chief beneficiaries) and offering love to those whom money will not help, he can expunge the guilt of his inherited wealth and his accidental murder of three German firemen during World War II.

The circumstances that have led Eliot to this intemperate response are chronicled in the opening chapters of the novel. He has returned to civilian life a hero, married a beautiful girl, earned a doctorate in international law, and taken over the Rosewater Foundation in its original, intended form, dispensing money for birth control clinics, cancer research, and college sabbaticals. The first evidence that something is wrong with him comes when he gets drunk and breaks in on the science-fiction writers' conference in Milford, Pennsylvania. From Milford Eliot goes to Swarthmore and delivers a tearful lecture in a bar on the dangers of breathing oxygen and the glorious fidelity of volunteer firefighters, and thence across the country, drinking with firemen, trading away his expensive clothes for Robert Hall suits and war surplus jackets, losing all his friends in the process.

> He drove away his rich friends by telling them that whatever they had was based on dumb luck. He advised his artist friends that the only people who paid any attention to what they did were rich horses' asses with nothing more athletic to do. He asked his scholarly friends, "Who has time to read all the boring crap you write and listen to all the boring things you say?" He alienated his friends in the sciences by thanking them extravagantly for scientific advances he had read about in recent newspapers and magazines, by assuring them, with a perfectly straight face, that life was getting better and better, thanks to scientific thinking.

Eliot was, as Vonnegut says, "a flamboyantly sick man."

After a brief rejuvenation through psychoanalysis, he cracks up again during a Rosewater Foundation-sponsored performance of *Aida*, when he yells to Aida and Radames not to sing in their airtight crypt. "You will last a lot longer if you don't try to sing," he tells them. A disappearance and more alcoholic peregrinations follow, until Eliot gets the idea to move to Rosewater County, Indiana, where he becomes Fire Lieutenant, and he and Sylvia snub the petit bourgeois in the town to "throw lavish banquets for morons, perverts, starvelings and the unemployed." The results of this quixotic gesture are predictable: Sylvia has a nervous breakdown, burns down the firehouse, and is sent away to a sanatorium; Eliot, to the further chagrin of his senator father and the respectable citizens of the county, moves from the mansion to an attic over a lunchroom and liquor store, and re-establishes the Foundation in different form. This time he will spend its money not from the top down, but from the bottom up. We see him, "an athlete gone to lard, a big man, six-feet-three, two hundred thirty pounds, pale, balding on all sides of a wispy scalplock. He was swaddled in the elephant wrinkles of war-surplus long underwear. Written on gold letters on each of his windows, and on his street-level door, too, were these words:

ROSEWATER FOUNDATION
HOW CAN WE HELP
YOU?

What has just been described is only the first fifty pages of the novel, its introduction. Again, as in *Mother Night* and *Cat's Cradle*, Vonnegut saves the main narrative until he can intensify the reader's curiosity and lay sufficient groundwork so that the chronological story can be told economically. The last three-quarters of the novel show Eliot in philanthropic action, fighting for his sanity, and to keep his wife from divorcing him, while and unscrupulous Lebanese attorney, Norman Mushari, works in the background to steer the Foundation money into the hands of Eliot's feckless cousin, Fred Rosewater. Fred Rosewater is Gloucester to Eliot's Lear. Although the novel is more than half over before he appears, he is fully drawn, and except for his cousin, the most interesting character in the book. Existing at a lower level than the tragi-comic Eliot, Fred leads a pathetic life, selling insurance in Pisquontuit, Rhode Island, ("pronounced 'Pawn-it' by those who loved it, and 'Piss-on-it' by those who didn't"), killing time in drug stores where he looks longingly at the pictures in girly magazines but buys *Better Homes and Gardens*. He looks as if "he had been kicked and kicked and kicked every day of his life." And indeed he has, spiritually, by the empty life he leads, and physically by his social-climbing wife's endtables strewn all through the house. His only happiness comes when naive brides, to whose husbands he has sold huge insurance policies, thank him for creating large estates for them. "God bless you, Mr. Rosewater," one says, in the most ironic sentence of the novel.

The final section of the novel concerns Eliot's next break-down, his year's incarceration in a sanitarium, and his final victory over Norman Mushari, which is accomplished simply by giving one hundred thousand dollars to the Pisquontuit Rosewaters and by acknowledging all the illegitimate children attributed to him in Rosewater County (fifty-six), none of which is actually his. "Let their names be Rosewater from this moment on. And tell them that their father loves them, no matter what they may turn out to be. And tell them—" Eliot fell silent, raised his tennis racket as though it were a magic wand. "And tell them," he began again, "to be fruitful and multiply."

Man's seemingly endless capacity for hate manifests itself in *Cat's Cradle* in the form of ice, but in *God Bless You, Mr. Rosewater* fire is the agent, and the fire department Vonnegut's symbol of the antidote, love. (As far back as *The Sirens of Titan* the fire department bell was used to herald the return to earth of Unk, the messiah.) Eliot, who has accidentally killed some German firemen—performing the hateful act of war—venerates firemen, because, as Kilgore Trout tells him,

> "Your devotion to volunteer fire departments is very sane, too, Eliot, for they are, when the alarm goes off, almost the only examples of enthusiastic unselfishness to be seen in this land. They rush to the rescue of any human being and count not the cost. The most contemptible man in town, should his contemptible house catch fire, will see his enemies put the fire out. And, as he pokes through the ashes for remains of his contemptible possessions, he will be comforted and pitied by no less than the Fire Chief."
>
> Trout spread his hands. "There we have people treasuring people as people. It's extremely rare. So from this we must learn."

During one of his binges Eliot expounds on the reasons that firemen are the saviors of the earth:

> He went into a small bar there, announced that anyone who could produce a volunteer fireman's badge could drink with him free. He built gradually into a crying jag, during which he claimed to be deeply touched by the idea of an inhabited planet with an atmosphere that was eager to combine violently with almost everything the inhabitants held dear. He was speaking of Earth and the element oxygen.

"When you think about it, boys," he said brokenly, "that's what holds us together more than anything else, except maybe gravity. We few, we happy few, we band of brothers—joined in the serious business of keeping our food, shelter, clothing and loved ones from combining with oxygen. I tell you, boys, I used to belong to a volunteer fire department, and I'd belong to one now, if there were such a human thing, such a humane thing, in New York City." This was bunk about Eliot's being a fireman. The closest he had ever come to that was during his annual childhood visits to Rosewater County, to the family fief. Sycophants among the townies had flattered little Eliot by making him mascot of the Volunteer Fire Department of Rosewater. He had never fought a fire.

With *Rosewater*, Vonnegut makes two advances thematically; he stops stewing about unanswerable questions concerning the purpose of life, and second, he proposes an individual, workable ethic for those who, like Rosewater and Vonnegut, are plagued by guilt about their roles in the tragicomedy of existence. As noted before, the ethic is neither original nor profound, but it is positive. Rosewater takes Malachi Constant's advice to "love whoever is around to be loved," and carries it to its logical conclusion—he will love those people whom it is impossible to love for one's own gain. His senator father and socialite wife are lovable for potentially selfish reasons, so he literally abandons them for the havenots and lowlifes of Rosewater County. After all, if there is no god to love them, who else will? The therapeutic effects of this indiscriminate love are less evident on the donor than on the recipients. Confronted with his father's accusations that he made a mess of his life and hated those two people closest to him, Eliot has a nervous breakdown that sends him to a sanitarium, but the possible benefit to others, as envisioned by Kilgore Trout, is immense:

> "It seems to me," said Trout, "that the main lesson Eliot learned is that people can use all the uncritical love they can get."
> "This is news?" the Senator raucously inquired.
> "It's news that a man was able to *give* that kind of love over a long period of time. If one man can do it, perhaps others can do it, too. It means that our hatred of useless human beings and the cruelties we inflict upon them for their own good need not be parts of human nature. Thanks to the example of Eliot Rosewater, millions upon millions of people may learn to love and help whomever they see."

Like Howard W. Campbell, war criminal, Eliot Rosewater, war criminal, holes himself up in a small room away from his own kind, but unlike Campbell, Eliot does not become a recluse. In quixotic fashion he tries to atone for his former hate by working and loving; Vonnegut's ethical modus operandi is, of course, nothing more than the work ethic mixed with early Christian love, and Eliot Rosewater's earthly success at applying it is no greater than was Christ's, a fact of which Vonnegut must have been cognizant when he wrote the ingenuously optimistic lines of Trout quoted above.

It is not difficult to place *Slaughterhouse-Five* (1969) in Vonnegut's cosmos, although the book represents both a step forward and one backward philosophically. *Slaughterhouse-Five* is a novel about which it might be said with only a bit of facetiousness that it is written entirely *in medias res.* After a non-fictional first chapter describing his problems in writing the book Vonnegut introduces the protagonist, Billy Pilgrim, with the statement, "Billy Pilgrim has come unstuck in time." From then on until the last of the book's 186 pages, we view Billy in Parmenidesian fashion, at the various stages of his life, but primarily three: his wartime nightmare, his postwar life as an optometrist in Ilium, New York, and his captivity on the planet Tralfamadore as a zoomate to Montana Wildhack, the former blue movie queen. These three settings switch constantly and usually without transition; no vital word or recollective scene such as triggered Benjy Compson's shiftings are needed. The purpose of this technique is not so much stylistic as ideational. Vonnegut, taking the stance of the Eliot of *Four Quartets*, is trying to show us that "all moments, past, present, and future, always have existed, and always will exist." We are all "bugs in amber," as his Tralfamadorian abductor tells Billy. But in Vonnegut's universe, unlike Eliot's, there is no free will, no good or evil. What is, is. When Billy tells a Tralfamadorian crowd that the most important thing he has learned on the planet is how to live in peace, after spending most of his life on savage Earth, the inhabitants laugh at him.

> "Would—would you mind telling me—" he said to the guide, much deflated, "what was so stupid about that?"
>
> "We know how the Universe ends—" said the guide, "and Earth has nothing to do with it, except that *it* gets wiped out, too."
>
> "How—how *does* the Universe end?" said Billy.
>
> "We blow it up, experimenting with new fuels for our flying saucers. A Tralfamadorian test pilot presses a starter button and the whole Universe disappears." So it goes.
>
> "If you know this," said Billy, "isn't there some way you

can prevent it? Can't you keep the pilot from *pressing* the button?"

"He has *always* pressed it, and he always *will*. We *always* let him and we *always will* let him. The moment is *structured* that way."

Actually, the most important thing that Billy learns is that no one really dies—"When a person dies he only *appears* to die. He is still very much alive in the past, so it is very silly for people to cry at his funeral." On these two rather ancient beliefs, then, the Objective Idealism of Parmenides and the concept of immortality in some form, Vonnegut bases the rational structure of his novel. They are, quite simply, the comforts which have enabled him to live with his wartime nightmare. In such a philosophical system, no single event, however horrible, can have great significance because it is not perceived as a fixed point in time, nor do the victims of death cease to have some kind of consciousness. Billy Pilgrim's own death, scheduled for February 13, 1976, is described in the novel as "simply violet light and a hum." Then Billy returns to life at an earlier time and place. All of Vonnegut's attempts to explain the sorry condition mankind is in, after the deep pessimism of *The Sirens of Titan*, can be viewed as slightly more optimistic than the previous. *Mother Night, Cat's Cradle*, and *God Bless You, Mr. Rosewater* are each slightly more hopeful than the preceding. *Slaughterhouse-Five* brings the author to mature, if still irascible, acceptance of the human condition. One of the Tralfamadorian maxims is that we should concentrate on the pleasant moments of our existence; indeed, their literature is based on this premise:

> Billy couldn't read Tralfamadorian, of course, but he could at least see how the books were laid out—in brief clumps of symbols separated by stars. Billy commented that the clumps might be telegrams.
>
> "Exactly," said the voice.
>
> "They *are* telegrams?"
>
> "There are no telegrams on Tralfamadore. But you're right: each clump of symbols is a brief, urgent message—describing a situation, a scene. We Tralfamadorians read them all at once, not one after the other. There isn't any particular relationship between all the messages, except that the author has chosen them carefully, so that, when seen all at once, they produce an image of life that is beautiful and surprising and deep. There is no beginning, no middle, no end, no suspense, no moral, no

causes, no effects. What we love in our books are the depths of
many marvelous moments seen all at one time."

The parallel between the Tralfamadorian literary method and Kurt
Vonnegut's in *Slaughterhouse-Five* is obvious.

The novel's tripartite plot needs little more description than has
already been given. Chronologically (which is, of course, not the way the
author intended us to read it) the wartime exploits of Billy come first. These
are divided into three segments: his wanderings in the Ardennes Forest
during the Battle of the Bulge, his capture and transportation back to
Germany, with a stopover at a prisoner-of-war camp inhabited by stiff-
upper-lip British officers, and his witnessing of the fire-bombing raid on
Dresden, on February 13, 1945. Billy, a chaplain's assistant still dressed in his
off-duty low cut shoes, is only dimly aware of what is happening to him. He
has no malice toward his enemies, feels no comradeship for his fellow
soldiers. His only urge is to survive, and even that is not too strong. When
he is put to work digging corpses out of the rubble of Dresden, he does it
without protest, although a Maori prisoner working with him dies of disgust.
The ghastly experience is simply too unreal for him to digest, and the full
shock of it does not come until he is back in civilian life, when he symbolically
returns to it again and again in his time-travels. Billy's middle-class life in Ilium
with a fat, uncomprehending wife, daughter, and Green Beret son, is noteworthy only for its occasional excesses of conduct—going on a radio talk show
in New York to tell of becoming unstuck in time, committing himself to a
mental ward of a veteran's hospital, or watching war movies backwards on television the night of his daughter's wedding (the same night he is kidnapped by
Tralfamadorians). His life on Tralfamadore is uniquely placid. Comfortably
cared for in the zoo, he fathers a child by the beautiful Miss Wildhack, and
continues his time-travels back on Earth. The novel ends during a Dresden
scene, which is appropriate, but hardly crucial to the book's structure.

Billy Pilgrim's (the theological implications in the name duly noted)
twofold discovery that man does not die but exists at several points in the
universe at the same time, similar to Winston Niles Rumfoord's encounter
with the chrono-synclastic infundibulum, and further that nothing that
happens on the earth will bring about the destruction of the universe, is
comforting and indicates additional maturation by the author, but, on the
other hand, the assertion that the universe *will* be destroyed by Tralfamadorian means and that it is determined to happen that way by an inscrutable
"structuring" brings one back to the fatalism of *The Sirens of Titan*. One
could say that since there *is* a structure, there must be a meaning, and that
since a fate for the universe has been preordained there must be a preordi-

nator, but the total lack of free will in this system and the utter fecklessness of our representative, Billy, combine to give the reader a less than optimistic feeling. It is the tone of the novel rather than the overt statements of the author which leads one to believe that Vonnegut has finally washed the horror and guilt of Dresden from his mind and has come to accept the previously unacceptable—man's capacity for evil, the tongue-in-cheek way this evil seems to be directed, or abetted, by some exterior force, and the helplessness of the individual to do much about either. Billy is battered but alive, and will continue to live. These facts, and the comfort they evidently give Billy's creator (his literary creator) produce the exact opposite of a fatalistic mood in the novel; if anything the book is sentimental.

The sixth novel is, unlike any of the others, completely without villains. Billy's German captors are only briefly and not unsympathetically delineated, his abductors from Tralfamadore are more mentors than kidnappers, and those with whom he comes in conflict in his life in America never possess the civilized savagery of Kroner, Hoenikker, Rumfoord, or Norman Mushari, nor the brute animosity of Dr. Jones, Krapptauer, or Senator Rosewater. The novel's subtitle, *The Children's Crusade*, has potentially the bitterest implication—the comparison of the Allied war effort in World War II to the infamous children's crusades in the middle ages, but this is only briefly accomplished, and in the non-fiction first chapter of the novel at that. The events of Billy's life are often horrible, to be sure, but to one who has read Vonnegut from the beginning, it is apparent that he has come to accept them as something it does no good to maunder about; Billy, the optometrist who fits people with glasses, has fitted Vonnegut with a pair which, if not exactly rose colored, have enabled him to see things in their proper perspective. A romp in bed with Montana Wildhack has just as much cosmic significance as an afternoon spent digging corpses out of the rubble of Dresden, no more, no less.

It would be foolhardy to try to construct a cogent, organized philosophical system from Vonnegut's writing; it simply is not there. Although it is obvious that he has taken his novels seriously from the beginning, and has sought meaningful content in each of them, his stance has always been more descriptive than analytical, his attitude comic rather than tragic, although a discussion of his themes tends to obscure this last fact. It seems evident also, that Vonnegut has said about all he has to say metaphysically—if *Slaughterhouse-Five* is any indication of the present state of his ethos. One can look for more time traveling from him, but probably back and forth over the old ground, a la Billy Pilgrim, and perhaps in the future novels his new, and old, characters will mirror the resignation apparent in the sixth novel. If this turns out to be true, the ironic indignation that made the early works so interesting will be missing, as it is to great extent in *Slaughterhouse-Five*. So it goes.

JAMES LUNDQUIST

Cosmic Irony

One of the stranger details Vonnegut gives us concerning the boyhood of Billy Pilgrim in *Slaughterhouse-Five* is that even though Billy was not a Catholic, there was a gruesome crucifix hanging on his bedroom wall. Vonnegut explains that Billy's mother, who was a substitute organist for several churches but a member of none, developed a powerful longing for a crucifix. So when she found one she liked in a Santa Fe knick-knack store while on a vacation trip out West, she bought it. "Like so many Americans," Vonnegut writes, "she was trying to construct a life that made sense from things she found in gift shops."

Vonnegut is a comic writer. His aside about Billy Pilgrim's mother and the Santa Fe crucifix is typical of his humor, which derives, as often as not, from the pathetically laughable attempts of human beings to either discover or impose order on the pluralistic universe in which they live. Mrs. Pilgrim has the same impulse so many of Vonnegut's characters have: she wants life to make sense. Vonnegut knows that it simply does not; and his readers soon learn that the answer is not to be found in Santa Fe. So Mrs. Pilgrim is a comic figure, and the allusion to the gift shop, with its pop-culture implications, adds to the "fun," such as it is. The term for this type of humor, and the term that works best overall in discussing Vonnegut's most distinctive feature, his comic vision, is cosmic irony—the laughable prospect

From *Kurt Vonnegut* by James Lundquist. © 1977 by Frederick Ungar Publishing Co., Inc.

of man's attempts to give order to the disorder of the universe through philosophies, theologies, or even scientific systems. In one way or another, each of Vonnegut's novels is an extended cosmically ironic joke.

Another term, black humor, has often been used in discussing Vonnegut's comedy and must also be taken into account in any extended consideration of his work even though black humor has never lent itself to the kind of definition that its suggestion of genre would, on face value, indicate. This is because black humor has its origin in a state of mind as much as anything—the state of mind that prevailed throughout most of the 1960s and received its impetus from televised body counts, assassinations, campus riots, and the drug culture. But the roots go back to the absurdities of the cold war, the disappointments of Korea, the rise of Joe McCarthy, the Kefauver crime hearings, Nixon's Checkers speech, the race riots in Little Rock, and even the hula-hoop craze. The question invited by all of this was how to react. One response was laughter of a sort that initially seemed either peculiar or disgusting.

The first use of black humor as a critical description was in an article by Conrad Knickerbocker, "Humor with a Mortal Sting," that appeared in *The New York Times Book Review* (27 September 1964). Main credit for making the term widely known is given, however, to Bruce Jay Friedman, who edited a paperback anthology, *Black Humor*, which was published in 1965. In addition to Friedman himself, the anthology included twelve other writers: Terry Southern, J. P. Donleavy, Edward Albee, Louis-Ferdinand Céline, Joseph Heller, Thomas Pynchon, John Barth, John Rechy, Charles Simmons, James Purdy, Vladimir Nabokov, and Knickerbocker. Oddly enough, Vonnegut, whose name is one of those now most often associated with black humor, was not represented in the original thirteen. This in itself suggests some problems with both Friedman's selection and his use of the term. The critic Robert Scholes, who elsewhere argues for the validity of the concept of black humor, admits that Friedman's employment of the term amounts to little more than making it into a sales-promotion label. And a quick look at Friedman's anthology suggests that black humor must incorporate the theatre of the absurd, existentialism, Irish whimsey, and that memorable phenomenon of the 1950s, the sick joke. As one commentator has said, black humor seems to cover "everything from a kind of generalized irreverence as in the macabre-joke movies of Terry Southern and George Axelrod, to a sense of doom so intense that the only possible reaction is horrified laughter."

But there are some stylistic features that Vonnegut and these writers share. They like to take tragic material and give it grotesquely comic treatment—the way Vonnegut depicts the end of the world in *Cat's Cradle* is an example. They like one-dimensional characters and comic-strip-simple settings—Terry Southern's *The Magic Christian*, and, to much the same extent, *Candy*, are examples here. They often use a narrative structure that reflects their disjunctive view of human nature and their refusal to accept the traditional conception of time. This is evident in Pynchon's *V* and *Gravity's Rainbow* as well as in Vonnegut's *Slaughterhouse-Five* and the time-tripping of Billy Pilgrim. They tend to blur fact and fiction, a tendency arising out of a suspicion that one's vision of reality is hardly reliable—this is at the center of Vonnegut's *Breakfast of Champions*. And they utilize a number of other stylistic devices: self-conscious artifice, a mocking tone, despair over the possibility of ever correcting human vices, and a tendency to draw imagery from the more fantastic manifestations of pop culture (blue movies, Buick LeSabres, Ramada Inns, Big Macs).

It may well be that, as Raymond M. Olderman maintains, "Black Humor as a term to describe the kind of comedy used in the fable of the sixties is as good as any other to explain a phenomenon difficult for most of us to comprehend. It is a kind of comedy that juxtaposes pain with laughter, fantastic fact with calmly inadequate reactions, and cruelty with tenderness. . . ." But behind most of the stylistic approaches and behind the laughter is a shared attitude that Vonnegut has perhaps made the most effective use of—suspicion of easy explanations and solutions to human problems, and the meaning of existence.

Vonnegut, like most of the other writers who have been labeled black humorists, is skeptical about the sufficiency of systems, be they metaphysical, theological, or psychological, in either comforting us or giving purpose to our lives. He consequently writes, most of the time, as an observer of the laughable despair that results from adherence to these systems. Vonnegut's universe is pluralistic—that is, there is no necessary plan behind it, no necessary interlocking of its parts according to a single logical scheme—and the only operative plan for man is to be ready to be pragmatic, to try out all possibilities until one that works is found. The difficulty with this approach to life is that from a cosmic standpoint, all human responses, since they are based on such a limited perspective, are laughable.

Vonnegut himself has defined this kind of humor as gallows humor—the humor of people laughing in the midst of helplessness. This is humor, he has said, that "goes against the American storytelling grain. . . . There is the implication that if you just have a little more energy, a little more fight, the problem always can be solved. This is so untrue that it makes me want to cry—or laugh." Crying will, alas, not help. But laughter might. For Vonnegut, it is the most effective reaction to the inevitable frustration of human schemes and desires. And since laughter is a response to frustration, the biggest laughs derive from the biggest fears and disappointments.

A good example of the kind of joke Vonnegut often deals with is in *Fortitude*, a screenplay for an unproduced short science-fiction film. Dr. Norbert Frankenstein, in response to the grief he feels over being unable to save his mother from cancer, becomes an expert in mechanical replacements for human organs. When the screenplay opens, he and his assistant, Dr. Tom Swift, are showing a visiting physician (the *Ladies' Home Journal* Family Doctor of the Year) around the laboratory.

The visitor soon learns, to his consternation, that Dr. Frankenstein is keeping a hundred-year-old woman alive by means of a room full of pumps and pipes and computers. All that remains of Mrs. Lovejoy's original body is her head, mounted on a tripod, beneath which are two mechanical arms and a tangle of plumbing. Mrs. Lovejoy desperately wants to die, but Dr. Franken-stein, who has told her that she has at least another five hundred years of life, has rigged her arms so that she cannot feed herself, poison, or turn a gun on herself. His interest in Mrs. Lovejoy is more than professional, however. He tells her that when he dies, he will be hooked up to the same machines and that the two of them will enjoy the marriage of marriages—they will share the same kidney, the same liver, the same heart. Their moods will always match, her downs will be his downs, her ups will be his ups. When she hears this, she pulls out a pistol her beautician has smuggled to her and shoots him six times.

Twenty-eight minutes later, Dr. Frankenstein's head is on a tripod beside that of Mrs. Lovejoy. Dr. Swift turns some dials and shoots the two of them full of martinis and LSD. As Dr. Frankenstein and his bride blissfully awaken, a record begins to play. It is Jeanette McDonald and Nelson Eddy singing "Ah, Sweet Mystery of Life." The joke, of course, is on Dr. Franken-stein; but it is also on anyone who hopes that death can be averted by twen-tieth-century medicine. Death itself is a bad enough joke on us; but human schemes to get around it are worse, as Vonnegut's cosmic irony shows.

Vonnegut's humor points toward mental health, toward life, and away from insanity and morbidity, even though in his technique he relies upon repulsive details and situations and his characters are often deranged. His purpose seems to be kindness, to help us gain the dignity that comes from being able to laugh at our own predicament. At the same time, as Vance Bourjaily emphasizes, Vonnegut, like Lawrence Sterne and Mark Twain, does not "exempt himself from the humanity whose extravagances and idio-cies are on review." His viewpoint is dictated by the objectivity of his cosmic stance, but this does not stop him from inserting himself as a character, or at least a presence, in most of his fiction—and this makes the beneficent poison in his constant joking easier to take.

The poison is not so strong in *Player Piano* as it is in the later novels. But it is there nonetheless, administered in typical Vonnegut fashion through a narrative that turns out to be the extended-joke structure Vonnegut returns to again and again.

The central character of *Player Piano* is Paul Proteus, whose name suggests his discontentment; his essential nature is changeable, but he lives in an unspecified future time when rampant technology has made change impossible. American know-how has led to an anti-utopia, in which machines do nearly all the work, and the dignity of human labor has been so devalued that all except the most talented engineers are relegated to government make-work jobs or to meaningless drill in a weaponless army.

The Ilium Works is an incredible complex designed to turn out refrigerators so automatically that the night shift consists of a single carload of employees. Paul, the brilliant manager of the Works, is vaguely disturbed by the smugness of his own managerial class and the unhappiness of the disenfranchised workers. Through the influence of a friend, Ed Finnerty, who has quit his prestigious job in Washington to foster revolution, Paul becomes a member of the Ghost Shirt Society, a radical underground Luddite movement that plans to smash the machines and establish a society that would offer satisfying employment for all.

But the joke is on Paul and his cohorts, who had decided that they would make Ilium a laboratory where they would demonstrate how well men could get along with a minimum of machines. They would heat and cook with wood, read books instead of watching TV; it would be a renaissance in upstate New York. As they are touring the city one day, they notice a crowd of people in the waiting room of the railroad station. They discover that the center of attention is a soft-drink machine that had been damaged in the uprising but was now being repaired by a mechanic. Paul realizes that all over the city, workers are instinctively putting back together the machines that had been smashed a few months before. The man repairing the pop machine "was proud and smiling because his hands were busy doing what they liked to do best, Paul supposed—replacing men like himself with machines. He hooked up the lamp behind the Orange-O sign. 'There we are.'" And there Paul and his revolution are—right back at the beginning.

The ending of the novel suggests, of course, the central metaphor of the book: not only has American know-how resulted in a society that is itself a huge player piano, but history is much like the music on a piano roll—it can only repeat itself. Just as Paul finds himself right back where he started, so will all revolutionists and schemers. What is so ironic about the frustration of his plans is that Paul had failed to realize that the very workers he wants to set free by smashing the machines are programmed machines themselves. The essential nature of man may well be protean, and like so many of Vonnegut's characters, Paul is anxious to change himself as well as to change others. He does undergo an inner change, but this has no ultimate impact on external matters. He ends up sadly and comically deluded, however enlightening his experience has been.

Much of the comedy in the novel derives not so much from Paul, however, as it does from the craziness of American society as viewed by a comic outside observer, the Shah of Bratpuhr, who is being taken on a guided tour of the country by a representative of the U.S. State Department. The Shah wants to find out what he can learn from the most technologically advanced nation in the world that would benefit his own backward principality. Naturally, he learns little of benefit as he encounters a soldier who dreams only of the day when he can retire and tell a general off, a housewife who combats boredom by doing the family laundry in the bathtub instead of using her state-provided automatic washer, and a super computer that can answer every question except an ancient riddle of life the Shah puts to it. But Vonnegut has a lot of sport with the translation problems the State-Department official encounters in trying to defend American ways against the Shah's shrewd comments.

Unfortunately, Vonnegut's humor does not quite carry *Player Piano*. While the stories of Paul and the Shah complement one another, they do not quite mesh. The Shah remains merely a device (and an old one besides) that enables Vonnegut to work in a commentary on the failures of American democracy. Another problem in the novel is that, even though the book is a warning about mechanization, there is something mechanical about the book itself.

Vonnegut's cosmic irony does, however, serve to bring out one of his major concerns. Like Bernard Malamud in *The Assistant* and John Barth in *The Floating Opera*, Vonnegut is dealing with problems of identity, individuality, and dehumanization. But unlike those of others, Vonnegut's characters are not so much forced into their crises by internal forces as by external ones: automation in *Player Piano*, space travel in *The Sirens of Titan*, Nazism in *Mother Night*, science in *Cat's Cradle*, the power of money in *God Bless You, Mr. Rosewater*, and the fire-bombing of Dresden in *Slaughterhouse-Five*.

An identity fable runs through Vonnegut's fiction and is outlined right at the start. Paul Proteus is troubled by the image of his father, who had been the nation's first National, Industrial, Commercial, Communications, Foodstuffs, and Resources Director, a position actually more important than the presidency of the United States. Paul is expected to live up to that image, but he is not certain that he can, and he eventually decides that he does not want to. But Paul as an American is also troubled by the image of America and the way of life that is forced upon him. He tries to seek a new identity through actions that will also change his country, but he is trapped.

"Partly because there are no escapes within the bounds of normalcy in the real world of the present," Peter J. Reed writes, "Vonnegut's characters frequently talk and act as if they were prisoners. Their being subject to incomprehensible forces in general, and to a social and economic structure which appears overbearing and unresponsive, also contributes to their sense of imprisonment. Cells, small rooms, oubliettes, fences, and prisons abound in the novels, underlying the air of confinement." The fence around the Ilium Works is symbolic of the fence that surrounds Paul's life. He has no more chance to escape than does the cat, early in the novel, who winds up fried on the charged wires.

But while Paul cannot overcome the circumstances of his life, he does, like Lewis's *Babbitt*, enjoy at least a slight victory. The central joke in the novel is at his expense because of his self-delusion, his belief that he and his fellow revolutionarists can establish a machineless agrarian state. When the novel ends, Paul understands that he has only been fooling himself. The nature of his identity becomes more clear to him as he raises a bottle for one last drink with his defeated comrades: "'To a better world,' he started to say, but he cut the toast short, thinking of the people of Ilium, already eager to recreate the same old nightmare. He shrugged. 'To the record,' he said, and smashed the empty bottle on a rock." It is here, where self-delusion becomes the theme and the mode approaches classical satire, that Vonnegut's comedy cuts the cleanest and gentlest.

Vonnegut's humor extends in many directions in *Player Piano*, however, and Vonnegut certainly relies on more than just cosmic irony for his effect. But the narrative movement inevitably gathers momentum toward the depiction of a laughter-provoking catastrophe that is funny only when viewed from the cosmic vantage point Vonnegut allows us.

Such humor does not seem very humorous to everybody, however, and the reviews the novel received tended to reflect this. Charles Lee, for instance, writing in the *Saturday Review of Literature*, expressed the opinion that *Player Piano* "has its bright side as entertainment, and its witty moments. But it's not funny." Granville Hicks was able to appreciate Vonnegut as "a sharp-eyed satirist." But it would be more than a decade and several novels later before Vonnegut's comic vision would be accepted, if not necessarily understood.

The Sirens of Titan, which appeared seven years after *Player Piano*, continues many of the same themes (especially the problem of self-delusion) and employs some of the same comedy as does Vonnegut's first novel, but it is a superior work in every respect.

Unlike *Player Piano*, *The Sirens of Titan* is narrated by a persona who is looking backward from the distant future when men have finally realized that human exploration should be directed inward, that the human soul, not outer space, is the true *terra incognita*. We are told a story set sometime between World War II and what Vonnegut vaguely terms the "Third Great Depression," when men still believed that it was human destiny to push toward the stars.

Malachi Constant, the richest man in the United States, is called to the estate of Winston Niles Rumfoord, who is scheduled to materialize from the "chronosynclastic infundibulum" into which his spaceship plunged while on a journey to Mars. The infundibulum—a gyre-like, intergalactic roller-coaster track on which Rumfoord and his dog, Kazak, are forced to travel around and around and up and down in space and time—enables Rumfoord to see into the future.

Malachi (whose name means "faithful messenger") is told that he will marry Rumfoord's wife, Beatrice, on Mars and that they will conceive a child. From Mars, Malachi will go to Mercury for a time and then return to earth. Eventually he will wind up on Titan, one of the moons of Saturn, with Beatrice and their son. (As characters always do in stories of this sort, both Malachi and Beatrice do what they can to escape the prediction of the oracle. But everything Rumfoord predicts does, of course, come to pass, even though Malachi must discover the details for himself.)

Malachi learns, while on Mars, that Rumfoord is training an army of kidnaped and electronically brain-washed earthlings to return to their mother planet as Martians in a suicidal attack that will serve to unite the warring peoples of earth through the threat of a common enemy. A secondary result of this unification will be the establishment of a new world-wide religion, the Church of God the Utterly Indifferent, based on the frank acceptance of the idea that God is not a big eye in the sky watching us, that he does not care at all, and that we are all simply the victims of accident.

Malachi does not take part in the invasion, however. He is instead shunted to Mercury, where he spends two years in a cave. When he does succeed in returning to earth, he is welcomed as The Space Wanderer, a messiah whose coming Rumfoord had predicted in founding the new religion. But—as he does at every turn in the novel—Malachi soon learns that the joke is on him. In a symbolic crucifixion/ascension scene, Malachi is sent to Titan with his wife and son. There he meets Salo, a robot from the planet Tralfamadore, who has been stranded on Titan for centuries because of a defective part in his spacecraft.

It is from Salo that Malachi learns the cruelest joke of all, that the Tralfamadorians have been directing human history so that the replacement part, which turns out to be a good-luck charm Malachi's son has been wearing around his neck for years, can be delivered to Titan. Even

Rumfoord, who thought he could see everything in the past and future, is under the control of the Tralfamadorians. And what is the purpose of Salo's mission? What could be so important that the Tralfamadorians would utilize some of the most magnificent achievements of man to send comforting messages to Salo? (The Great Wall of China, for example, simply told him to be patient, the Golden House of Nero meant that they are doing the best they can for him.) He is carrying a square of aluminum on which there is a single dot. The meaning of the dot is Greetings. It is this that Salo is to carry to the far edge of the universe.

The explanation Salo gives for the purpose of human history illustrates more clearly than anywhere else in Vonnegut's work the extent to which his novels are structured around cosmically ironic jokes. Scholes explains that "This novel suggests that the joke is on us every time we attribute purpose or meaning that suits us to things which are either accidental or possessed of purpose and meaning quite different from those we would supply." Through the joke, we can also see the extent of Vonnegut's absurdist vision. *The Sirens of Titan* is an expression of the belief that we are imprisoned in a universe that lacks meaning and that there is no way to make sense of the human condition. Even the Tralfamadorian explanation is ultimately inadequate because it raises the larger question of what the Tralfamadorians are for. Who is controlling them?

But despite this statement of human absurdity, the main thrust of Vonnegut's humor is not negative. Vonnegut paradoxically transcends meaninglessness by showing everything as meaningless, thus simultaneously cancelling out both pride and self-pity. In other words, since man is not at the center of creation, he is not responsible for evil. He cannot have fallen (nor can he rise) since there is no place to have fallen *from*. This idea is offered as comfort because it gives us one less reason to feel alienated from ourselves.

Vonnegut's view is that absolute answers are what get people into trouble—trouble that provides him with most of his comic scenes. Accordingly, one of his main themes is the illusions man finds to live by, illusions that fall into two categories.

The first type of illusion is found in both *Player Piano* and *Sirens of Titan*—illusions such as racial and national superiority, social Darwinism, the puritan ethic, and so on, all of which make human existence unnecessarily miserable.

The second kind of illusion, the illusion of a purposeful universe, is, of course, more central to *The Sirens of Titan*. This kind does sometimes work to overcome despair. But it also leads to the formation of dogmatic notions about what the purpose of the universe is. These notions almost always lead,

in turn, to inquisitions, witch burnings, and worse things, such as those practiced in Hitler's Germany—one of Vonnegut's main concerns in his next
novel, *Mother Night*, published in 1962.

Mother Night, the purported confessions of an American Nazi, is,
despite Vonnegut's characteristic debunking tone, one of his grimmest novels
in its implications. And it is the only one lacking his fanciful and usually satirical science-fiction devices.

Howard W. Campbell, Jr., a successful playwright in Germany
(where he grew up after his father's transfer from the General Electric plant
in Schenectady), is persuaded to become an American spy. He infiltrates the
Nazi party and becomes a vicious broadcaster of propaganda beamed by
German radio at the English-speaking world. But Howard actually is trans-
mitting secret messages to the Allies through a code based on the pause
patterns of his speech. His beloved actress wife, Helga, is lost while entertaining troops on the eastern front. After the war is over, Howard surrenders
to American forces.

He is quietly allowed to take up residence in New York City's
Greenwich Village and lives in seclusion for years. But his identity is eventually discovered. To escape from Israeli agents, who want to try him as a war
criminal, he takes refuge in an American Nazi cell, the Iron Guard of the
White Sons of the American Constitution.

The Iron Guard mysteriously produces Helga. But Howard learns,
in one of the many jokes on him, that the girl is actually Helga's younger
sister, Resi. He also learns through Frank Wirtanen, the U.S. Army officer
who had persuaded Howard to become an American agent in the first place,
that the Iron Guard and Resi are part of a mysterious communist plan to
abduct him to Moscow. Resi insists, nonetheless, that she has fallen in love
with Campbell, and commits suicide to prove the point.

Wearied by the pressures he has lived under for so long, Howard
surrenders to the Israelis and is taken to Jerusalem for trial. Wirtanen is
willing to provide evidence of Howard's true role, but Howard hangs himself
(or says he will) in his cell. He finds out too late the moral of his life
(suggested in Vonnegut's 1966 Introduction to *Mother Night*) that "We are
what we pretend to be, so we must be careful about what we pretend to be."

Like Paul Proteus, and to a certain extent Malachi Constant,
Howard's problems begin with a kind of willful self-delusion. Despite his
success as a playwright, Howard is blind to what is going on around him in
the Germany of the 1930s, or at least he chooses to ignore it. He writes
nothing but medieval romances, all based on the illusion that life can be
given meaning through rescuing a maiden, living up to the code of chivalry,
and acting under the twin impulses of love and religious faith in a clearly

defined cosmos that is divinely planned and ordered. This would at first seem to be as removed from Nazism as one could get. But, ironically enough, Hitler saw Germany's aggression in terms of a crusade; and he actually had a portrait painted of himself as a questing knight, thus piling illusion upon illusion. So in pretending to ignore Hitler and his programs by writing escape literature, Howard is actually appealing to the spirit of the times. And the very popularity of his plays means that the joke is on him.

On the day he is recruited to become an American agent, he is sitting on a park bench in the Tiergarten in Berlin contemplating his next play, *Das Reich der Zwei*. It is about the love he and his wife have for one another: "It was going to show how a pair of lovers in a world gone mad could survive by being loyal only to a nation composed of themselves—a nation of two." This, as the plot summary of *Mother Night* has already shown, is a hopelessly romantic notion, and the play never gets written. Instead, Howard writes *The Memoirs of a Monogamous Casanova*, a diary of his erotic life with Helga during the first two years of the war. His intention is to show the many different ways a married couple could please one another sexually by assuming numerous roles (again the matter of identity and illusion). To his laughable outrage, he finds out, after he has been taken to Jerusalem, that a Russian corporal, an interpreter, obtained a copy of the diary and succeeded in getting it published in Budapest (with illustrations). It has become an underground bestseller in the Soviet Union. Again, the joke is on Howard, and all he can do is rage that "The part of me that wanted to tell the truth got turned into an expert liar! The lover in me got turned into a pornographer! The artist in me got turned into such ugliness as the world has rarely seen before."

Much of the humor in *Mother Night* turns on just such compounded absurdity; Vonnegut likes to twist the knife more than once. A writer such as Terry Southern is usually equal to Vonnegut in the use of single absurdities, but Vonnegut's superiority is evident in his ability to handle multiple layers of dark comicality. A good example occurs elsewhere in *Mother Night* when Howard comes home and discovers a hangman's noose left in his apartment by representatives of the American Legion. Resi throws the noose into the garbage. The garbage collector actually hangs himself with it because he has discovered a genuine cure for cancer and nobody will listen to him. Vonnegut piles absurdity upon absurdity until the noose that symbolizes the punishment Howard deserves for war crimes he did not commit figures in the self-destruction of a disappointed trashman.

These layers of absurdity contribute to the depth of the darkness Vonnegut sees behind human motivation and the murkiness that surrounds the outcome of all human events. Try as we will, he seems to say, we can never escape the darkness that surrounds our every act. This theme is stated in another way by Mephistopheles in Goethe's *Faust:* "I am a part of the part that at first was all, part of the darkness that gave birth to light, that supercilious light which now disputes with Mother Night her ancient rank and space, and yet can not succeed." The title of the novel is thus a fitting choice for the story of a man who admits that he "served evil too openly and good too secretly, the crime of his times."

Mother Night may be bleak in its implications, but it is not bleak reading. As Richard Schickel wrote when the book was reissued in 1966, it "is on the contrary, a wonderful splash of bright, primary colors, an artful, zestful cartoon that lets us see despair without forcing us to surrender to it. There is no self-pity at the core of Vonnegut's work, only the purifying laughter of a man who has survived that stage."

Vonnegut's laughter is purifying for reasons outside the larger ones of cosmic irony and multiple layers of absurdity. There are dozens of funny lines, bizarre images, and smart remarks in the novel. Some of the funniest moments involve commentary on writers and writing. Here are two examples. Near the beginning of his confessions, Howard recalls meeting Rudolf Hoess, Commandant of Auschwitz, at a New Year's Eve party in Warsaw in 1943. Hoess suggests that he and Howard collaborate on some stories after the war. "I can talk it," Hoess says, "but I can't write it." Much later, when Howard is in prison in Jerusalem, he receives a note smuggled to him from a prisoner being held in Tel Aviv. The prisoner is Adolf Eichmann, who is writing the story of his life and asks Howard, "Do you think a literary agent is absolutely necessary?" Howard's reply: "For book-club sales in the United States of America, absolutely."

Cat's Cradle abounds in humor of this type partly because the narrator is again a writer, although hardly an author of medieval romances or monogamous pornography. John, a free-lance writer who prefers (for all too obvious symbolic reasons) to be called Jonah, is researching a book about the sixth of August, 1945, the day the atomic bomb was dropped on Hiroshima. The book is to be titled *The Day the World Ended*. His investigation takes him to the laboratory of the late Dr. Felix Hoenikker, the man who could most fully claim to be the father of nuclear weapons. He learns that Dr. Hoenikker, at the time of his death, was trying to discover a way to make water freeze at a higher temperature—so the Marines could fight on top of mud instead of in it. But Jonah does not immediately discover whether or not Dr. Hoenikker was successful.

Some time later, Jonah, in order to write a magazine article, goes to San Lorenzo, an impoverished Caribbean island run by Papa Monzano, the chief of state, who is secretly and mysteriously influenced by Frank Hoenikker, Dr. Hoenikker's long-vanished son. We eventually learn that

Frank bought favor with Papa by revealing that not only had Dr. Hoenikker's project succeeded but that Frank possessed some *ice-nine*, which if released into the ocean or placed in contact with any water anywhere, would solidify it instantly. Frank gave Papa a vial of the substance, which Papa wore on a necklace.

Of course, the inevitable happens. Papa, suffering horribly from cancer, commits suicide by swallowing the *ice-nine* and instantly turning into an *ice-nine* statue. The next day an airplane crash causes Papa's castle and Papa himself to slide into the sea. The ocean freezes, and the sky is filled with tornadoes. Jonah, along with the girl of his dreams, Mona Aamons Monzano, Papa's adopted daughter, takes refuge in a bomb shelter. Like so many other Vonnegut characters, Jonah is thus the victim of an ironic joke. He sets out to write a book about the day the world ended, and he winds up living through that day himself.

San Lorenzo has something stranger than *ice-nine*, however—the outlawed religion of Bokononism. Its founder, Bokonon, a black man from Tobago, arrived on San Lorenzo years before as a castaway with Earl McCabe, a deserter from the United States Marines. The two of them manage to take control of the island. To maintain order and to take the minds of the people off their wretched economic condition, they concoct an ersatz religion based (among other ideas) on translating good vibrations from one believer to another by pressing the soles of the feet together. Bokonon himself lives in the jungle, where he composes the calypsos that comprise Bokononist scripture.

After Jonah emerges from the bomb shelter, he finds that Bokonon is one of the few other survivors. Bokonon hands Jonah a piece of paper on which is written the final sentence for *The Books of Bokonon:* "If I were a younger man, I would write a history of human stupidity; and I would climb to the top of Mount McCabe and lie down on my back with my history for a pillow; and I would take from the ground some of the blue-white poison [the *ice-nine* crystals] that makes statues of men; and I would make a statue of myself, lying on my back, grinning horribly, and thumbing my nose at You Know Who." Jonah's narrative turns out to be just that "history of stupidity." As part of the joke, the metaphoric title he started out with, *The Day the World Ended*, turns out to be literally true.

One of Vonnegut's persistent lessons involves how to take a joke. The conclusion of *Cat's Cradle* certainly presents one of his most graphic illustrations. Just as Bokonon and McCabe have perpetrated a joke on the islanders in their comic scheme for maintaining order through a phony religion, so some greater power has perpetrated a joke on all mankind—the notion that the physical world will remain stable, that water will always solidify at the same temperature, that the climate will always remain hospitable in the warm southern seas. But when all this ceases to be the case, when the punchline is delivered, Bokonon can take the joke because he has enjoyed a few jokes of his own making.

Bokonon, with his religion based on "foma," or harmless lies, is in contrast to Dr. Hoenikker, who is the unwitting cause of the humorous apocalypse with which the novel ends. Vonnegut's scientist, with his childlike inquisitiveness, his inability to respond emotionally to others (one morning he left his wife a tip underneath his breakfast plate), and his amorality ("What is sin?" he asks at one point), is too much a caricature to be taken any way except as a straw man in a rigged sermon. But he is a pivotal figure in the cosmic view of the human condition that Vonnegut is trying to give the reader. Dr. Hoenikker's laboratory is littered with children's puzzles and toys, suggestive of the scientific impulse toward reductionism, the notion that only through concentrated simplification (the movement toward the understanding of basic principles, elemental relationships), can knowledge be advanced. Dr. Hoenikker's mistake is that he chooses not to consider the expanded implications of any of his discoveries. "What hope can there be for mankind," Jonah asks, "when there are such men as Felix Hoenikker to give such playthings as *ice-nine* to such short-sighted children as almost all men and women are?" Bokonon's answer is that there is no hope.

Yet *Cat's Cradle* is ultimately a humane and hopeful novel. "Ironically, its concentrations on the design of the end is a gently humorous program for a new and less pretentious beginning," John R. May writes in his study of the theme of apocalypse in the American novel. "The reasons for its imagined apocalypse are patent: the pastiche of uncontrolled invention and absolutized religion. Bokononism, cutting religion and man down to size, is the contour of our hope. And if the hope is slender, it is nevertheless genuine."

Bokononism, with its cult language of *wrang-wrang, karass, vin-dit, wampeter, boko-maru,* and *foma,* accounts for much of the popularity *Cat's Cradle* brought Vonnegut. The language itself is amusing, but it serves to outline an approach to life that has considerable appeal as a way of averting catastrophe. Bokononism was born out of pragmatism and the kind of pop-culture ridiculousness that figures so often in Vonnegut's fiction. Bokonon (whose real name was Lionel Boyd Johnson, his initials an oblique suggestion of a conceptual connection involving Lyndon Baines Johnson) concludes, after reading about the principle of "dynamic tension" (pitting one muscle against another) promoted by Charles Atlas in his mail-order body-building school, that the best way to maintain a humane society on perpetually impoverished San Lorenzo is to artificially establish a state of dynamic tension between religion and government—"pitting good against evil, and . . . keeping the tension between the two high at all times." Bokonon accordingly arranged that he and his religion be outlawed, and that those caught practicing it be killed. The resulting tension gave both Bokononists and government officials a sense of purpose, something Bokonon considered essential for happiness and survival.

It is out of this conviction that the more mystical aspects of Bokononism arise. One of the tenets of the religion is "that humanity is organized into teams, teams that do God's Will without ever discovering what they are doing." The term for each of these teams is *karass*. The Bokononist spends most of his life trying to discover the nature of his *karass* and what work it is doing. This is the process of discovery that is behind the book Jonah (who reveals himself as a converted Bokononist) writes.

As it turns out, he and Bokonon are on the same team. But to what purpose? Other than to learn how to take the ultimate joke, there is no answer. And in the end, Bokononism, like all systems Vonnegut describes, is foolish. Bokonon believed that someone was trying to get him somewhere for some reason, that there is something special about his own destiny. This, it seems, is an essential mistake; and the result, from Vonnegut's cosmic viewpoint is inevitably ludicrous. But even though Bokononism is as wrong as the belief of Billy Pilgrim's mother in the efficacies of gift-shop crucifixes, it is helpful in that it works to give both Bokonon and Jonah the dignity they need to take the joke well.

Bokononism and science work against one another in the book to create dynamic tension of another sort. This is symbolized by the child's game with string that serves as the novel's title. One of Dr. Hoenikker's children recalls his disappointment at being shown a cat's cradle by Dr. Hoenikker and discovering that it does not contain a cat and is not even a cradle; it is just an arrangement of string stretched between two hands. The import of the book is that there are two kinds of cat's cradles—scientific models (the lines, angles, and frame of the string game suggest this) and philosophical and religious systems. Both are artificial representations of reality. The question is, which "cradle" is most helpful in promoting happiness. Vonnegut is clearly on the side of Bokonon and his *foma*, if for no other reason than that Bokonon and Vonnegut agree on what must be held sacred: Man himself.

Another reason for his sympathy with Bokonon is that Vonnegut, in continuing a line of humor from *Mother Night*, sees writers as traffickers in helpful lies. Jonah learns that a writer is a "drug salesman," that perhaps his most useful purpose is to write "some kind of book to read to people who are dying or in terrible pain." Later, Jonah says, "When a man becomes a writer,

I think he takes on a sacred obligation to produce beauty and enlightenment and comfort at top speed." At no point is truth mentioned; the comfort of lies in a world of pain is more important.

But while Vonnegut emphasizes the usefulness of Bokonon's lies, Bokonon is nonetheless a comic figure. "Wherever possible," Jonah writes of Bokonon, "he had taken the cosmic view, had taken into consideration, for instance, such things as the shortness of life and the longness of eternity." The problem is in the "wherever possible." As helpful as Bokononism is, as devoid of false pieties as it is, as concerned as it is with human decency and the necessity of having a sense of purpose, it only enables Jonah to "find some neat way to die." And that seems to be the final message of Bokonon, Vonnegut's most famous messiah, who ends up barefoot, sitting on a rock, and wearing a blue bedspread with blue tufts, his farewell appearance pointing toward Vonnegut's other messiah, the even more ludicrous figure of Eliot Rosewater.

Eliot spends most of his time in *God Bless You, Mr. Rosewater* sitting around in his long underwear in a squalid one-room office in Rosewater, Indiana, where he serves as a combination notary public, volunteer fireman, and comforter of the poor. On the door of his office is a sign, "Rosewater Foundation, How Can We Help You?" And by his cot are two telephones, one of which is red for fire calls. The black one is for calls from the distressed citizens of the surrounding county—from Diana Moon Glampers, "a sixty-eight-year-old virgin who, by almost anybody's standards, was too dumb to live," and who suffers from a paranoid fear of electricity and imagined kidney pains; from a suicidal man who says he "wouldn't live through the next week for a million dollars" but who agrees to go on living when Eliot gets him down to a hundred; from Sherman Wesley Little, an unemployed tool-and-die maker whose second child has cerebral palsy; and from various other people.

Eliot mistakenly believes that these "were the same sorts of people who, in generations past, had cleared the forests, drained the swamps, built the bridges, people whose sons formed the backbone of the infantry in time of war—and so on." These are the people who are now forgotten in a money-mad United States, Eliot reasons, and he tries to help them as best he can. He sometimes prescribes an aspirin and a glass of wine for his callers. At other times he advances modest sums of money known as Rosewater Fellowships. And when those he has helped want to repay him, he organizes therapeutic fly hunts in his screenless office.

How Eliot got to be this way is a complicated matter, and the plot structure of *God Bless You, Mr. Rosewater* is extremely complex, perhaps because the central concern—money as a "psychological germ-carrier"— affords so many opportunities for humor. "A sum of money is a leading character in this tale about people," Vonnegut writes in his opening sentence, "just as a sum of honey might properly be a leading character in a tale about bees." So from the start, Vonnegut sets the novel up as a fable that moves from lesson to lesson down through a series of cosmically ironic moral points concerning the insane wisdom of his messianic fool.

The Rosewater Foundation consists of much more than Eliot's one-room office, and Eliot as president of the Foundation is much more (or was much more) than his long johns would indicate. On June 1, 1964, the Rosewater wealth consists of $87,472,033.61, a sum that produces an income of $3,500,000 a day. Like most American fortunes of its sort, it was produced through speculation and bribery during and after the Civil War. Now channelled into the Rosewater Foundation, the money is beyond taxation. The oldest son in the direct line of succession in each generation accedes to the presidency.

From 1947 through 1953, Eliot was a model president. His education at Loomis and Harvard (a doctorate in international law) was superb. He had served admirably in Europe during World War II. He had married a beautiful wife in Paris, Sylvia DuVrais Zetterling. And he had directed the Foundation money toward research projects in cancer, mental illness, racial prejudice, "and countless other miseries." But then Eliot disappears for a week and crashes a convention of science-fiction writers being held in a motel in Milford, Pennsylvania.

What Eliot admires about science-fiction writers is their cosmic outlook. "The hell with the talented sparrowfarts who write delicately of one small piece of one mere lifetime, when the issues are galaxies, eons, and trillions of souls yet to be born," he says. The science-fiction writer Eliot most admires is Kilgore Trout, the neglected author of eighty-seven paperback books and now, at the age of sixty-six, a stock clerk in a trading-stamp redemption center in Hyannis, Massachusetts. The Kilgore Trout book Eliot most admires is *2BR02B*, a title that turns out to be the famous question asked by Hamlet. Trout, who is Vonnegut's alter ego (the two full names contain the same number of letters), has as his favorite formula one not unlike Vonnegut's own—to describe a grotesque society and then suggest ways of changing it. In *2BR02B*, Trout writes about an America, somewhat similar to that of *Player Piano*, in which all the work is done by machines. Because of the eradication of disease, the United States suffers from an over-population problem, which is being solved by Suicide Parlors (located at all major intersections). As one of Trout's characters is being eased into death on a Barca Lounger with Muzak in the background, he asks the stewardess who is attending him a central question for both Vonnegut and Eliot, "What in hell are people for?"

Eliot, like most other Vonnegut characters, is in turn forced to ask what *he* is for, a question that is complicated by his past. Eliot is oppressed by the example of his father, Senator Lister Rosewater, who has spent all of his adult life in the Congress of the United States teaching the morality of reactionary Republicanism, a morality of cruelly enforced, repressive laws that is offensive to Eliot. Eliot is also obsessed with what happened to him during the war when he shot and killed three volunteer firemen (two old men and a fourteen-year old boy) whom he mistook for S. S. troops in a burning building. The incident led to what was diagnosed as battle fatigue and Eliot had to be evacuated to Paris. In addition to all this, Eliot has to cope with his responsibility for the death of his mother in a sailing accident that happened when he was fourteen. As the psychiatrist who treats him after his return from the science-fiction convention (and the several carousing trips that followed) tells Sylvia, "Your husband has the most massively defended neurosis I have ever attempted to treat." The treatment, as one would expect, does not work, and Eliot disappears again.

Ten days later, Sylvia gets a letter from Elsinore, California, where Eliot has gotten involved with the Volunteer Fire Department. It is in this letter that Eliot reveals the flaw that always leads to comedy in a Vonnegut novel. "Maybe I flatter myself when I think that I have things in common with Hamlet," he writes, "that I have an important mission, that I'm temporarily mixed up about how it should be done. Hamlet had one big edge on me. His father's ghost told him exactly what he had to do, while I am operating without instructions." Eliot believes that he is being sent some-where for some purpose, and, given Vonnegut's omnipresent cosmic perspective, such assumptions can only result in dark comedy.

Unknown to Eliot with his confused sense of mission, there is an intrigue against him. Norman Mushari, a young lawyer whose boyhood idol was Senator Joe McCarthy, has learned one important lesson at Cornell Law School from his favorite professor, Leonard Leech: a lawyer should always be looking for situations where large amounts of cash were about to change hands. Mushari, who learns that the Rosewater Foundation President can be deposed if proved insane, gets an idea. Since Eliot is obviously out of his mind and since Eliot is the only son of Lister, Mushari persuades Fred Rosewater, the head of another branch of the family, to initiate a court action that would make the Rosewater millions his.

This introduces a long subplot involving Fred, a sexually frustrated life-insurance salesman, his bisexual wife, Caroline, and the inhabitants of Pisquontuit, Rhode Island. Among them are the Buntlines, whose ancestors made a fortune out of a broom factory that employed disabled Civil War veterans (thus providing Vonnegut with another case history of wealth). The ironic thing about Fred's claim to Eliot's position is that the Pisquontuit Rosewaters represent the honest branch of the family. Fred is descended from George Rosewater, the younger brother of Noah Rosewater, Eliot's direct ancestor. Unlike Noah, George did not avoid serving in the Civil War by buying a substitute. He rose to the rank of brigadier general and was blinded at Antietam. After the war, he went east and became a foreman in the Buntline broom factory.

Meanwhile, Eliot continues his life in Indiana until, under the pressure of divorce proceedings, he agrees to go to Indianapolis for a meeting with Sylvia in the hope of arranging a reconciliation. While reading a Kilgore Trout novel on the bus, he sees a vision of Indianapolis in flames, a reminder of the firestorm that followed the bombing of Dresden, and he passes out. A year later, he awakens in a mental hospital and learns that he has spent twelve months playing tennis. Apparently he has recovered from his madness—and just in time, because the sanity hearing brought on by Mushari and the Pisquontuit Rosewaters is scheduled for the next day. Eliot's father has hired Kilgore Trout as a consultant, and Trout wants Eliot to claim that he had been experimenting in ways to make technologically obsolete people feel loved. But Eliot gets an idea of his own when he finds out that Mushari, anxious to discredit him in any way possible, has bribed people to say bad things about him. As a result, fifty-seven women have brought paternity suits against Eliot—something he is able to turn to his advantage, however. Since Fred would have no chance if Eliot had an heir, Eliot asks that papers be drawn up acknowledging that every child in Rosewater County said to be his *is* his and that they all have the rights of inheritance. Fred Rosewater gets a check for $100,000, and no more. Eliot then proclaims of his "children": "Let their names be Rosewater from this moment on. And tell them that their father loves them no matter what they may turn out to be. And tell them . . . to be fruitful and multiply."

So Eliot has the last laugh on Fred Rosewater and Mushari, but is, in a way, the butt of his own joke. His newly adopted descendants may multiply, and be fruitful in that sense; but the picture Vonnegut has drawn of them in an automated America underscores their uselessness. And how can Eliot love them if he is incapable of loving either his father or his wife? As Vonnegut emphasizes, Eliot had wrecked the life of a woman whose only fault had been that she loved him. Eliot's self-delusion, which reaches its highest point in the godlike conception of himself projected in his final pronouncements, goes back to his essential mistake—that he has an important mission. This, more than his absurd attempts at being a good samaritan, is an indication of his insanity.

But even though he is tripped up at the end, Eliot tries to move toward the cosmic perspective that will lead to sanity. This is evident not only in his interest in science fiction, but is also indicated in an unfinished novel he began on the evening when he first realized that his wife would never come back to him.

Eliot's novel is structured around a reincarnation theme, with human souls returning again and again to earth because heaven is so boring. They have to take their chances on how they will return, however. Kublai Khan, for instance, is now a veterinarian's wife in Lima, Peru. And Richard the Lion-Hearted is "a pitiful exhibitionist and freelance garbageman in Rosewater, Indiana." But lately, more and more souls do not want to return to earth, even those who had a relatively easy time of it last time around. The narrator of the novel, who was executed as a witch in 1587 in the Austrian village of Dillingen, and who herself has had no burning desire to take her chances in this world again, decides to seek another incarnation to find out what horrible thing has been happening of late to the reborn souls on earth. When the novel breaks off, she has learned that she is to be sent to Rosewater.

Here Eliot tries for the long view of the centuries and an outside perspective on human life. He does come up with an answer to the problems of dislocation and depersonalization that plague him, one that seems workable to him.

This answer is presented in the baptismal prayer he says over a set of twins born to Mary Moody, one of the useless nobodies he tries to help: "God damn it, you've got to be kind."

Vonnegut thus strikes an uncertain balance between the cosmic and the pragmatic in his characterization of Eliot Rosewater, and the result is his most thoroughly funny novel. "It's a tribute to Kurt Vonnegut, Jr.," Daniel Talbot wrote in his review of the book, "that he has covered such a large territory of human follies in so short a book . . . the author has literally taken on the late Norbert Wiener's book title—*The Human Use of Human Beings*—and fashioned a black satire out of its implications. His technique of presenting this material is fascinating—an amalgam of short comic strip-like takes, dada dialogue . . . no characterization, minimal plot, and straight dramaturgy. The net effect is at once explosively funny and agonizing."

The explosiveness, if not the agony, of Vonnegut's humor also extends into the thinly and somewhat strangely veiled topical satire on the 1964 Republican presidential candidate, Barry Goldwater, whose name and family background of wealth as well as his political conservatism, are satirized in the depiction of Senator Lister Rosewater.

But as funny as *God Bless You, Mr. Rosewater* is, it is not a well-structured novel. There is an awkward movement from the present to the past as

Vonnegut fills the reader in with the Rosewater family history, and the focus on Eliot and his problems is lost when Fred Rosewater's story is told. There is a problem too in Eliot's response to his wartime experience. His adulation of volunteer firemen and his conception of the earth as a planet with an atmosphere that, because of its oxygen, "was eager to combine violently with almost everything the inhabitants held dear" is comic in a pathetic way. But this obsession somehow does not seem to be a satisfactory response to the trauma that triggered it in the burning building during the war. Vonnegut's next novel, *Slaughterhouse-Five*, which features Eliot Rosewater and Kilgore Trout as well as Howard W. Campbell, Jr., is a corrective on this point.

Slaughterhouse-Five is several stories in one, all told simultaneously. The main part of the novel deals with the central character, Billy Pilgrim, what happens to him during the Battle of the Bulge, how he survives the fire-bombing of Dresden, and how he leads his life after World War II. In those postwar years he becomes a successful optometrist and imagines he travels by flying saucer to the planet Tralfamadore. But it is also the story of Vonnegut himself and his experiences at Dresden and what happened to him afterward. In addition, it is a story about the difficulty of writing a novel that deals adequately with the horror of our times. It is with this problem that Vonnegut begins.

The book starts and ends with an autobiographical frame. Vonnegut explains that ever since the late 1940s he has been telling people that he has been working on a book about Dresden. He lived through the surprise raid on what was assumed to be a safe city. Since it contained few targets of military importance, it was assumed that Dresden would not be massively bombed. As a consequence, its population had been doubled by prisoners of war and by refugees from the eastern front. But on the night of February 13, 1944, eight-hundred Royal Air Force Lancaster bombers, striking in waves, dropped high-explosive bombs followed by over 650,000 incendiaries, causing a firestorm that could be seen more than two hundred miles away. On February 14, American B-17 Fortresses carried out a second raid, followed by P-51 Mustang fighters, which completed the destruction of the city with strafing missions. The official death count is the figure 135,000 listed by the Dresden police chief. But some estimates indicate that more than 200,000 people were either killed outright, burned to death during the conflagration, or died afterward. Vonnegut, a prisoner of war like Billy Pilgrim, was herded with other POWs into the underground cold-storage area of a slaughterhouse, and emerged after the raid to see the city looking like the face of the moon. Vonnegut tried to obtain the air force report on the raid when he wanted to begin writing about Dresden, but he was told that the information was still classified.

Being denied access to the report was not the main problem for Vonnegut in writing the book, however. And, in a sense, he was able to begin work on it long before *Slaughterhouse-Five* materialized. As Jerome Klinkowitz has pointed out, the matter of Dresden furnished the informing principle for *Player Piano, Mother Night*, and *God Bless You, Mr. Rosewater*. But until *Slaughterhouse-Five*, Vonnegut was not able to deal with Dresden directly, and he was not able to come up with an approach that would work to exorcise what had become his private demon.

His first step in coming up with that approach was to visit an old friend, Bernard V. O'Hare, who had been with him at Dresden. O'Hare's wife, as Vonnegut recounts in his opening frame, was suspiciously hostile to the projected book because she feared that what he wanted to do was to write a novel glorifying war, something that John Wayne and Frank Sinatra could star in when it was made into a movie. The truth of the matter, she points out, was that Vonnegut, O'Hare, and most of the other men actually involved in the war were little more than children at the time. "So then I understood," Vonnegut writes. "It was war that made her so angry. She didn't want her babies or anybody else's babies killed in wars. And she thought wars were partly encouraged by books and movies." Vonnegut calms her down by telling her that he will subtitle the book, "The Children's Crusade," after the infamous idea, concocted in 1213 by two monks, to raise armies of children in France and Germany, march them to North Africa, and sell them as slaves (30,000 children were actually recruited—half got to North Africa and were sold, most of the others drowned on the way).

Vonnegut later recounts how he receives a Guggenheim Fellowship and returns to Dresden with O'Hare. They make friends with a cab driver who takes them to the slaughterhouse. The driver sent O'Hare a postcard the next Christmas, writing "I wish you and your family also as to your friend Merry Christmas and a happy New Year and I hope that we'll meet again in a world of peace and freedom in the taxi cab if the accident will." The phrase, "if the accident will," determines the order of events and their significance in the novel. As much as Vonnegut would like to see order and significance in what happened at Dresden and afterward, it all comes down to a matter of accidents—some fortuitous, most not. All the accidents, from school girls being boiled alive in a water tower to the assassinations of Martin Luther King and Robert Kennedy, are followed by the catchphrase, "So it goes."

Vonnegut also recounts how, to kill some time while in a motel room, he looked through the Gideon Bible for tales of destruction. There he read the passage in Genesis about God raining fire and brimstone on Sodom and Gomorrah and Lot's wife being turned to a pillar of salt when she looked back as she and her husband were fleeing the condemned cities. Vonnegut says that in looking back at Dresden, he too has been turned into a pillar of salt, that perhaps the essential mistake is to try to account for what had happened. There is no way that he, as a participant, can obtain the cosmic view necessary for clarification or even for coherence. So Vonnegut tells the story of Billy Pilgrim by haphazardly moving back and forth in time and concentrating on the accidents that make up the extended dark joke of the Children's Crusade that World War II is for Billy.

Billy was born in 1922 (the same year as Vonnegut), and, like most other Vonnegut protagonists, is in conflict with his father. (His father once tried to teach him to swim by throwing him into a swimming pool and letting him sink. Billy's father was later shot and killed on a deer-hunting trip.) Billy does poorly in college, enters the army, and becomes a chaplain's assistant—a service assignment that establishes Billy as a Christ figure, a symbolic connection that is maintained throughout the rest of the narrative. He is stranded behind enemy lines during the Battle of the Bulge, and, along with a tank gunner named Roland Weary, is captured and marched toward Germany. Billy and Weary are eventually loaded into a boxcar with a crowd of other prisoners and begin rolling eastward. Weary dies of gangrene on the journey and irrationally blames Billy for his fate. Paul Lazzaro, a vicious paranoid who believes Weary to be his only friend, vows to kill Billy.

The prisoners are taken to a camp in Germany where they are greeted by a group of British officers. They are well-fed and in good health because, through an error, they are receiving five hundred Red Cross packages a month instead of the fifty they are supposed to get. The British prisoners-of-war give Billy and his fellow prisoners a big welcome dinner and put on a show for them—all of which so overwhelms Billy that he winds up in sick quarters. A few days later the Americans are marched to Dresden, where they are put to work bottling a vitamin supplement for pregnant women and are housed in slaughterhouse number five. Howard W. Campbell, Jr., shows up and tries to talk them into joining the Free America Corps and help the Germans fight the Russians. The Dresden raid ends all such talk, however, and Billy and his comrades are subsequently put to work "mining" bodies in the devastated city. It is here that the most horrible joke in the novel is told. A schoolteacher named Edgar Derby takes a teapot from the ruins and is arrested for plundering. "I think the climax of the book will be the execution of poor old Edgar Derby," Vonnegut tells O'Hare in the prefatory chapter. "The irony is so great. A whole city gets burned down, and thousands and thousands of people are killed. And then this one American soldier is arrested in the ruins for taking a teapot. And he's given a regular trial, and then he's shot by a firing squad."

Billy returns to Ilium, New York, after the war ends and marries the daughter of the founder of the optometry school in which he enrolls. Billy and his wife have two children, one of whom becomes a Green Beret and fights in Vietnam. Billy's business prospers and he drives a Cadillac with John Birch Society stickers on its rear bumper. But he has gotten so addicted to becoming "unstuck in time," as a consequence of his war experiences that, at one point, he has himself committed to a mental hospital. There he meets Eliot Rosewater and through him becomes acquainted with the novels of Kilgore Trout. Later he meets Trout and invites him to his eighteenth wedding anniversary. Trout shows up, and, "gobbling canapes . . . talking with a mouthful of Philadelphia cream cheese and salmon roe," is the hit of the party.

Obviously influenced by the novels of Trout, Billy imagines, on the night of his daughter's wedding in 1967, that he is kidnapped by a Tralfamadorian flying saucer and taken to a zoo on Tralfamadore. There he is mated with Montana Wildhack, a Hollywood sex symbol whose mysterious disappearance had been played up in the news. Billy and Montana lead an almost idyllic life and have a baby. But the most significant thing that happens to Billy on Tralfamadore is that his captors explain their concept of time to him.

While still in the flying saucer, Billy asks where he is and how he got there. "It would take another Earthling to explain it to you," says a voice from a speaker on the wall. "Earthlings are the great explainers, explaining why this event is structured as it is, telling how other events may be achieved or avoided. . . . All time is all time. It does not change. It does not lend itself to warnings or explanations. It simply *is*. Take it moment by moment, and you will find that we are all, as I've said before, bugs in amber."

The Tralfamadorians add that all moments exist simultaneously, hence nothing can be done to change the past or the future because, technically, there is neither past nor future. When someone is dead, it simply means that he is in a bad condition at that moment but that at another moment he is alive and well and possibly happy. There is thus no such thing as free will, and the best Billy can do is to accept the message inscribed on the locket that dangles between Montana's breasts (and is also displayed on a wall plaque in his office on earth): "God grant me the serenity to accept the things I cannot change, courage to change the things I can, and wisdom always to tell the difference."

Billy gets back to earth and survives an airplane crash only to learn that his wife has died of carbon-monoxide poisoning. When he gets out of the hospital, he succeeds in getting on radio talk-shows to tell what he has learned from the Tralfamadorians. He eventually becomes famous and is in demand as a speaker, giving speeches (after the manner of Vonnegut himself) on space travel and Tralfamadorian time theory. On the twenty-first anniversary of the Dresden raid, he is gunned down by a hired killer while speaking in a Chicago arena. The paranoid friend of Roland Weary, Paul Lazaro, is responsible.

The novel ends with Vonnegut, after mentioning the recent deaths of Martin Luther King and Robert Kennedy, musing about what the Tralfamadorians taught Billy. "If what Billy Pilgrim learned from the Tralfamadorians is true," Vonnegut writes, "that we will all live forever, no matter how dead we may sometimes seem to be, I am not overjoyed. Still—if I am going to spend eternity visiting this moment and that, I'm grateful that so many of those moments are nice." Vonnegut is, as the events recounted in the novel surely indicate, being sarcastic here. And what he does is to make his "famous book about Dresden" into something of a shaggy-dog story with a horrible twist—if we all live forever, so too will the fire-bombing of Dresden go on forever.

But even though this is the cosmic implication of what Billy learns and Vonnegut posits, Tralfamadorian time theory does have pragmatic value in dealing with the crises they have both been through. What Billy does in his imagined travels to Tralfamadore is what Kilgore Trout and the other science-fiction writers do—that is, to try "to re-invent themselves and their universe," to come up with some new lies so they can go on living. Billy is unhinged to the point of madness by what happens to him in the war, and he can no longer control his time-tripping, so he invents the Tralfamadorians to make his madness accord with some vision of reality. His life is thus given a certain order and pattern and he does attain "serenity." But how seriously does Vonnegut take this and what practical value does it have for him? Here is a significant statement: "When I think about my own death," he writes, "I don't console myself with the idea that my descendants and my books and all that will live on. Anybody with any sense knows that the whole solar system will go up like a celluloid collar by-and-by. I honestly believe, though, that we are wrong to think that moments go away never to be seen again. This moment and every moment lasts forever."

Vonnegut apparently takes Billy seriously as a messiah, as a bringer of a message that can be applied to the question of how to deal with catastrophe and go on living. Vonnegut's seriousness is indicated in the large number of parallels he draws between Billy and Christ. Roland Weary makes Billy into a scapegoat, and he is reviled by the other prisoners while on the journey to the prisoner-of-war camp. He is forced to stand up most of the way, hanging from a crossbar in the boxcar. And, two days after the war ends, he is sleeping, still in Dresden, when he is slowly awakened by the sound of a man and a woman speaking in German somewhere nearby. "Before Billy opened his eyes," Vonnegut writes, "it seemed to him that the tones might have been those used by the friends of Jesus when they took His ruined body down from His cross. So it goes."

Even though Billy is a comic figure in many scenes, he is nowhere near as ludicrous as Eliot Rosewater in the role of messiah. Billy has more to say than simply, "God damn it, you've got to be kind." He says you've got to reinvent yourself and your universe. As Scholes wrote in his review of *Slaughterhouse-Five*, "Only Billy's time-warped perspective could do justice to the cosmic absurdity of his life, which is Vonnegut's life and our lives."

But, as do all of Vonnegut's protagonists, Billy nonetheless lives a life that is an extended joke. Like all of them, he is comic because he is a victim of his illusions. We know that Tralfamadore does not exist and that Montana Wildhack is just a dream. His life is a series of accidents, most of which can only be seen as manifestations of some grotesquely sick sense of humor that is behind it all (although this too is an illusion). What should we expect of Billy when he regains consciousness as the sole survivor of an airplane crash and learns of his wife's absurd death but that he gets himself on crackpot talk-shows? He is crazy, an unwitting clown, and it is only fitting that a maniac should arrange his assassination.

Yet Billy is the character toward whom Vonnegut worked ever since Paul Proteus; he is the one central character who is able to be protean, to successfully change himself for survival. At the end of the novel, O'Hare tells Vonnegut that by the year 2000, the world's population will double to seven billion people. Vonnegut replies sarcastically, "I suppose they will all want dignity." They most certainly will, and one way they may find it is through the example of Billy Pilgrim. Or, to repeat what Vonnegut said in his 1973 *Playboy* interview, "It may be that the population will become so dense that *everybody's* going to live in ugliness, and that the intelligent solution—the only possible solution—will be to change our insides." And that is just what Billy does, fool though he may be, messiah that he is—he rescues himself and arranges his resurrection through a work of his own imagination, a rationalizing fantasy.

Near the conclusion of his preface to *Slaughterhouse-Five*, Vonnegut states that "I've finished my war book now. The next one I write is going to be fun!" The next one turned out to be *Breakfast of Champions*, and it does turn out to be fun even though it is, like *Slaughterhouse*, a partially autobiographical, partially therapeutic work, that has its basis in manic depression, and, in its own way, is a rationalizing fantasy of another sort.

Breakfast of Champions has its genesis in Vonnegut's efforts at dealing with his own self-acknowledged manic-depressive tendencies. In the late 1960s, he was suffering from periodic fits of depression. His doctor prescribed Ritalin, an amphetamine, and Vonnegut's depression lifted. "I used to think I was responding to Attica or to the mining of Haiphong," he said. "But I wasn't. I was obviously responding to internal chemistry. All I had to do was take one of these little pills." This experience impressed Vonnegut with the degree to which human motivation and behavior is influenced by physiological factors, how a pill no larger than the head of a pin can alter personality.

The cosmic view that thus emerges in *Breakfast of Champions* is based on the idea, hinted at but not very fully explored in the earlier novels, that we are robots or machines made up of rubbery tubes with boiling chemicals inside. In the opening section of *Breakfast of Champions*, Vonnegut writes that "it is a big temptation to me, when I create a character for a novel, to say that he is what he is because of faulty wiring, or because of microscopic amounts of chemicals which he ate or failed to eat on that particular day." The hitch is (as in *Slaughterhouse-Five*) that Vonnegut has to look at himself as a chemically fueled machine when he enters the novel as a fellow "character," programed the same way the other people in the book are. This can hardly be an upbeat approach to one's depression, and Vonnegut admits that "suicide is at the heart of the book." But at the same time, Vonnegut manages to find a pragmatic solution that makes it possible for him to go on living even if it is not true and even if it makes himself into a comic figure.

Vonnegut begins *Breakfast of Champions* by indicating he is writing the novel as a fiftieth birthday present for himself, trying to clear his head of "all the junk in there" by getting rid of the characters that have been haunting him for years. What he does is to contrive a meeting between Kilgore Trout and Dwayne Hoover, a middle-aged Pontiac dealer in Midland City who is suffering from a brain full of bad chemicals.

Although he does not know it, Dwayne is about to go berserk. A major cause will be the ideas he learns from one of Trout's novels, *Now It Can Be Told*. The core of these ideas is that the reader of the book is the only creature in the universe who has free will. All other creatures are robots (a common fantasy, by the way, that occurs in exaggerated form among paranoid schizophrenics). At the end of *Breakfast of Champions*, Dwayne suffers from the same delusion that other deluded Vonnegut characters do—the idea that he is unique, the idea that his life must be something special, the idea that he alone has some purpose to fulfill. Given Vonnegut's cosmic viewpoint, whatever Dwayne does and why he does it under this delusion is the stuff of comedy because he makes the mistake that he and he alone has free will—a laughable assumption for any character in a Vonnegut novel to make.

What brings Trout and Dwayne together is an invitation Trout receives to speak at a festival celebrating the opening of the Mildred Barry

Memorial Center for the Arts in Midland City. Trout has been invited upon
the recommendation of Eliot Rosewater (who else?), who agrees to loan the
Center an El Greco worth three million dollars if the chairman of the festival
will hire Trout as a speaker. Trout, whose novels are still being published as
filler material in pornographically illustrated books and magazines, is living
in a basement apartment in Cohoes, New York, and working as an installer
of combination storm windows when he gets the letter from Midland City
and a check for a thousand dollars.

Trout goes to Manhattan (with half of his honorarium pinned to his
underpants) to look through the porno shops for some of his novels to take
along. (His publishers never bother to send his complimentary copies.) He is
mugged on a handball court underneath the Queensboro Bridge on Fifty-
ninth Street and loses all but ten dollars of his travel fund. He is forced to
hitchhike west, getting a ride in a truck that is hauling 78,000 pounds of
Spanish olives. Trout talks to the truck driver about conservation, politics,
friendship in the modern world, and aluminum siding.

Meanwhile Dwayne is becoming increasingly insane. He sees a
monstrous duck directing traffic. He sees eleven moons in the sky. He insults
his sales manager, Harry LeSabre (who wrongly suspects that Dwayne knows
of his fondness for dressing up in women's clothing on weekends). Dwayne
goes home and puts the muzzle of a .38-calibre revolver into his mouth.
Then, on second thought, he decides to shoot the flamingo on his bathtub
enclosure instead. He goes out, gets into a black Plymouth Fury he had taken
in trade, and drives crazily to the new Holiday Inn, of which he is part owner.
He climbs the stairs to the roof of the motel and stands there, asking himself
where he is. He has forgotten almost everything; he has even forgotten that
his wife had killed herself by eating Drano and that his son, Bunny, who plays
piano in the cocktail lounge of the Inn, is one of the most notorious homo-
sexuals in Midland City.

The conversation between Trout and the truck driver continues on
through Pennsylvania and West Virginia as Vonnegut describes the landscape of a dying planet—topsoil gone, hillsides collapsing into the strip-mine
pits, and rusted Cadillacs capsized in muddy creeks.

Dwayne's chemicals, meanwhile, are seething. He develops echolalia
and compulsively repeats the last word of whatever he has just heard: "When
the radio said that there had been a tornado in Texas, Dwayne said this out
loud: 'Texas.'" And he reacts like a coiled rattlesnake when he incorrectly
concludes that his receptionist and mistress, Francine Pefko, is being nice to
him only so she can sweet-talk him into buying her a Colonel Sanders
Kentucky Fried Chicken franchise. (What she actually longs for is radial tires
for her car.)

Trout finally arrives in Midland City, enjoying the last leg of his journey in a Ford Galaxie (he asks the driver what it is like to steer something a hundred-thousand light years in diameter). Dwayne is sitting in the cocktail lounge of the Holiday Inn on a zebra-skin banquette as Bunny plays the piano. Another person, Vonnegut himself, is looking on through the silvered lenses of one-way sunglasses. Vonnegut is drinking a Black and White and water and mouthing the word *schizophrenia*. When the cocktail waitress brings Dwayne his drink, a House of Lords martini, she makes her customary remark, "Breakfast of Champions," a remark that often accompanies the serving of drinks in the mid-west.

Dwayne is hoping that the artists who have come to Midland City for the festival will tell him some new truths about life that will enable him to keep out of the mental ward of the Midland County Hospital. Rabo Karabekian, the "minimalist" painter, whose work, *The Temptation of St. Anthony*, consisting of a vertical stripe of orange reflecting tape on a field of green wall paint, delivers a lecture that would seem to offer some hope for Dwayne.

Sensing antagonism toward him in the cocktail lounge when he enters (he had been paid fifty-thousand dollars for *The Temptation of St. Anthony*) Karabekian defends his masterpiece. It shows all that is important about life, he argues; it represents the "I am" in every animal, the receptor to which all messages from the outside are sent. "It is unwavering and pure, no matter what preposterous adventure may befall us," Karabekian says. "A sacred picture of St. Anthony alone is one vertical, unwavering band of light. If a cockroach were near him or a cocktail waitress, the picture would show two such bands of light. Our awareness is all that is alive and maybe sacred in any of us. Everything else about us is dead machinery." Karabekian's words cause Vonnegut, who has suicidally come to the conclusion that we are all just machines doomed to collide with one another repeatedly, to feel himself "born again." But Dwayne Hoover gains nothing from the lecture; he sits hypnotized by the beads of lemon oil on the surface of his martini.

When Trout shows up carrying a copy of *Now It Can Be Told*, Dwayne's hypnotized eyes fix on him. Dwayne staggers up to Trout and asks for a message. He sees the novel, grabs it, and begins to speed-read it. His reaction to the news that he is "an experiment by the Creator of the Universe" and that he is the only person in the cocktail lounge or anywhere else not to be a robot, "the only creature in the entire Universe who has free will," is to walk over to his son at the piano and to pound Bunny's head up and down the keyboard. Then he socks the cocktail waitress, runs across the street to his Pontiac showroom and breaks Francine Pefko's jaw and three ribs. As he continues his rampage, he bites off the topmost joint of Trout's ring finger and assaults more than a dozen other victims. Vonnegut tries to stay out of his way, but someone else jumps back and breaks Vonnegut's watch crystal and his big toe. Two state policemen eventually subdue Dwayne on the median of the Interstate highway and haul him off to jail. The resulting lawsuits will bankrupt him and he will wind up on Midland City's skid row, Vonnegut tells us.

In the epilogue to the novel, Vonnegut rents a Plymouth Duster from Avis and goes to intercept Trout as the science-fiction writer returns from the hospital where he had his finger bandaged up. Vonnegut parks the car near the supply yard of the Maritimo Brothers Construction Company and gets out to wait. Vonnegut suddenly sees a huge Doberman pinscher leaping at him from behind the supply-yard fence. Vonnegut, for all his being born again through his new conception of himself as an unwavering band of light, reacts like a machine. A message is sent from his eyes to his brain, which in turn contacts the hypothalamus, and on down the chain of switches and reactions until he receives a massive charge of adrenaline. He retracts his testicles into his abdominal cavity and leaps over his car. The dog hits the fence and is thrown back. The joke this time is on the author. He can no more control his responses than can the characters in his novel.

Trout, who watches all of this, starts to run away. Vonnegut chases him and tells him that he is only a character in a book and that his creator will reward him for all his suffering with the Nobel Prize for Medicine. "I am approaching my fiftieth birthday, Mr. Trout," Vonnegut anxiously explains. "I am cleansing and renewing myself for the very different sorts of years to come. Under similar spiritual conditions, Count Tolstoi freed his serfs. Thomas Jefferson freed his slaves. I am going to set at liberty all the literary characters who have served me so loyally during my writing career." He adds that Trout is to be the only character so informed, and Trout, ironically, is stuck with the burden that destroys character after character in Vonnegut's novels—the burden of being told he has free will even though Vonnegut again and again demonstrates the impossibility of the very concept. As Vonnegut somersaults into the void, he hears Trout's distant voice requesting only one thing—to be made young.

Several layers of irony thus run through the novel and the humor is compounded many times. Vonnegut shows Dwayne going insane while Vonnegut cuts back and forth from the zany adventures and conversations of the world's most neglected writer making his way west. The climactic confrontation becomes all the more comic when Dwayne grabs Trout's schizophrenic novel and thinks *Now It Can Be Told* is a message intended for him alone. But Trout and Dwayne are not the only ones suffering from delusion, the delusion that they are not machines and that they may act as they wish. When Vonnegut enters the story, we soon learn that he is as deluded as the rest. He feels that he is a new person after Karabekian's speech, but then he reacts mechanistically when the dog jumps at him. Again the point is that any comforting assumption or belief, even Vonnegut's own, is laughable when looked at cosmically. But as false as it is shown to be, Karabekian's message does have pragmatic value—it does help Vonnegut (the character, at any rate) deal with his schizophrenia, even if it does not keep him from being a comic figure.

Karabekian's ideas, however central they are to Vonnegut's vision, no more oppressively dominate *Breakfast of Champions* than does the manic wisdom of Eliot in *God Bless You, Mr. Rosewater*, the only other Vonnegut novel that is funnier. The extended cosmic jokes (and especially the central one on Vonnegut) are there but much of the humor in *Breakfast of Champions* derives from Vonnegut's synopses of Trout stories and various gag situations. There is also the matter of Vonnegut's illustrations, made with a felt-tip pen and included as if the audience has lost the ability to read. (It is significant that Trout is to take part in a seminar on the American novel and its future in the age of McLuhan.) The illustrations also suggest that the book is intended as an artifact, as something of a Rosetta Stone with its pictures of beaver, hamburgers, and Volkswagens, to be discovered by explorers from another planet long after the earth is dead.

Much of Vonnegut's comedy is also aimed at Midland City with its Sacred Miracle Cave and its Cathedral of Whispers (in which thousands of people have been married), its white boulder painted to resemble Moby Dick, and a skeleton said to be the remains of Jesse James. Vonnegut's emphasis on such bizarre Americana and all of the insanity in the flatlands can only remind one of Sherwood Anderson's *Winesburg, Ohio*, or Hamlin Garland's *Main-Travelled Roads*, or sections of Vonnegut's fellow Indianapolitan, Booth Tarkington. Vonnegut depicts the midwest, a region of supposed conservatism and sanity, as a place of madness. But it is only by returning to such a place to face his past and his own self-destructive impulses that Vonnegut can himself be freed. At the end, he holds a mirror up to his eye (Trout thinks mirrors are leaks into another universe) and sees a single teardrop falling—a tear of sadness, a tear of relief, and a tear of laughter all in one, the Vonnegut response to the terrors that surround us all.

The same terrors and the same response are present in *Slapstick*, a work that seems more an afterthought than an important novel, despite Vonnegut's claim in the prologue that it is the closest he will ever come to writing an autobiography. The book is dedicated to Laurel and Hardy by way of explaining the title. Life, Vonnegut points out, is a slapstick comedy based on a "fundamental joke." The joke comes out of constantly being asked to do our best at all times and then bungling everything because of our limited agility and intelligence. Vonnegut knows this joke well, he writes, because he "was so perpetually intoxicated and instructed by Laurel and Hardy" when he was growing up during the great depression. He also knows it because of the unfortunate example of his sister, Alice, who died of cancer at the age of forty-one, two days after her husband had been killed in a train wreck. Four children, the youngest only a year old, were orphaned. "Soap opera!" Alice had said in commenting on her life. "Slapstick."

Vonnegut's relationship with his sister was close, and he confesses that she is the audience he has been writing for all along. Out of this relationship comes a dream that occurs as Vonnegut is flying to an uncle's funeral in Indianapolis with his older brother, Bernard. The dream provided Vonnegut with the story he eventually turned into *Slapstick*.

The hero-narrator of the novel, which opens in Vonnegut's typically indefinite future, is Dr. Wilbur Daffodil-11 Swain, the final (as well as the tallest) President of the United States, sitting in a clearing in a jungle on Manhattan Island. He is wearing a purple toga made from draperies that once hung in the Americana Hotel. The bridges to the mainland are down, the tunnels are blocked, and the island is a quarantine area because of a mysterious plague known as the Green Death.

Wilbur then tells us his story. He and his twin sister, Eliza, were mistaken for Mongolian idiots when they were born, and they were isolated by their parents (the father a Mellon, the mother a Rockefeller) in a mansion near Galen, Vermont. But the twins are actually a new type of human being, "Neanderthaloids," over seven feet tall by the age of ten with twelve fingers, twelve toes, and four nipples each. They are also supremely intelligent. But their most important characteristic is that they "were born with the capacity and the determination to be utterly happy all the time." Given Vonnegut's cosmic irony, his sense of slapstick, such a capacity is bound to lead to trouble—and it does.

Wilbur and Eliza can only be happy when they are together, and they can think as geniuses only when their heads are within a few feet of each other. They are separated for their education, however, and except for a few encounters that turn out to be more traumatic than happy, circumstance forces Wilbur and Eliza to remain apart for the rest of their lives. Eliza is locked up for many years in an institution for the feeble-minded (as brilliant as she is, she is unable to read or write). She somehow manages to obtain a lawyer (Norman Mushari, Jr., from *God Bless You Mr. Rosewater*), sue her family for damages, buy a half-interest in the New England Patriots of the National Football League, and move into a condominium in Machu Picchu, the ancient Inca capital in Peru.

Wilber goes to Harvard Medical School and then becomes a practitioner of rural medicine. He runs for Senator and even becomes President, proposing a scheme for happiness that he and Eliza thought up when they were children. They concluded that American society is a cold and unhappy one because nobody has enough relatives any more. The solution, which has been alluded to in chapter one, is to assign everyone thousands of relatives by computer. Each American will get a new middle name and number. The middle name—Daffodil or Chipmunk or Peanut or whatever—would indicate the artificial extended family. The number would indicate individual relationships within the family—two people with the same number would be siblings, those with different numbers would be cousins. Wilbur's campaign button reads, "Lonesome No More."

But because there are complications beyond Wilbur's control, and because of his limited agility and intelligence, "Lonesome No More" (like all of the comic schemes for happiness Vonnegut satirizes) does not get much of a chance to work out.

By the time Wilbur is elected, the United States has so far exhausted its resources that the harbors are used mainly by sailing ships and the farm-work is being done with horses. There is so little fuel left to run the generators that Wilbur is forced to raid the National Archives for paper to burn in the power plants so that computers can be used to put "Lonesome No More" in operation. He starts with the documents from the Nixon administration, then he moves on to those of the Grant and Harding administrations. The middle names do get assigned, however, and Wilbur believes that Americans are happier than ever. But then people begin to die of the Green Death and another ailment called the Albanian Flu. The United States breaks up into the "Kingdom of Michigan" and various territories controlled by the armies of such upstarts as the "Duke of Oklahoma."

There are some foreign problems as well. The Chinese have created millions of geniuses by teaching groups of telepathically congenial specialists to think as one mind. The Chinese learn how to miniaturize themselves to save resources, carrying out the process until they become microscopic—and this, it turns out, is the cause of the Green Death. The Chinese, "who were peace-loving and meant no one any harm," Vonnegut explains, "were nonetheless invariably fatal to normal-sized human beings when inhaled or ingested."

The Albanian Flu is also blamed on the Chinese, who have developed a way of sending people to Mars without using a space vehicle. The flu germs are Martians who are brought to earth on the return trip. It is also suspected that the Chinese have been playing around with the force of gravity, which has become strangely variable. Some days it is so heavy that movement is nearly impossible. On other days it is so slight that all males have continual erections. But by this time, American society has become so chaotic that nothing matters to most of the people except a new religion, The Church of Jesus Christ the Kidnapped. Its adherents are recognizable by their rapid and anxious movements as they keep a nervous eye out for the Saviour, who has supposedly returned to earth but has been abducted by unspecified evil forces.

Wilbur's presidency ends, for all practical purposes, two-thirds of the way through his second term, and he dies before he is able to finish his story. *Slapstick* thus becomes another putdown of utopian schemes, and in this, as well as in its depiction of a paranoid culture hellbent for destruction, it echoes the earlier novels. The difficulty is that it is too much of an echo. Wilbur's purple toga reminds one too directly of Bokonon's blue bed-spread with the blue tufts. Wilbur's repetition of "Hi ho" after every ironic turn in the narrative sounds too much like the "So it goes" of *Slaughterhouse-Five*. And the miniaturization of the Chinese along with the tidal shifts in gravity sounds like something Vonnegut would ordinarily ascribe to Kilgore Trout. But like all Vonnegut books, *Slapstick* is wildly funny and disturbing in places, and it is full of wry comments on American life, comments that enable it to succeed even though it is, to the longtime reader of Vonnegut, essentially repetitive.

In "The Literature of Exhaustion," John Barth writes this about the contemporary novelist: "His artistic victory . . . is that he confronts an intellectual dead end and employs it against itself to accomplish new human work." This is certainly what Vonnegut accomplishes through his cosmic irony as he moves consistently from his absurdist view of man's meaningless place in the universe and the comic prospects in all human systems and solutions (such as "Lonesome No More") toward a paradoxical emphasis on the worth of having some useful rationalizing fantasy.

"True reality, if it does exist at all," writes one commentator on Vonnegut's outlook, "can never be known since it consists of the sum total of all individual points of view. Given such a Universe, the best man can do is to try to survive by being pragmatic, by applying a moral test to help him decide his course of action." Vonnegut comes down to this point in each of his novels, ending up as something of a cosmic moralist as he turns Barth's intellectual dead end (or phrenic asteroid belt) into a type of novel that indeed does blend pop-culture artifacts and contemporary fable into new human work.

LAWRENCE R. BROER

Cat's Cradle: *Jonah and the Whale*

> Too much sanity may be madness,
> and the maddest of all is to see life as
> it is and not as it should be.
> —*Man of La Mancha*

> I realize today that nothing in the
> world is more distasteful to a man
> than to take the path that leads to
> himself.
> —Herman Hesse, *Demian*

Cat's Cradle, a novel Vonnegut himself awards an A+, shows a world so devastated by forms of mechanistic insanity that only a cynical religion like "Bokononism" will serve to make existence tolerable. Frustrated in the attempt to achieve meaningful social reforms in a society that has become unmanageable and eventually doomed by technological horrors such as "Ice-9," an ultimate doomsday device, Bokonon offers a solution based upon "a bitter disappointment for which no remedy exists unless laughter can be said to remedy anything." Proposing that "everything happens as it is meant to happen, Bokonon encourages the population of San Lorenzo to turn away

From *Sanity Plea: Schizophrenia in the Novels of Kurt Vonnegut* by Lawrence R. Broer. © 1989 by The University of Alabama Press.

from thinking about things as they are and to live in harmony with seemingly harmless comforting lies or illusions that make their remaining, darkening moments less terrifying. The challenge awaiting the protagonist on San Lorenzo is to discover that the moral advantages of lying about reality and surrendering to Bokononist fatalism are tragically mistaken. Relieved of having to deal with complex experience, the protagonist is threatened by the moral and physical petrification that has turned San Lorenzans into puppet-like creatures who expedite their own demise. To be true to the courage and conscience of his predecessor Howard Campbell, Jonah must reject defensive self-deceptions and act against the totalitarian machinery that threatens to engulf him.

To understand the narrator called "Jonah," whose psychic drama comes to the fore in the second half of *Cat's Cradle*, we must backtrack briefly to the fictional city of Ilium, New York, and a particularly hellish caldron called the General Forge and Foundry Company, birthplace of the atomic bomb and an equally deadly substance called "Ice-9" that threatens the end of life on earth. At General Forge science is worshiped as the strongest and most beneficial force in the life of mankind; its practitioners, especially pure researchers like Nobel Prize winning Felix Hoenikker, are viewed practically as gods. Felix is the father of the atomic bomb and of "Ice-9" but also of three very strange children whom Jonah, collecting material for a book to be called "The Day the World Ended," has come to interview. It is in the course of these interviews that a less charitable image of the saints of pure science begins to form in Jonah's mind.

Suggesting the perversion of natural, life-directed processes by such mechanistic activities as characterize Felix's so-called pure research, the brother of the research director at General Forge explains to Jonah,

> I know all about how harmless and gentle and dreamy he was supposed to be . . . how he was so innocent he was practically a Jesus . . . but how the hell innocent is a man who helps make a thing like an atomic bomb? And how can you say a man had a good mind when he couldn't even bother to do anything when the best-hearted, most beautiful woman in the world, his own wife, was dying for lack of love and understanding. . . . Sometimes I wonder if he wasn't born dead. I never met a man who was less interested in the living.

Felix and Thanatos are directly related. Felix's lack of interest in his wife (he once leaves her a tip for preparing his breakfast) indirectly causes her death and Newt's deformity. She dies in an accident caused when she picks up the car Felix abandons in a "glacier" of automobiles. Her grave marker is an "alabaster phallus . . . plastered with sleet." Ice-9, a device that once set in motion can turn the world into a solid glacier and its inhabitants into statues of ice, proves a compelling symbol for the coldness and lovelessness bred into Felix Hoenikker who, caring only for his work, passes the effects of his coldness to all those around him. The impersonal processes at General Forge have rendered the workers there so vacant and dull-witted that they almost welcome the mindless, robotlike functions assigned to them by "faceless voices of scientists on dictaphone records." One secretary decides that she will go crazy on the spot if anybody asks her to do any thinking. In effect, the black elevator operator named Lyman Enders Knowles, who grabs his own behind and cries, "Yes, yes!" whenever he feels that he's made a point, has made a point indeed when he asks, "How come they got to build a building like this . . . and fill it with all these crazy people?"

Suggestive of the novel's pervasive water imagery, the souls of the women in the foundry's "girl pool" have been drowned in the loveless, mechanized swirl of their "deathlike jobs." So the three Hoenikker children, grotesquely victimized by parental lovelessness and likened to "babies full of rabies," turn into ice-chips off the family block of ice represented by Felix. The youngest son Newt is a four-foot-tall midget to whom his father has hardly ever spoken. Equally misshapen, Angela is a giantess worn out by age twenty-two from having to mother Felix as well as her two brothers. Frank Hoenikker is so hollowed of identity that he is referred to as "a man with a paper rectum," a man with almost no experience of talking to anyone because of a totally furtive existence. All in all, what has been done to the Hoenikker children is described by the plastic picture folder in which Angela keeps "all the people I love." They have been trapped in plexiglass like fossil beetles in amber, frozen or petrified into objects incapable of growth.

The emotional and physical deformity of the Hoenikker offspring is even more tragic because of thwarted artistic potential. Newt, described as "shrewdly watchful" and capable of "amiable grace," is a talented artist who can paint only morbid pictures; Frank's architectural genius, which he finally realizes only as a puppet-sycophant to a dictator, is diverted into years of masturbating and building model airplanes. And Angela plays the clarinet so beautifully but with such pain that the narrator senses "the depth, the violence, and the almost intolerable beauty" of her "disease." "Such music from such a woman," says Jonah, "could only be a case of schizophrenia or demonic possession." A form of schizophrenia is doubtlessly the correct diagnosis of the disease that has claimed the Hoenikker children and the workers at General Forge, and that stalks the narrator throughout the course of the novel. Eros, the instinct to love and create, has been petrified in the

Hoenikker children by such unfeeling, mechanized forces as represented by Felix, Asa Breed, Ice-9, and the deathly, impersonal life at General Forge, which spreads like proliferating Ice-9 to the Hoenikker home. In effect, Newt, Frank, and Angela have been caught up in the dehumanizing mechanism of a "cat's cradle," symbolized in this novel and throughout Vonnegut's work by insidious spirals, tunnels, clocks, caves, staircases, and mountain rims, which appear to entrap unwary individuals and send them spinning toward certain doom. Whether these mechanistic traps represent structures of control that are economic, religious, philosophic, militaristic, environmental, psychic, or biological, their chief evil is that they offer the kind of illusory protection and security that lure Paul Proteus, Malachi Constant, and Howard Campbell, while locking them into cycles of action indifferent to individual will or aspiration. Such is the spiral of lovelessness that reproduces itself in the Hoenikker family, or that of Ice-9 or the nuclear arms race that assumes a deadly momentum toward global destruction. Notably, Jonah is in a tombstone salesroom, a room of death, when he first hears of the labyrinthine miseries of the Hoenikker children. Feeling himself drawn into the spiraling mechanisms that have destroyed them, Jonah senses the room tipping and its walls and ceiling transforming into "the mouths of many tunnels." Frank Hoenikker has a wiry pompadour, "a sort of cube of hair" that rises to an incredible height.

Laing's paradigm for schizophrenic loss of self becomes the central expression of Jonah's plight—engulfment in the form of drowning or petrification. Hence it is that Jonah feels strongly drawn toward the girls in the girl pool. As he contemplates the devouring mechanisms at work in the foundry, he sees his own fate reflected by that "sea of pale faces" into which Dr. Breed benignly peers. Felix himself is "facing the sea" when he dies from Ice-9 poisoning. What Vonnegut is telling us about cat's cradles is conveyed by the fact that such drowning imagery occurs in this novel whenever individuals lend themselves passively to mechanistic systems, entrapping spirals that they believe themselves helpless to resist, or when they believe themselves to be mysterious agents in the working out of destinies they are not to question. In short, those who out of moral inertia rationalize cat's cradles are as responsible for such apocalyptic nightmares as Hiroshima, or that which befalls ill-fated San Lorenzo in this novel, as are the amoral scientists who dissociate themselves from the potential horror of their playful creations. The sea of futility in which they drown is one they themselves have made. The fact that Felix was found constructing a cat's cradle with a piece of string the day the atom bomb was dropped on Hiroshima suggests that, while both activities originate from an impulse more playful than devious, cat's cradles like atom bombs can become the deadliest of adult realities, especially if their use is determined by such warped and childishly irresponsible people as the Hoenikker children prove to be.

The precise nature of the challenge facing the novel's narrator comes in the image of poor Frank Hoenikker, wanted by the Florida police, the FBI, and the Treasury Department for running stolen cars to Cuba, washed up onto the shores of the Republic of San Lorenzo in the Caribbean after his pleasure craft has sunk. Heedless of the man-eating sharks that make ominous spirallike circles in the water around him, Frank observes, "I raised my eyes to my Maker, willing to accept whatever His decision might be. And my eyes alit on a glorious mountain peak above the clouds. Was this Fata Morgana—the cruel deception of a mirage?" That Frank should consider Mount McCabe or his deliverance to the rocky shores of diseased, poverty-ridden San Lorenzo as an act of God, as something glorious, is a mirage more deceitfully cruel than this spiritual ostrich will ever know. The fact is that in his pathetic need to believe that he is finally to play an important role in an experiment that is humanly meaningful—helping to build a utopian society as Minister of Science and Progress in San Lorenzo—Frank comes to the destitute banana republic unwittingly to complete the process of moral petrification his father had begun in Ilium. By relinquishing what is left of his frozen soul to the totalitarian forces on San Lorenzo, he becomes transformed into a totally subservient, puppetlike creature who expedites his own doom while initiating global destruction. Linking the cat's cradle of scientific progress in Ilium with the cat's cradle of totalitarianism in San Lorenzo, he brings with him to this second Ilium the Trojan horse of Ice-9.

Following his journalistic instincts that all is *not* as promised in the ad in the New York Sunday *Times* about the "healthy, happy, progressive, freedom-loving, beautiful nation" of San Lorenzo, Jonah looks up Fata Morgana and learns that it *was* in fact a "mirage" named after Morgan le Fay, a fairy who lived at the *bottom* of a lake. "It was famous for appearing in the Strait of Messina, between Calabria and Sicily. Fata Morgana was poetic crap, in short." On the one hand, Jonah's realism reveals to us his determination at the beginning of the story to tell about "the human rather than the technical side of the making and dropping of the bomb on Hiroshima," the human costs of irresponsible technology. To be true to his purpose he must above all else remain free from the defeatism and the self-imprisoning fantasies of paradise on San Lorenzo that have swallowed up Frank Hoenikker. The problem is that for reasons of moral comfort Jonah is tempted by the same pain-killing, womblike illusions of contentment and security that shipwreck Frank. Coming from a past as wasteful and degenerate as that which demoralizes Malachi Constant, Jonah describes himself early in the novel as feeling "bristly, diseased, cynical," his soul seeming "as foul as smoke from burning cat fur." Too much involvement with cat's cradles has evidently taken its psychological toll. It has been "two wives . . . 250,000 cigarettes . . . 3,000 quarts of booze ago" that he had begun his book. His second wife had left him "on the ground that I was too pessimistic for an optimist to live with." When he attempts to put his thoughts in order to conduct his interviews, he finds, he says, "that my mental health had not improved. . . . I found that the public-relations centers of my brain had been suffocated by booze and burning cat fur." It is not surprising then that Jonah's commitment to truth should be so compromised by a potentially incapacitating pessimism that he should state his intentions as examining "all *strong* hints as to what on Earth we, collectively, have been up to," as if in his dazed condition to look carefully at more subtle hints is more than he is capable of. We wonder too at the lassitude behind his statement that "when a man becomes a writer, I think he takes on a sacred obligation to produce beauty and enlightenment and comfort at top speed." The comfort may only be Jonah's if the truths he tells are superficial. When asked on San Lorenzo if a writer may not be a drug salesman, Jonah answers, "I'll accept that. Guilty as charged." When further asked if he has written anything like that, Jonah says, "Not yet."

Both *Mother Night* and *Cat's Cradle* focus Vonnegut's concern with fiction as a form of play that can be constructive or destructive. In the editor's note to *Mother Night*, Vonnegut writes that lies told for the sake of artistic effect can be the most beguiling form of truth. Kraft tells Howard Campbell that future civilizations will be judged by the strength of their artistic will, and by the quality of their creations. Whether Jonah is to be as a writer and a human being a drug salesman, a dispenser of quick and easy answers to complex questions, an evader of painful realities like the spurious prophet Bokonon, rather than the honest writer we feel he would like to be, is a main conflict in Jonah as well as in all Vonnegut's artist-protagonists. His essential challenge is to learn to distinguish good or bad "lies" or fictions that, as David Ketterer says, either encourage the forces of aggression and death or abet the forces of life—of hope, compassion, and engagement. The writer (or prophet) who lies to escape pain or to encourage others to do so is as mad as the scientist who blithely engages in research designed to make doomsday weapons. When a character by the name of H. Lowe Crosby refers to caricatures used for target practice by the San Lorenzan Air Force, saying, "They got practically every enemy that freedom ever had out there," the truth, for Jonah at least, is that the enemy is the one within, the agonizing split in his soul represented by the voice of fatalism on the one hand and the voice of affirmation on the other. By the start of the story, we see that Jonah has already embraced the will-sapping philosophy of the bogus holy man

Bokonon, whose religion, though outlawed, constitutes the pervasive faith of all those on San Lorenzo. "I am a Bokononist now," he tells us on page 1, which in effect means one who believes in "the folly of pretending to discover, to understand," hardly a fitting prerequisite for a reality seeker. Rather than truth, the cynical Bokonon, whose social utopianism had failed to alleviate the suffering of San Lorenzans, encourages the population to turn away from thinking about things as they are and to live in harmony with *seemingly* harmless, comforting lies called "foma" that make their remaining, darkening moments less terrifying. The Bokononist faithful do not have to worry about reality because reality is too terrible to contemplate, and because, says Bokonon, "everything happens as it was meant to happen," because "it is impossible to make a mistake," and because "each of us has to be what he or she is." What no one on San Lorenzo seems to notice is that this supposed holy man (Felix has been identified as a modern "holy" man too) and his hide-from-it-if-it-hurts philosophy has turned San Lorenzans into hopelessly conforming, petrified statues as effectively as Ice-9 could have done. In the meantime Bokonon lives a cozy existence in the jungle, where he writes all day and eats the good things his disciples bring him. Not as Edenic for Bokonon as it sounds, however, since his corrosive pessimism and the mask of gentle holy man behind which has been hidden a complex and fragmented spirit have driven him insane.

Because Jonah is a Bokononist, one who "would have agreed gaily to go anywhere anyone suggested," who believes that "somebody or something . . . has compelled me to be certain places at certain times without fail," his susceptibility to cat's cradles on San Lorenzo may put him into a deep spiritual sleep and produce the fate of his biblical namesake. The narrator captures his penchant for the easy way in his very first words to us: "Call me Jonah. My parents did, or nearly did. They called me John. Jonah—John— if I had been a Sam, I would have been a Jonah still." Jonah receives his first "very personal shove" in the direction of Bokononism by imagining that "God Almighty knew all about me . . . that God . . . had some pretty elaborate plans for me." But if his religious delusions, his belief that his thoughts or actions are controlled by others, may lead him straight into the mouth of the whale of moral oblivion, John, his real self, the voice of conscience, his anti-Bokononist voice, is still sufficiently alive and alarmed over the dubious consolations of Bokononist fatalism to fight for the narrator's divided soul. The key to the novel's ultimate moral affirmation is that Jonah's story, like Howard Campbell's, is told in retrospect, and though the narrator is still under the influence of Bokononist thought, we get the feeling that, as the story unfolds, the drug has begun to wear off, that John has come increasingly to suspect that the benefits of Bokononism are as dubious as those of technological progress offered by Felix Hoenikker. In less than reverent tones, Jonah's narrative is an imaginative reconstruction of events that led to Jonah's Bokononist conversion with a chance to reexplore their meaning. This defies the deathly stasis of Bokonon's own view of human and societal structures. When Jonah suggests an improvisation of Bokonon's Twenty-Third Psalm, Bokonon cannot change a single word. That a growth in awareness has indeed taken place is indicated by the narrator's observation near the close of the story that "I turned to the Books of Bokonon, still suffi-ciently unfamiliar with them to believe they contained spiritual comfort somewhere." Evidently he has learned better.

The nature of Jonah's particular brand of schizophrenia is that his spiritual self, that affirmative voice that wants to tell the truth, is so effec-tively counterbalanced by the voice of futility that a kind of stasis results, reflected in "the cruel paradox of Bokononist thought" about the heart-breaking necessity of lying about reality. The part of him that prefers foma to reality interviews the demented Julian Castle with the view, "I knew I wasn't going to have an easy time writing a popular article about him. I was going to have to concentrate on his saintly deeds and ignore entirely the satanic things he thought and said." It is also the part that allows him to be used as a puppet-president of San Lorenzo by Minister of Science and Progress Frank Hoenikker and threatens, so to speak, to put the *ice*ing on the cake of his schizophrenic dilemma, making him as morally dead as Frank or Felix Hoenikker or Bokonon. As a machine, he experiences no libidinal energy, hence no creativity, at all. He mourns that he has no "sex urge left," thus "no dreams . . . nothing." At first, when the cancer-ridden dictator of San Lorenzo decides to commit suicide with the Ice-9 Frank has given him and to take the rest of the world into the frozen sea with him, and Jonah is asked to rule the doomed island, his resistance is firm. "Nuts," he tells Frank. When Frank says "You haven't really thought about it," Jonah answers, "Enough to know it's crazy." Frank knows Jonah's moral evasiveness and pleads, "Come on. Be president of San Lorenzo. You'd be real good at it, with *your* personality." Suggestive of the soulless political machinery to which Frank wants Jonah to be a mindless accomplice, "Frank made his fingers into gears again. 'We'd work together,'" he says. "'I'd be backing you all the time.'" In effect Frank invites Jonah to become the public side of himself so that each is but half a human being—a mechanical being at that. When Franks tells him they could really hit it off, that they "mesh," Jonah notes: "I was grateful when he took his hand from my shoulder. He meshed the fingers of his hands like gear teeth. One hand represented him, I suppose, and the other represented me." "We need each other," Frank continues, wiggling his fingers to show how the gear worked. Frank explains that Jonah is a worldly person good for public show and he himself is a technical person who works best behind the scenes. Jonah feels that watery oblivion threatening him as his will weakens, aided by the bribe of a hundred thousand dollars a year and a palace of his own where he will drink out of gold goblets every night and eat off of gold plates. Jonah observes, "Frank was frantic for me to complete his thought, to do it enthusiastically, but I was still at sea." Increasingly powerless to resist, Jonah says that Frank has made Jonah's will as irrelevant as the free will "of a piggy-wig arriving at the Chicago stockyard." Jonah then sums up the combined forces that have depleted his will for years and made him a prime candidate for Bokononism.

> And the time of night and the cave and the waterfall—and the stone angel in Ilium. . . . And 250,000 cigarettes and 3,000 quarts of booze, and two wives and no wife. . . . And no love waiting for me anywhere. . . . And the listless life of an ink-stained hack. . . . And Pabu, the moon, and Borasisi, the sun, their children . . . [Bokononist cosmology]. . . . All things conspired to form one cosmic vin-dit, one mighty shove into Bokononism, into the belief that God was running my life and that He had work for me to do. And, inwardly, I sarooned, which is to say that I acquiesced to the seeming demands of my vin-dit. Inwardly, I agreed to become the next President of San Lorenzo. Outwardly, I was still guarded, suspicious.

Jonah has adopted the same false self system of previous heroes, resulting in an increasingly depleted inner being. When Frank dissociates himself from the pending destruction of San Lorenzo, making Jonah the new president with the words, "You're the boss, sir," Jonah reflects: "each time he said those words they seemed to come from farther away, as though Frank were descending the rungs of a ladder into a deep shaft, while I was obliged to remain above." Jonah realizes with chagrin that agreeing to be boss, secretly withdrawing his true self, he has freed Frank to do what his father had done: to receive honors and creative comforts while escaping human responsibilities. Frank was accomplishing this by going down a "spiritual oubliette." While Jonah is appalled at Frank's sudden abdication from human affairs, he himself escapes into a spiritual oubliette both literally and figuratively by becoming a Bokononist stooge, a "stuppa," a "fogbound child." Literally he flees down the manhole cover of an oubliette into the "rock-womb" of his castle's cozy bomb shelter to escape the gnashing, gobbling mouths of tornadoes spewing the poisonous bluewhite frost of Ice-9. Repeatedly, as Jonah allows himself to be carried along by the mindless momentum of what he assumes is his unmistakable destiny, we see him headed toward a watery grave at the end of entrapping tunnels, staircases, caves, shafts, mountains, some form of devouring cat's cradle. When he accepts the puppet role of president, it is in "a cave that was curtained by a waterfall"; he experiences "the ragged rim of oblivion . . . now inches from my curling toes." "I looked down," he says. "My lukewarm sea had swallowed all." Ominously he notes, "I was a respectful stranger to my own voice. My voice had a metallic authority that was new. I was already starting to rule."

It is of course the Frank Hoenikker or Bokonon part of his personality that has started to rule, rule *him* as well as the island, abetted by a golden-haired creature named Mona Aamons, the adopted daughter of the island's dictator who automatically belongs to Jonah as the island's new leader. Jonah's diffused will is no match for this latest siren. Says Jonah,

> While I didn't feel that purposeful seas were wafting me to San Lorenzo, I did feel that love was doing the job. The Fata Morgana, the mirage of what it would be like to be loved by Mona Aamons Monzano, had become a tremendous force in my meaningless life. I imagined that she could make me far happier than any woman had so far succeeded in doing.

Jonah fantasizes that Mona is not only the most heartbreakingly beautiful girl he can ever hope to see, but also "luminously compassionate and wise." He is more than willing to trade his writer's integrity for Mona's "warm and creamy soul . . . peace and plenty forever." After all, he reasons, "She was all there was to understand. Mona was the simplicity of the All."

Jonah is thrilled, heartbroken, hilarious, and most significantly, "insane," over Mona, immune to reality while enjoying the catatonic, orgiastic rigidity of boko-maru with her—the kissing of souls by mingling the bottoms of their feet together. Under her anesthetizing influence he is less likely than ever to know what is real. But it is the discovery that she is as false a mother as she is a lover that engenders a moral awakening and delivers Jonah from the mouth of the whale. He recognizes not only that her love is promiscuously mechanical but that, as with Felix, Frank, or Bokonon, compassion is unknown to her. After the "pool pah," the shit storm, has struck, after Ice-9 has left nearly everyone dead or threatened by eternal winter, Mona looks down from Mt. McCabe at thousands upon thousands of dead San Lorenzans who, at Bokonon's command, had gathered themselves together first to practice boko-maru and then to commit suicide by Ice-9 poisoning. The transition from mechanical love, a form of death-in-life, to literal death is simply achieved. Not only does she not cry; in fact, says Jonah, "she seemed to verge on laughter." Then, with an actual laugh that strikes Jonah as "startlingly deep and raw," "strolling down among the petrified thousands," still laughing, she says, raising her arms lazily, "It's all so simple, that's all. It solves so much for so many so simply."

While Mona finishes up as insane as Bokonon, Jonah's new self-assertiveness suggests *his* sanity may be returning, his splintered soul on the mend. He announces that, in case anyone was interested, he was willing to answer tough questions about what had gone wrong—"where and how." Telling his story about the human rather than the technical side of the bomb, one exactly like that in which he appears, provides the therapy and self-discovery he needs to resist the cat's cradle that had always been his personal nemesis—overwhelming pessimism. The fact that Jonah's mysterious last name may be "Vonnegut" suggests that this story is Vonnegut's too. A German immigrant had once ordered an angel to mark the grave of his diseased wife. Marvin Breed says that the last name on the marker, "a screwy name," was probably Americanized to Jones or Black or Thompson. "There you're wrong," Jonah assures him. When Marvin asks if Jonah knows some people by that name, Jonah says, "The name was my last name, too." The book by Jonah and the one by Vonnegut, or the one by Jonah Vonnegut, are incomplete . . . directing our attention to "what might yet be, if the world would thaw." If John and Jonah remain split, the John and Jonah in Vonnegut are closer to whole, closer to fulfilling Jonah's ancient role of warning the world against self-destruction. Jonah's battle for awareness and self-possession continues in what is Vonnegut's prototypal schizoid hero, Eliot Rosewater.

PETER J. REED

Hurting 'Til It Laughs: The Painful-Comic Science Fiction Stories of Kurt Vonnegut

> As for the story itself, it was entitled "The Dancing Fool." Like so many Trout stories, it was about a tragic failure to communicate.
>
> Here was the plot: A flying saucer creature named Zog arrived on Earth to explain how wars could be prevented and how cancer could be cured. He brought the information from Margo, a planet where the natives conversed by means of farts and tap dancing.
>
> Zog landed at night in Connecticut. He had no sooner touched down than he saw a house on fire. He rushed into the house, farting and tap dancing, warning the people about the terrible danger they were in. The head of the house brained Zog with a golfclub.
>
> —*Breakfast of Champions*

Kilgore Trout's "The Dancing Fool" typifies Kurt Vonnegut's use of science fiction, above all in being funny. But beyond its being comical, it shows some other characteristics frequently seen in Vonnegut's short stories and in the science fiction episodes in his novels. Note, for example, that while this curt account provides a minimum of context, of "how" or "why," it includes the mundane detail that Zog's landing was in Connecticut. While comical, the story has a touch of pathos in Zog's ill-deserved fate. The humor relies on hyperbole, on comic exaggeration, for much of its effect, and is highly visual. One source of the humor is in disparity, particularly that between Zog's lofty purpose in visiting Earth and the manner of its communication, and between his noble intent to save lives and his ignominious braining. These are all characteristics frequently seen in Vonnegut's science fiction short stories. They may be even more obvious in the science fiction interludes, such as the Trout inventions, in the novels. Typically, "The Dancing Fool" is not essential to its novel's main plot: used in *Black Garterbelt* magazine as filler, it could be about anything. It is comic interjection. It does have thematic connections, however, in being about communication and failures of communication. That becomes a major theme in *Breakfast of Champions*, from the failures of Rabo Karabekian's art to communicate to its audience, to Dwayne Hoover's inverting the message of Trout's "Now It Can Be Told." The story serves, then, not only as comic interlude, but in its thematic implications, as comic fable (perhaps for the moral that "No good deed goes unpunished"). All of these features are characteristic of Vonnegut's use of science fiction, evident from his earliest short stories to the later novels.

While Vonnegut has been characterized all too often as a "black humorist" and has been exaggeratedly classified as a science fiction writer, what remains distinctive in his method is the combining of these approaches. Vonnegut's recourse to science fiction, be it in a short story entirely in that mode or simply as interjection within a larger "realistic" work, is invariably comedic and usually humorous. While it often displays the properties of farce, as in "The Dancing Fool," his science fiction frequently has a tragicomic tone. Much of it may be described aptly as "painful comedy," where the comical vies with the hurtful. Sometimes it derives its humor from an existential sense of the absurd, in the incongruity between human (or even robot) efforts and the forces that they strive to master. Good comedy holds within it the potential for tragedy, and derives its cathartic value from alleviating broadly perceived threats or dangers. That is certainly true of many of Vonnegut's stories.

Reflecting their times, they deal with Cold War fears, the Damoclean threat of the Bomb, the lurking dangers of overpopulation and food shortage on the one hand and on the other government's Big Brotherly efforts to assuage them. The threats to the individual, of being dehumanized in an anonymous technological world, of loss of identity, purpose, or power of choice, are implied repeatedly in even lightly humorous stories. Science fiction plots provide the perfect mode in allowing Vonnegut to treat these topics without becoming bogged down in the quagmires of logic that often inhibit their more serious discussion. He can touch upon issues of free will, population control or race and gender relations, for example, with hyperbole and humor. He can thus express a philosophical point of view or make moral judgment in a manner that may avoid the resistance argumentation might invite. He gains the freedom to play both sides of an issue, and by his humor he can enlighten or provoke while entertaining. Hence, these stories often function as parables, comic and fantastic, but with moral purpose.

The novels are the most familiar of Vonnegut's writings to the majority of his audience, and painful-comic science fiction appears in them from the start. *Player Piano* (1952) has its share of both pain and humor written into its dystopian world. Its science fiction episodes usually adhere to the novel's theme of the human in combat with the machine: Paul Proteus' challenging "Checker Charley" at chess, and winning after Ed Finnerty hobbles the machine, or the Shah of Bratpuhr's challenging the mighty EPICAC XIV with a rhyming puzzle as incomprehensible to the machine as to anyone else. Sometimes "animal vs. machine" dramatizes the human conflict. The plant cat's surviving the robot sweeper only to die scaling the fence roughly parallels Paul Proteus' course in this novel, much as the luckier animal in the short story "Deer in the Works" amplifies the situation of that tale's protagonist.

The second novel, *The Sirens of Titan* (1959), moves further into the realm of science fiction, and the painful comic elements become even more conspicuous. One of the central science fiction creations of this novel is the Tralfamadorian robot Salo. This remarkable machine is described as "eleven million Earthling years old" and "four and a half feet tall." He has "a skin with the texture and color of the skin of an Earthling tangerine" and "three light deer-like legs." His inflatable feet enable him to walk on water or up walls. Salo has no arms, three eyes, and a head that is round and hung on gimbals. When anxious he lifts his feet up and down, making a squelching sound. He has been stranded on Titan for centuries for the lack of a part as simple as a beer can opener, and his Odyssey across the universe has been "a fool's errand"—his closely guarded secret message is simply "Greetings." The comic aspects of his plight are enhanced by the messages the Tralfamadorians send him by manipulating massive human constructions on Earth. Stonehenge reads "Replacement part being rushed with all possible speed." The Kremlin walls spell out, "You will be on your way before you know it." While often the source of comedy, Salo also brings sentiment, even pathos, to the novel. He is loyal, compassionate, and feeling, emotions stronger in him than in the humans around him and that bring him to self-destruct. But in true comedic fashion he is repairable, and he creates the novel's happy ending by leaving Malachi Constant with a heart-warming illusion of reunion with his old friend Stony Stevenson and the message that "somebody up there likes you."

While less familiar to most readers, the short stories are worth examining because many come early in Vonnegut's career where he evolves and develops his science fiction technique. Also, the short stories sometimes contain more sustained employment of science fiction than occurs in the short episodes, like the Kilgore Trout plots, that are found in the novels. There are marked similarities, however, and the characteristics briefly noted as occurring in "The Dancing Fool" emerge early in Vonnegut's work. In those early years he was working for the General Electric Company where, as he has said, he saw new technology and its implications for the future emerging all around him. As a high school and college journalist Vonnegut had often used fantasized and hyperbolic renditions of events to make commentary. Combining that bent with projections of an evolving technological society quickly leads to his own style of comic but dystopian science fiction. In the early stories the technique sometimes seems aimed at engaging the interest of an audience still in the grip of a postwar "can-do" faith in scientific innovation. Later it more often expresses cynicism, anger, or even ridicule, its laughter more bitter. It can become sharper, compressed, and more fantastic as the pretense of plausibility yields to the rapidly sketched plots of Kilgore Trout. But that is to jump ahead, and it is best to start at the beginning, with Vonnegut's first published short story.

"Report on the Barnhouse Effect," which appeared in *Collier's* on February 11, 1950, records the experiments of Professor Arthur Barnhouse as presented by his assistant. Barnhouse achieves what he calls "'dynamopsychism,' or force of the mind," by following a "thought train that aligned the professor's brain cells." He then has the power to move physical objects. He begins by manipulating dice; eventually he becomes "about fifty-five times more powerful that a Nagasaki-type atomic bomb," able to destroy objects thousands of miles distant. The professor wants to use his power for peaceful purposes such as "moving cloud masses into drought areas," but the armed services become "interested in dynamopsychism as a potential weapon." Barnhouse resists sharing the secret of his powers, but agrees to a demonstration, destroying fleets of aircraft and warships. But in the midst of his triumph he slips away into hiding and sets about destroying the weapons of the world's powers in an effort to bring about global peace. Barnhouse's endeavors are threatened by the efforts of governments to hunt him down and by the fact that he is "of short-lived stock." While his death would mean the end of his single-handed imposition of peace, at the end of the report the writer reveals that he has decoded the last message Barnhouse left him and is now increasingly able to exercise "dynamopsychism" himself. With the clear implication he will take up Barnhouse's role, he ends the report with a simple "Good-bye."

Much of the humor in this story resides in its far-fetched plot, which nevertheless retains enough plausibility to sustain interest and suspense. Fascination with the potential of psycho-kinetic powers tends to persist, recurring in fiction and even fueling rumors of Russian experiments with it for military purposes. Its use in this story injects an element of the American "tall tale" tradition, coupling the comic use of science fiction with an established and familiar form of humor. Typically, Vonnegut quickly dispenses with seemingly logical explanations of "dynamopsychism," offering simply the throwaway note that Barnhouse achieves his power by "aligning the brain cells." The title of the process—"dynamopsychism"—is another example of Vonnegut's love of inventing comic words and language. Comic descriptions are scattered throughout the story, such as the notation that at one point Barnhouse "had the range and power of a 37-millimeter cannon, perhaps." The scale of the ultimate experiment is itself comic in its sheer excess, with everything carried to a hyperbolic extreme, a carnage of ships, planes and rockets, as the delighted general chortles, "Well, sir, by George, by George, by George!" like a gleeful Sidney Greenstreet.

Barnhouse's escape and solo campaign to disarm the opposing forces before any of the competing sides can capture him and avail themselves of his powers creates the suspense in the story and is heightened with the revelation of Barnhouse's coming from "short-lived stock." That circumstance inserts a genetic joker into the plot, and introduces a human element into a science fiction setting. The solution to the problem is easy and predictable: the young narrator will carry on the professor's work. It is a surprise turn in the plot at the end that is not really a surprise, and that in itself is a comic device. Vonnegut's short stories often have a sudden turn in events that has the appearance of a surprise ending, but that we have been let in on earlier. We gain the double satisfaction of the relief that a last minute reversal typically gives, plus the rather smug satisfaction of having suspected what was to come.

The story functions as comedy in that it confronts the familiar "bogey-men" of that Cold War era and overcomes them. The pervasive fears of war, the Bomb, a military-industrial complex or an intrusive Big Brother government are dispelled—and by a human power. The professor remains invulnerable—except to his own humanity. Just as in *Player Piano*, it is human failings that at once thwart the revolution but affirm its humanity, so here Barnhouse's genes confirm his humanity against the dispassionate forces of science and militarism. Barnhouse's potential mortality threatens to turn the story toward tragedy. But the emergence of the underling, the student who will by cunning thwart the figures of authority, is a reversal in the best traditions of comedy.

"Report on the Barnhouse Effect" embodies science fiction with para-psychological overtones, and "Thanasphere," which appeared in *Collier's* on September 2, 1950, takes this direction further. Major Allen Rice, an astronaut in orbit two thousand miles above the earth, begins complaining of hearing voices that drown out those from mission control. When the ground personnel check out names that Rice hears mentioned, they find that the speakers he hears are dead. It emerges that Rice has entered a sphere populated by the spirits of the dead. These spirits bombard Rice with messages for people living on earth. Much of the humor derives from the mounting obsession of Rice with the phenomenon he has encountered played against the hysterical frustration of the ground team. The latter find the prospect of Rice possibly going crazy or that he is sane and his discovery will be revealed universally through the radio operators trying to listen in equally appalling. Once again there is the comic figure of a blustering general, yelling at the astronaut, "I don't know what your angle is, but I do know I'll bring you back down and slap you on a rock pile in Leavenworth so fast you'll leave your teeth up there." The tension mounts when the spirits later manifest themselves as beautiful shimmering phantoms, with Rice's late wife Margaret appearing among them. While the ground crew try to keep the mission a secret, they can do nothing except jam the transmissions and bring Rice down.

Their fears that the orbiting Rice may prefer to crash and thus join his wife are duly realized. His death provides a macabre comic resolution of the story, ensuring the continued secrecy of the mission and of the existence of the "Thanasphere," and permitting Rice to rejoin his wife. Vonnegut inserts an ironic underlining to the comic nature of the story by having the supervising scientist of the project tell the suspicious newsmen, "You people read too many comic books."

Being written more than a decade before the first manned space flight, some aspects of "Thanasphere" may appear accidentally humorous to us now. But humor is implicit in the science fiction elements of the story. The whole concept of a "dead zone," where spirits compete to be heard by an astronaut, is comic in itself. The particulars, like the late Hollywood actor trying to rectify his nephew's tampering with his will, and the amateur radio operators trying to make sense of this when they intercept a transmission, add delightful touches of the absurd. This will not be the last time Vonnegut will entertain with comic visions of an afterworld or communications with it. Other renditions occur in the play *Happy Birthday, Wanda June* (1970), where scenes are set in a shuffleboard-playing heaven, and in *Slapstick* (1976), where the scenes of Wilbur Swain communicating with his dead sister via the "Hooligan" take on the character suggested by the novel's title.

"EPICAC," which first appeared in the November 25, 1950, *Collier's*, owes its genesis to Vonnegut's inevitable involvement with technology while working for General Electric. In his *Playboy* interview he says, "There was no avoiding it, since the General Electric company was science fiction." EPICAC, the subject of the story, is a huge computer that cost $776,434,927.54 and occupies "about an acre." It is intended to "plot the course of a rocket from anywhere on earth to the second button from the bottom of Joe Stalin's overcoat, if necessary." Its great size in itself seems comic in an era of microcircuitry. So does the specific figure of its cost, down to the last cent. Moreover, EPICAC falters in its task because it is unhappy in its work. Until, that is, its operator tells it of his love for Pat Callaghan, a woman colleague. The machine then writes copious romantic poems that the narrator claims as his own and uses to woo Pat. EPICAC has fallen in love. When the narrator tells EPICAC that Pat believes that the poems are from him and that she cannot love a computer anyway, EPICAC commits suicide.

One might argue that Vonnegut shows characteristic foresight, and that a situation like this might yet arise in the interaction between humans and artificial intelligence. One advantage to Vonnegut's comic shaping of science fiction is that he can be predictive without the same requirements of plausibility or technical accuracy that might be expected of serious science fiction. Most of the specifics of this plot take on their character because of the dependence of this story's humor on comic exaggeration. "EPICAC" is another story that invites suspension of disbelief, again given touches of brass-tacks plausibility. One such—itself comic—is that the mathematically accomplished operator and the supercomputer can come up with no more sophisticated means of communication than "a childish numbers-for-letters code: 1 for A" and so on. There is comic hyperbole in the sheer volume of poetry that EPICAC produces, in the computer's astronomical price, even in the devastation produced by its suicide.

"EPICAC" depends heavily upon the effectiveness of its narrative persona. A factual, third-person omniscient reportage of the events would fall flat. So Vonnegut establishes a characterization behind the narrative voice from the first sentence: "Hell, it's about time somebody told about my friend EPICAC." The careless informality creates a different level of acceptance from that applied to an objectively stated story. It makes the giving of EPICAC gender, personality, and relationship plausible, too. Further, the narrator saves the story from succumbing to its sentimentality. The emotions are his: we may share in them, but are not asked to be the primary receptor of them as would be the case without his presence. Vonnegut sometimes seems sentimental in his earlier work. Frequently, though, he undercuts the sentiment with humor and with something rather off-handed or rough-hewn in the narration, as in "EPICAC." The machine's falling in love, its being told it cannot be loved because it is a machine, and that it is inferior because it is not protoplasm is poignant—but still a joke.

"The Euphio Question" (*Collier's*, May 12, 1951) is presented as a report to the Federal Communications Commission about a physicist who has picked up radio signals from space. The hiss that emanates from his equipment induces a state of supine euphoria in the listening audience. The physicist and two friends, their sights set on making themselves fortunes with a scheme to market guaranteed happiness, come up with a "euphoria-phone" and run a home test. The scene that results becomes a mix of Laurel and Hardy and the Three Stooges, as more and more people arrive and fall under the sound's spell. In careless abandon they trash the house and would continue in their hypnotic state indefinitely, it seems, but for a tree's falling on the power lines to cut off the machine. The end of the story has a characteristic Vonnegutian twist. The unscrupulous radio announcer giving the FCC report plans to push ahead with the euphoriaphone and mounts a demonstration model in the hearing room. We are left to imagine the consequences.

"The Euphio Question" illustrates a theme frequent in Vonnegut's work: the downside of the pleasure principle, or the Utopian becoming nightmare. While that theme obviously has serious implications, Vonnegut relishes treating it with comic exaggeration in slapstick scenes. While once again the science fiction concept—beaming a universal soporific from space—is comic, much of the story's humor derives not from the science fiction itself but from the slapstick events that ensue from it. Additionally, the comic resolution of "The Euphio Question" evades answering the moral issues the situation has raised. In that sense, "The Euphio Question" repre- sents a variation on the shaggy dog story, the form explicitly invoked in Vonnegut's next story.

"Tom Edison's Shaggy Dog," which first appeared in *Collier's* on March 14, 1953, while not strictly science fiction, makes use of science for its main comic episode. Two retired men share a bench in a Florida park. Harold K. Bullard chatters endlessly of his past business successes. His captive listener merely wants to sit and read, but Bullard's dog keeps nuzzling his suspenders, while Bullard relentlessly pursues his self-aggrandizing monologue. The victim's move to another bench fails to deter either the dog or Bullard. In self-defense the stranger launches into a story of his own. He tells how when he was a boy he lived next door to Thomas Edison's laboratory. He made friends with Edison's dog, Sparky, which one day led to his meeting the great man. Edison showed him a black box called an intelligence analyzer. As a test they attached it to Sparky's head, and it at once read off the scale. It seems that dogs had been smarter than humans all along, giving humans the worry and stress of providing for them while they lived in comfort. To repay Edison for keeping this secret, Sparky told Edison to use carbonized cotton thread as a filament for the light bulb, and gave the boy the stock tip that had made him wealthy for the rest of his life. The unfortunate Sparky, however, was killed by a pack of dogs who had overheard him reveal the secrets of man's best friend.

Vonnegut has flirted with the shaggy dog story form before, but this self-proclaimed example is a classic. It is, after all, a shaggy dog story about a dog—and within a frame story also involving a dog. Part of our enjoyment comes from seeing the tables turned on the boring Bullard and his intrusive dog, and in watching his mounting incredulity as the stranger's story escalates. The climax of the stranger's tall tale sneaks up delightfully. Edison is lamenting that he has been working for the last year, "'Slaving to work out a light bulb so dogs can play at night.' 'Look, Mr. Edison,' said Sparky, 'why not—' 'Hold on!' roared Bullard." The purple-faced Bullard's finally being caught as the story takes its last step over the edge of credulity is a masterfully contrived moment. Beside being one of the most amusing short stories with a science fiction element, "Tom Edison's Shaggy Dog" is noteworthy in another respect. By using within the narrative a storyteller who mixes scientific history and the far-fetched, this short story points toward the eventual use of Kilgore Trout and his vignettes in later novels.

"Unready to Wear" was the first of two stories Vonnegut would publish in *Galaxy Science Fiction*. A fine example of Vonnegut's comedic uses of science fiction, it appeared in the April 1953 issue and was subsequently reprinted in both *Canary in a Cathouse* and *Welcome to the Monkey House*. It depicts a future in which people have learned, thanks to a Professor Konigswasser, how to escape their bodies. Such people are called amphibians, in that they are like the first creatures that learned how to leave the water and live on land. Ironically, Professor Konigswasser has discovered how to do this by walking into water. Ever absentminded—in fact, his absentmindedness is seen as the first step to his leaving his body—he has walked into a lake. Later he walks back out, sees a rescue team resuscitating a decrepit body, and realizes it is his, so to spare people any inconvenience, he gets back into it and walks it home. From then on he mostly leaves his body in a closet, keeping it on low maintenance. He writes a book on how to do all of this and soon has millions of followers, among them the narrator of the story and his wife Madge. The amphibians store some bodies for people to check out when they want. Despite discarding their bodies, some of the amphibians remain ironically obsessional about them. For the annual Pioneers' Day parade even old Konigswasser checks out the body of a tall, blond cowboy who crushes beer cans between his fingers. Madge shows a penchant for the body of a platinum blonde burlesque queen.

The amphibians' enemies are those humans who have resisted becoming amphibian. One day Madge and the narrator discover that the humans have built an elaborate body storage center, like the ones the amphibians maintain. Madge decides the enemy has seen the light and plans to become amphibians. She spots an irresistible body, "six feet tall and built like a goddess. . . . The body had copper-colored skin, chartreuse hair and fingernails, and a gold lame evening gown." But it proves to be a trap. The ankles are tied so that an amphibian cannot take the first few steps required to leave a body. Trying to help Madge, the narrator enters another body that is also a trap. The humans stage a trial and convict the two trapped amphibians of desertion, but the amphibians counter that this will mean war, that other amphibians surround the building, and that if the two of them are not released amphibians will enter the humans' bodies and march them off the edge of a cliff. This, the narrator confides, actually would be impossible, since only one person can inhabit a body at a time! The bluff works, and the amphibians escape the bodies and human capture, but not before Madge has left instructions for the copper-colored char-treuse-haired body to be sent to her.

Once again, the central science fiction ingredient in the plot of this story is a throwaway device. The few absentminded steps necessary to set the would-be amphibian walking out of a body have about the same plausibility as Barnhouse's aligning his brain cells. The "how" of this central phenom-enon is not important—Vonnegut needs only to establish the situation of "what if" humans could escape their bodies? It is the kind of "what if" comic situation he delights in creating, as we see later in *Slapstick's* variable gravity or *Cat's Cradle's* Ice-Nine, and in which science fiction serves him so well. Konigswasser is also a set-piece comic figure for Vonnegut, the absent-minded professor in the mold of Barnhouse or *Cat's Cradle's* Felix Hoenikker. There is other stock humor in this story, such as the descriptions of the bodies amphibians choose and how they behave in them, the Pioneers' Day parade, and the trial, with its parody of a McCarthy hearing.

While its plot is almost farcical, "Unready to Wear" nevertheless touches on some serious social issues such as overpopulation and the effects of biochemistry on human behavior. Konigswasser vainly delights in assuming the "macho" image of the husky cowboy and crushing beer cans. Women, we are told, relate identity even more to the body, and delight in trying new bodies and costuming them and making them up like oversized dolls. But bodies are the source of most human problems. "The moment you get in, chemistry takes over—glands making you excitable or ready to fight or hungry or mad or affectionate, or—well, you never know what's going to happen next." This is the first instance of Vonnegut's speaking of people's being controlled by chemicals, something that he returns to quite often in later fiction. That concept becomes a major component of the plot of *Breakfast of Champions* and *Slapstick*, where chemicals' control of human behavior is seen as sometimes reducing them almost to being robots. That also touches on the issue of free will, and how much of it humans actually enjoy, which is another perennial topic with Vonnegut. While its subjects are comically treated, this story proves another example of Eliot Rosewater's grounds for complimenting science fiction writers in *God Bless You, Mr. Rosewater*: "You're the only ones who'll talk about the really terrific changes going on."

"Unready to Wear" works well as a comic parable about overpopulation while reveling in its own implausibility, in effect celebrating its own fictionality. Vonnegut rather resembles Konigswasser (who may even be seen as another German-named author-surrogate within a story) in his adolescent irreverence for the determined conditions of existence and the imagination to explore, if only in fun, what might happen if they were changed. This shows the same imagination that can conceive water that freezes at room temperature in *Cat's Cradle*, variable gravity in *Slapstick*, or chrono-synclastic infundibula in *The Sirens of Titan*. We recognize the parallel between Konigswasser's amphibian and the disembodied fictional character that an author creates, and just as the person "trapped" in a body and controlled by biochemistry lacks free will, so the fictional character faces the comic dilemma of being at the mercy of the author-creator. Vonnegut gives that situation extended treatment in the ending pages of *Breakfast of Champions*, in the amusing scene where Kilgore Trout and his creator come face to face.

The other story in *Galaxy Science Fiction* (January 1954, included in *Canary in a Cathouse* and *Welcome to the Monkey House* with the new title, "Tomorrow and Tomorrow and Tomorrow") similarly gives comic treatment to serious social issues, returning in its primary focus to the one of overpopulation. Set in 2185 A.D., "The Big Trip Up Yonder" depicts a world where the invention of anti-gerasone has enabled people to stop the aging process, resulting in overpopulation and the rationing of food and space. Life becomes miserable for most people, yet they remain reluctant to leave it, abandon their anti-gerasone, and take "The Big Trip Up Yonder." Lou and Emerald Ford share their grandfather's apartment with twenty-three other relatives. The 172-year-old Gramps rules the household ruthlessly, using the tyranny of his last will and testament, which determines who will succeed to his bedroom and who meanwhile will sleep on the prized daybed. Others sleep crowded on mattresses on the floor. Rivalries for favor in Gramps' eyes or to end his rule lead to subterfuges like attempts to dilute his anti-gerasone. Eventually Gramps uses a ruse of his own wherein he vanishes and appears to leave a suicide note dividing his belongings equally among all his descendants. This precipitates a riot among them that leads to them all being arrested. At the end Lou and Em are luxuriating in private eight-by-four prison cells with their own wash basins. They are hiring a good attorney to get them the longest sentence possible. Gramps retains his apartment, which is private at last, and sends off for the new Super-anti-gerasone, which not only stops aging but enables the user to recover youth.

Incidental humor abounds in this story, in addition to its central comic treatment of overpopulation. It satirizes the advertising world's promotion of the desire among people to look young and alike: "Wouldn't you pay $5,000 to be indistinguishable from everybody else?" the Super-anti-gerasone commercial asks. Even soap operas are satirized; "The McGarvey Family" has been running for at least 102 years. The situation in Gramps' apartment and the childish shenanigans of the five generations trapped there are sheer slapstick. The jailer threatens the celebrating family inmates with eviction if they do not keep quiet, and with lifelong exclusion if they ever disclose how good conditions are in prison. The post office box number for Super-anti-gerasone is 500,000! Only Gramps gets to eat real food; the rest get "buckwheat-type processed sawdust cakes" or "egg-type processed seaweed." The Indianapolis 500 has become the 5,000-mile Speedway Race. Typically, then, the humor depends heavily on hyperbole and the inversion of normal expectations. Traditional comic elements such as the cunning and tyrannical old patriarch, the resourceful younger couple, the treacherous snitch, and the surprise reversal that turns potential tragedy into a happy ending, all contribute to this story's appeal.

The two *Galaxy Science Fiction* stories give the Cassandra in Vonnegut freedom to alert his readership to issues confronting society, but also allow the comedian to enjoy comic situations and childlike deconstructions of traditional assumptions about life. He can use science-fictional terms and futuristic settings with a comic hyperbole that banishes resistance to their implausibility. These are stories that prefigure some of the earlier novels like *The Sirens of Titan* and *Cat's Cradle*, where the same combination of science fiction tropes and comic hyperbole produces energetic novels that both entertain and educate.

"Harrison Bergeron" appeared in the October 1961 issue of *Magazine of Fantasy and Science Fiction* and was reprinted in *National Review* on November 16, 1965, and then in *Welcome to the Monkey House*. It is a dystopian portrayal of a society premised on an idealistic vision that has turned into nightmare. The events take place in the year 2081 when "everybody was finally equal," as ensured by "the 211th, 212th, and 213th Amendments to the Constitution" and "the unceasing vigilance of the agents of the United States Handicapper General." The story is set in the home of George and Hazel Bergeron. Average Hazel remains unhandicapped, but clever George wears bags weighted with bird shot and an ear radio that transmits brain-shattering noises to diminish his powers of thought. The Bergerons' four-teen-year-old superhuman son, Harrison, has been arrested by the Handicapper General, Diana Moon Glampers. As the Bergerons watch a ballet on television, an announcer interrupts to say that Harrison Bergeron, dangerous athlete and genius, has escaped. At once Harrison makes a dramatic appearance on screen and, declaring himself "the Emperor!" tears off his handicaps, selects a ballerina to be his Empress, and proceeds to dance with superhuman grace and strength. As they kiss while suspended in an unimaginable leap, Diana Moon Glampers herself bursts in armed with a shotgun and shoots them down. George and Hazel return to watching the resumed program. Tears stain George's cheek, but with the sound of a riveting gun blasting in his ear, he has no idea why.

Visual humor dominates "Harrison Bergeron." Most of the action—all of that involving Harrison, the dancers and Diana Moon Glampers—appears on the Bergerons' television. Harrison enters looking "like a walking junk yard," required to wear "a red rubber ball for a nose, keep his eyebrows shaved off, and cover his even white teeth with black caps at snaggle-tooth random." When he dances with the ballerina they defy "the law of gravity and the laws of motion as well," leaping to kiss the thirty-foot ceiling until finally "they remained suspended in air inches below the ceiling, and they kissed each other for a long, long time." It is then that Glampers enters with her shotgun. "She fired twice, and the Emperor and the Empress were dead before they hit the floor." The sheer implausibility and exaggeration of all of this—the handicaps, Harrison's size and prowess, the astronomical leaps—create the comic spectacle. The story celebrates its very fictiveness: we know these things cannot happen. In depicting the action in a representational manner the story actually subverts its claims to realism by its sheer exaggeration. Rather than pretending to realism it actually declares its fictionality. Having the dramatic events within the story presented on television, two removes from reality, emphasizes this fictionality.

The "serious" topic that the story declares itself to be concerned with is equality. It satirizes an obsession with equalizing; the predominant images are of the ludicrousness of the mental and physical handicaps, the grimness of reducing a population to its lowest common denominator, and the Big-Brotherly oversight that results. But the topic's main emphasis is comic. "Harrison Bergeron" may be a satirical fable, like George Orwell's *Animal Farm*, but the balance between comical rendering and moral message in the fable becomes almost the opposite in the two stories. Take Vonnegut's view of what passes as average in America: "Hazel had a perfectly average intelligence, which meant she couldn't think about anything except in short bursts." The observation on the ballerinas continues the undercutting humor: "They weren't really very good—no better than anybody else would have been, anyway." There is heavy irony in the plodding Hazel's missing the point, as when she sympathizes with the stuttering announcer for trying "real hard" to do his best, or when she suggests George might remove some of his weights in the evenings. Compounding the irony she says, "'I think I'd make a good Handicapper General.' 'Good as anybody else,' said George." The range of sounds and the comic brutality of their effect provides another source of humor. We may recall that Vonnegut as a youth enjoyed the often painful comedy of such teams as Laurel and Hardy, Abbot and Costello, and the Three Stooges, whose physically violent slapstick was often accompanied by appropriately barbarous sounds. One of George's winces prompts Hazel to ask the cause. "Sounded like somebody hitting a milk bottle with a hammer," he replies. Another sounds like a twenty-one gun salute that leaves George "white and trembling" and two of the ballerinas on the floor clutching their temples. The final one is a riveting gun.

> "Gee—I could tell that one was a doozy," said Hazel.
> "You can say that again," said George.
> "Gee—" said Hazel—"I could tell that one was a doozy."

So "Harrison Bergeron" represents another of Vonnegut's painful comic renderings of a dystopian vision. Its technique on this occasion might be more accurately described as fantasy than as science fiction, particularly with its handsome, super-humanly endowed young hero who liberates his lovely young empress. The elements of dance, music, and staging all suggest that mode, as does the wicked witchlike presence of Diana Moon Glampers. But as with the science fiction, the fantasy tropes are transformed by slapstick undercutting and hyperbolic distortion.

"2BR02B" appeared in *Worlds of If* in January 1962 and returns to the portrayal of a dystopian future world governed by a good idea gone mad. (Vonnegut will use "2BR02B" again as the title of a Kilgore Trout story in *God Bless You, Mr. Rosewater.*) The good idea carried to excess is population control. As in "The Big Trip Up Yonder," a way has been found to stop the aging process, necessitating laws requiring that no child can be born until the parents can certify that someone else agrees to die. This story also features Ethical Suicide Studios staffed by efficient and welcoming young "gas chamber hostesses" who wear purple. A dispirited husband sits in a waiting room of the Chicago Lying-in Hospital, while above him a "sardonic" old painter works on a stepladder. The painter is completing a mural of a formal garden, with gardeners dressed in purple. Among those depicted stands Dr. Benjamin Hitz, the Chief Obstetrician, who at this point in the story actually enters the room in person. He announces to the waiting husband that his wife as expected has delivered triplets, and asks if the family has found three candidates for the Ethical Suicide Studios. The husband has found only one, so faces having to choose two of the triplets to die. But instead he produces a gun, shoots Hitz, and then himself. The old painter, having watched silently from above, descends, picks up the gun, lacks the nerve to shoot himself, and instead calls "2-B-R-0–2-B," the telephone number of the ethical suicide service. The answering hostess arranges an appointment, then delivers the story's ironic final lines: "Your city thanks you; your country thanks you; your planet thanks you. But the deepest thanks of all is from future generations."

As in "The Big Trip Up Yonder," Vonnegut uses painful comedy rather than didacticism to point out the dangers of overpopulation and, through the distortions of hyperbole, some of the difficult choices it imposes. In this story, the imposition of population control averts a disastrous situation where drinking water was already running out and people were eating seaweed. The negative aspects of population control are epitomized in the necessity to kill a baby if no volunteer for death can be found, and by the references to the euphemistically named Ethical Suicide Studios as gas chambers, calling up all the horrors of Nazi exterminations. The hyperbole heightens both sides of the issue to the point of absurdity. The story, like others on this topic, draws attention to one of the most serious issues facing human kind, but one that governments, religions, politicians, and people generally show a remarkable reluctance to consider. Vonnegut's dark humor permits an approach to a topic that generally invites instant resistance.

Some of the circumstances of "2BR02B" are repeated or extended in a Kilgore Trout story in *God Bless You, Mr. Rosewater* and in "Welcome to the Monkey House" some six years later, including what become Ethical Suicide Parlors. The hostesses wear purple there, too, and in each case the unnaturalness of this reversal of their human maternal functions is signaled by their unsexing. In "Welcome to the Monkey House," chemicals stop all feeling below their waists, while in this story they all develop facial hair— "an unmistakable mustache, in fact"—after a few years in the job. Vonnegut uses the name of his Shortridge High School chum, Ben Hitz, who was later best man at his first wedding, for one of the characters. Dr. Hitz stands seven feet tall, another instance of Vonnegut's use of hyperbole for comic effect. He creates other seven footers, such as Harrison Bergeron, or Wilbur Swain of *Slapstick*, and some midgets, too, like Newt Hoenikker of *Cat's Cradle*.

Despite the rather grim consequences in this story, "2BR02B" is told brightly, with a cheery tone and brisk, short sentences. The relative brevity of the story, combined with its pace, prevents its taking on the dour quality to which its content could lead. The opening sets the tone:

> Everything was perfectly swell.
> There were no prisons, no slums, no insane asylums, no cripples, no poverty, no wars.

The comic note is established early. The waiting husband, we are told, is a "mere stripling" being fifty-six where the average age is one hundred and twenty-nine. Then there are the lyrics of a currently popular song in which a lover threatens to go to "a girl in purple" if he is rejected. The mural on the hospital wall is ironically titled "The Happy Garden of Life." The Suicide Studios are run by a "Federal Bureau of Terminations," and the popular sobriquets for them include "Easy-go," "Catbox," "Kiss-me-quick," and "Why Worry." As with the other stories dealing with over-population, much of the humor derives from hyperbole and inversion, and there is an exuberance in treating serious subjects with flippancy. The ending falls short of the comic resolution of "The Big Trip Up Yonder," but is less clouded than that of "Welcome to the Monkey House." While the latter story (which appeared in *Playboy* in January 1968) has a futuristic setting, ethical suicide parlors, anti-aging pills and overpopulation, it appears less science fictional than social, and less comic than satiric. Its resolution, with the main female character having been raped for her own good, in effect, remains troubling, and diminishes the sparkle of the incidental humor along the way.

A short satirical piece written in 1962 is called "HOLE BEAU-TIFUL: Prospectus for a Magazine of Shelteredness," published in *Monocle* (Vol. 5, no. 1). This satire presents another comic banishing of the current Cold War fears. The proposed magazine's title obviously derives from *House Beautiful*, and its subject is fallout shelters and activities surrounding them. It will be "the magazine of gracious survival." As a general public relations consultant the magazine would employ "a leading undertaker" who, "with his valuable experience in the field of putting people under-ground, will be helpful in overcoming the negative image that death has in this country." Singing commercials might include "Hole is where the heart is" or "There's no place like hole." The publisher would be a separate corporation called Subterranean Publications, Inc., with offices in Mammoth Cave, Kentucky. "Cost per issue will be 50¢ in subways and $1.00 above ground." Because of negative connotations, the word "bomb" will never be used and instead it will be referred to as "the Big Fella." The editorial policy will be to oppose the government's community shelter program with the aid of the American Medical Association's attack on it as "socialized sheltering." The magazine would promote "Shelter Hopping Kits" designed to gain access to other people's shelters in time of attack by using various devices such as Cyklon-B gas or imitations of the pleadings of a beloved family pet. A sample theater review focuses on the theater's emergency exits, lighting, and proximity to a fallout shelter. Editorials projected include "Unilateral Disarmament by the Russians—Does It Violate the American Sense of Fair Play?" So it goes on, irreverent and inventive, in the best comedic tradition of meeting society's worst fears head on with laughter. Once the premise has been established, much of the humor of this piece depends on the evolving details, and it is not difficult to see how this text could have become one of the comic subplots that often run through the novels.

Those comic subplots are well illustrated by the science fiction portions of *Slaughterhouse-Five* and *Slapstick*. Significantly, the main plots of these two novels are among the most bleak in Vonnegut's canon, with settings of war, destruction, and death. In *Slaughterhouse-Five*, the Tralfamadorian segments provide the reader with relief from the war scenes much as they do for the protagonist Billy Pilgrim himself. While humorous, the science fiction subplot is shorn of the painful elements so often present in the short stories. Billy's life under the Tralfamadorians' geodesic dome, safe from the acidic atmosphere outside and with every need provided for, is pure wish fulfillment. Its humor—the watching plumber's-friend Tralfamadorians and their wishes to see the humans mate, the night cover, Billy's startled awakenings from time-traveling—seems mellow and reassuring in its contrast to the war scenes. Admittedly, the Tralfamadorian subplot includes a vision of the end of the world and the perpetuation of war, but these seem distant threats compared with the miseries of battlefield, prison camp, and firestorm. The Tralfamadorian philosophy of coping with life by thinking only of the good times seems less cynical than healing in this context. The incorporation of the science fiction subplot in such a way that it could all be read as Billy's imagining underscores the sense that the human mind can only tolerate so much pain. Thus, science fiction fulfills a similar role within Billy's personal drama that it often does in Vonnegut's fiction.

In *Slapstick*, the science fiction is not always as benign in its comic contributions. Variable gravity is one of the science fiction devices that sets up much of the plot of the novel, much as Ice-Nine does in *Cat's Cradle*. Both of these transformations of nature have their comic potential as well as their catastrophic consequences. Both display Vonnegut's characteristic tendency to ask the almost childlike question that challenges adult assumptions—what if ice could be frozen at room temperature? what if gravity varied, like the wind? The questions are comic in essence and may seem absurd, but they underline that we do, day in and day out, in effect gamble that such assumptions hold true until they do not—until the stable earth beneath us buckles in earthquake or sinks in flood, or the unnoticed breeze becomes a life-shattering tornado. Thus, variable gravity destroys bridges and crushes tunnels. But it also can be humorous in its effects, as when we learn that "All males have erections on days like this. They are automatic consequences of near-weightlessness." The fantastic events of *Slapstick* include Chinese who can miniaturize themselves, a new solution to the perennial overpopulation problem. There are rampant diseases like the Green Death and the Albanian Flu, the former caused by inhaling miniaturized Chinese. There is also the invention of "the Hooligan," a device that accidentally permits communication with the dead, whose world we learn sounds like a badly run turkey farm. The protagonist Wilbur Swain and his sister cut fantastic figures, being Neanderthaloids over seven feet tall with extra fingers, toes, and nipples. *Slapstick* then, abounds in the comic hyperbole that typically embraces pain and laughter—and that may lead to instruction—so often found in his science fiction and fantasy.

Beyond such subplots that carry science fiction motifs throughout their novels, however, there is a continuation of the short stories in the form of vignettes, plot outlines, or allusions within the novels. These sometimes function as parables and are frequently the invention of the ubiquitous Kilgore Trout. "The Dancing Fool," with which this chapter began, is a typical example. Kilgore Trout himself, of course, in his various shabby manifestations, might be seen as the embodiment of painful comedy. His plight as neglected science fiction writer, ever-accepting of the wonders of life, expecting the worst but always undaunted, surprised only by recognition, makes him the ideal persona through whom Vonnegut can insert his science fiction mini-stories when needed.

An example of how the Trout stories in the later fiction work much like parables is one in *Timequake* called "The Sisters B-36." It tells of three sisters, two pleasant and one evil, on a matriarchal planet named Booboo. One of the good sisters is a painter, while the other is a writer. The third is a scientist who talks mostly about thermodynamics. People find her boring and shun her. In an obvious parallel to humans, Booboolings' minds are programmed by what they are told in words during their infancy. Booboolings are thus trained how to look at pictures or print, and they develop circuits that Earthlings would call "Imagination." To make her own impression on Booboolings, the bad sister, "Nim-nim B-36," invents television. Booboolings then no longer need imagination, and only the older ones, whose circuits were formed before television, can appreciate pictures and writing. The two good sisters are reduced to feeling abandoned and neglected, just as B-36 wished, but still no one appreciates the scientific sister. So B-36 invents the land mine, barbed wire, the machine gun, the flame-thrower, the computer, and automation. Then Booboolings kill one another other readily, feeling nothing because they had no imaginations. They had lost the ability of their forebears to see a story in the face of another person, to vicariously feel what others might feel. Hence, they had lost any capacity for mercy.

"The Sisters B-36" is clearly a parable about our own society, where young people kill one another on the streets in extraordinary numbers, and where political bombings and other acts of violence proliferate. It urges the crucial role that writing and other arts play in the development of the imagination. It proclaims the dreadful cost to the culture and to the individual of the loss of the imagination and the capacity to recognize and respect the feelings of others. It reiterates Vonnegut's frequent denunciations of the negative impact that television has on society. It also returns to two even older themes in Vonnegut's work—pacifism, and the failure of the public to respond with understanding to scientific knowledge. It is a classic example of the insertion of a painful comic science fiction story into a novel to introduce at once laughter and message.

Naturally, the larger the role Trout assumes in the novel, the more frequently his stories appear, and hence they occur most often in *God Bless You, Mr. Rosewater, Slaughterhouse-Five, Breakfast of Champions*, and *Timequake*. Other science fiction tales, or at least episodes, occur in the novels, though few so specifically in this mode as in the Trout stories. In *Galápagos*, for instance, when the collapse of the international financial structure precipitates chaos and conflict, Vonnegut makes use of a typical science fiction perspective on things. From the violence people were doing to each other, and to all other living things, a visitor from another planet might have assumed that the environment had gone haywire, and that people were in such a frenzy because Nature was about to kill them all.

In like mode, a war is started when radars misidentify a meteorite shower as incoming missiles, and the earth is depopulated by a corkscrew-like virus that destroys human ovaries. Cruel jokes, indeed, but characteristic macabre humor. Also in that vein is the placing of asterisks beside the names of characters who will die in the course of the novel. In lighter tone, the computer Mandarax supplies wryly appropriate quotations for various occasions, in a manner reminiscent of the Tralfamadorian messages in *The Sirens of Titan*. Thus, when Peruvian rockets wipe out Ecuador, Mandarax quotes: "Happy is the nation without a history. Cesare Bonesana (1738—94)."

In sum, the more frequent characteristics of the comic science fiction short stories carry through into the science fiction subplots and the mini-stories contained in the novels. They share the same mix of the humorous, be it ironical or slapstick, and the painful, be it pathetic or threatening. They make use of hyperbole and disparity, and in so doing often invite visualization. The other-worldly or fantastic in their fundamental elements are often counterbalanced by mundane details that connect the situation with the familiar and add plausibility. That connection is enhanced where there is a narrator or a voice that assumes a persona, these typically adopting some of the folksy tone of the yarn-spinner. Such affirmation as occurs in these stories may stem from the sense of undiminished human aspiration that often runs through them. Vonnegut has written of his admiration for Laurel and Hardy for their invariably "bargaining in good faith with destiny." He recounts his fondness for the cartoon that shows two prisoners chained at ankle and wrist to a dungeon wall, with only the smallest barred window far above, and one saying to the other, "Now here's my plan." Similarly, there is that persistent voice that keeps asking "What if?" in the face of the comfortable assurances and platitudinous answers.

Our age questions whether tragedy can still be written, but the times are scarcely more kind to comedy. In many respects, though, Vonnegut's science fiction stories meet the classic requirements. Perhaps they can because they so often offer an alternative world. But the alternative worlds are almost always closely connected with our own, in theme and moral if not in feature, and their threats identifiable with those we know. While Vonnegut's fiction may serve to remind us of the nature and severity of those threats, it will also, in the best comic tradition, manage to surmount them with laughter or a momentary triumph. For Vonnegut, the reminder is frequently the important thing, calling attention to our neglect or overconfidence. As Northrop Frye wrote many years ago, "Comedy is designed not to condemn evil, but to ridicule a lack of self-knowledge." Sometimes, as in "Report on the Barnhouse Effect" or "The Big Trip Up Yonder," we even see the classic pattern of the younger man triumphing by his wits over the patriarchal figure who embodies a corrupted social status quo. Often the story will reach a formal comedic resolution even if the portended circumstances left at the end are not promising. While Vonnegut is often satirical, many of the short stories, lacking specific targets of satire, fit that categorization less well than that of a comedy that, encompassing the threats and dissonance of a contemporary chaotic world, remains painful. The metaphorical distinction drawn by James Hall still stands: "comic novels find garlic and sapphires in the mud, satiric ones find mostly garlic and blame it for not being sapphire."

What does the science fiction ingredient contribute to this brand of comedy? It certainly affords Vonnegut a greater freedom in addressing issues. While he shows little reluctance to address current social issues directly, science fiction becomes an effective device for achieving distance from which to address an issue that, close up, may be too controversial or confused. Issues projected into a science fiction setting can be simplified and exaggerated to expose or highlight their characteristics. They can be removed sufficiently from the controversies of their immediate contexts to be examined with detachment, and the consequences on one, the other, or both sides of the issue may be projected to extremes that reveal or emphasize their true nature. Science fiction becomes the perfect mode for allowing Vonnegut to move the examination of such issues into a realm where they can be treated, often hyperbolically, without the constraints normally attending their discussion. Science fiction, and the use of humor, allows him to speak of overpopulation, voluntary suicide, governmentally imposed contraception, or pacifism, for example, without necessarily invoking the entrenched resistance often surrounding such topics. In the short stories placed in the wide circulation glossy magazines, using science fiction enables him to extend the scope afforded him by the traditional domestic subjects, or to render them in a new light.

What I have called Vonnegut's painful comic science fiction writing has become, by whatever appellation, perhaps the most characteristic and identifying aspect of his work. To a great many readers Vonnegut is either a comic writer or a science fiction writer or both, and the works they are most likely to remember him by are *Cat's Cradle, Slaughterhouse-Five, Breakfast of Champions,* or maybe an anthologized "Harrison Bergeron." Perhaps it is ironic that the classification of Vonnegut as a science fiction writer tends to persist. Ironic, anyway, that it tends to persist as a narrowing definition, one that pigeonholes him when, in effect, his uses of science fiction have enabled him to broaden the scope of his work. In the short stories it is the science fiction plots, or elements in the plots, that are most likely to reach beyond the kinds of domestic dramas that constitute the stuff of most of his other stories. It is the science fiction that transcends the local to look at the future consequences of global patterns of human behavior, or of technological change, or of new knowledge. In the novels, the interjection of science fiction episodes extends their scope beyond their main plot and setting. It gives the freedom to amplify and broaden, to extend the context in which issues are presented and to create new perspectives. Even where the science fiction interludes seem largely for comic effect, which Vonnegut has spoken of as being like sending in the clowns, the comedy is often like that of the Fool in *King Lear*, seeming folly but with a moral message.

Vonnegut's mode of science fiction has proved an excellent medium for him, a principal component of a postmodern technique for dealing with a postmodern world. For Vonnegut, chaos theory must seem not an abstraction but a reality manifest in the startling deaths within his family and in his own wartime experiences. He has seen the operations of chance in the hazards of war, with its random meting out of death and destruction. Well may his characters ask, "Why me?" Even the peace has been chaotic, from the Great Depression of his youth to an era of constantly accelerating change reflected in ever-more dramatic scientific insights into the nature and origin of our universe and the dizzying rapidity of technological evolution. At a time when, on the one hand, individual human destiny is being seen more and more as genetically determined and when, on the other, many people seek to escape the anguish of an incomprehensible world in chemical dependency, Vonnegut's focus on biochemistry and human behavior seems all the more appropriate. While science fiction helps Vonnegut to observe and comment on such a universe, his painful comic rendering of the form acknowledges not just the suffering existence may impose, but the essential absurdity of the situation in which its randomness and incomprehensibility frequently place us. Vonnegut persists, nevertheless, in seeing the funny side of that situation. The comedy in his fiction expresses a resistance to accepting the logic of the horrors it depicts. His ability to create comedy from the frightening implications of the human condition as he sees it may only be a form of gallows or trench humor. But it may imply some measure of confidence that the same aspiring human spirit that so often lands us in trouble can say once more, "Now here's the plan."

LOREE RACKSTRAW

The Paradox of "Awareness" and Language in Vonnegut's Fiction

> Do I contradict myself?
> Very well then
> I contradict myself,
> I am large, I contain multitudes.
> —Walt Whitman

The writer may invent a story as a way of looking at the world—only to find, like Jorge Luis Borges, that the world he portrayed "traces the image of his face." Nonetheless, imaginative literature distills the experience of a culture into images that can shape its identity and transform its future. It can subvert the power of an enemy who would destroy and move a reader to rebellion or introspection, to laughter or to tears. Even if we may doubt the Aboriginal belief that the world must be sung into existence, most of us are still awed by the mysterious generative power of the word.

Persons outside academic institutions may not know (or care) that a renewed concern about the nature of language, reality, and literature has been blustering about the academy in the past decade or so. The speech of English professors at traditionally tedious meetings has been known to grow strident over the issue of whether words can refer to anything other than themselves. Recently, a stormy concern about the need for cultural literacy and a common national language has even made its way onto political ballots.

From *Kurt Vonnegut: Images and Representations*, edited by Marc Leeds and Peter J. Reed. © 2000 by Marc Leeds and Peter J. Reed. Reprinted with permission of Greenwood Publishing Group, Inc., Westport, CT. All rights reserved.

A confused observer of this tempest, which seems to recur periodically in literate cultures, may study difficult critical theories about the nature and function of language and literature, theories like that of Jacques Derrida's "deconstructionism" that drifted across the Atlantic from France in the 1970s. Or one can avoid the philosophical bluster and instead consult novelistic versions of what Kurt Vonnegut might call "colorful weather maps" to see whether they offer any insight into the prevailing conditions.

That has been my pleasant task since first being introduced to "nontraditional fiction" as a student of Vonnegut in the mid-1960s at the Iowa Writers' Workshop in Iowa City. It was then that I first became intrigued with Vonnegut's form of mind, his endlessly playful way of viewing the world.

That period was also a time of tempestuous concern about language on university campuses. Part of the distress came then, as now, from the recognition of the impending information explosion and acceleration of technological change—as described in *Future Shock* by Alvin Toffler in 1970. But part also came from a related recognition of the importance of diversity: the cultural richness of racial plurality and gender distinctions made visible by civil rights movements; the differences in kinds and relationships of species needed to maintain ecological systems; and new political complexities that arose from the growing United States involvement in Vietnam. Language was inevitably a dynamic participant in these recognitions—articulating, altering, and being transformed by them. It was in that context that I came to appreciate what was for me a dramatically different and valuable way of seeing and being in the world that Kurt Vonnegut and his fictions represented.

Then, it was no more unusual on a late fall afternoon than it is now at the University of Iowa to see students protesting on the central campus or listlessly dozing in the lounge of the Memorial Union. As a student in the Writers' Workshop, I was walking through the Union after class with Vonnegut, my Workshop mentor, when he pointed out Nelson Algren, then also on the Workshop faculty, motionless and prone on a couch back in a corner of the lounge. His slight frame was spotlighted by a floor lamp. Vonnegut suggested a detour to be sure he was all right. In a less benign setting, Algren might have been a park bench bum on one of those Chicago streets he knew so well. His pale, wizened face was softened by sleep into an uncharacteristic innocence. One arm dangled to the floor with his hand curled on the cover of the book he was reading—*In Cold Blood* by Truman Capote.

"That's sweet—he's reading Capote," whispered Vonnegut. We walked on. "There ought to be some kind of pension fund for poets so they wouldn't have to grow old like this," he said quietly.

Somehow that little cameo of a scene stays in my mind as a harbinger of the change that was occurring in literature as well as in the culture as a whole. In literature, here was Nelson Algren, one of America's best writers of modern realism, nodding over the "new journalism" that Capote's *In Cold Blood* heralded, a book Vonnegut regarded as very significant to 20th-century literature. Both writers would become friends of Vonnegut, then a little recognized author and, at the time, working on his *Slaughter-house-Five*, a novel that would shake the American literary traditions Algren and Capote helped establish.

In fact, within the next five years, Vonnegut would become a nationally known campus guru for youngsters struggling with the absurdities and paradoxes of global cultural change that were more insistent and destructive than those of the usual sophomoric crisis. But in 1965, with *Slaughterhouse* still resisting its liberation onto the page, he caused only a minor stir on the Iowa campus. It is true that he took a different approach to writing than other Workshop lecturers from whom one enjoyed the assurance that writing was a nearly sacred profession and way of life. Instead, he seemed to regard fiction-making more practically—as a respectable enterprise like any other business. He said any writer had an obligation to fulfill certain expectations for the reading customer, and there surely was no reason to write if one did not have "something"—and publication—on one's mind. He even was skeptical about the self-effacing voice of Henry James, a Workshop idol whose soul hovered almost visibly in the warm moist air of the World War II Quonset huts that housed writing classes.

On the other hand, he had an extraordinary creative intelligence that resonated, if whimsically, with universal profundities of world literature. His conversations and writings celebrated the fundamental creative process in all its forms—whether it was operating in the body or cultural change or scientific inventiveness or in the literary and fine arts. He loved music, and played clarinet in occasional jam sessions at fellow Workshop lecturer Vance Bourjailly's country schoolhouse studio with other pick up musicians who found their way out to the farm. Indeed, jazz was one of the happier ways he found to celebrate life rather than take it seriously.

These were serious times, however, and he listened with grim and sympathetic outrage to a young student, Steve Smith, the first of the university protesters to burn his draft card in renunciation of U.S. involvement in the Vietnam War. He contributed canned goods to a campus program sending aid to voter registration activists who were at that time being gravely threatened in Selma, Alabama.

Nonetheless, his playful way of looking at the world—his form of mind as expressed in the ideas and structures of his novels—seems prophetically intertwined with changing visions about the nature of consciousness occurring in the humanities as well as in the sciences. Despite a dark concern for the future of the planet, his vision celebrates the diversity and adaptability so important for sustaining life, and it invents models of reality that are life enhancing rather than life controlling. They recapitulate current scientific models of a dynamic cosmos in its eternal processes of self-organization, rather than the static, mechanistic models of 17th-century Newtonian science.

While an emphasis upon the artifice of language and life is now an important focus in contemporary literary criticism, it was not in academic vogue in American universities when Vonnegut was making his way into literary history. Thus, it is worth noting that Vonnegut was one of the first American writers to make explicit through his self-reflective fiction the irony that he was using language to explore the curious and powerful and sometimes even dangerous nature of language itself—how it functions as "signs" or symbols that can influence our perceptions and what we take to be real, and thus can actually shape our system of values and ethics.

One can see the beginnings of this concern in his earliest novels— for example in *Mother Night* (1961), with the dilemma of American counterspy, Howard W. Campbell, Jr., a popular American playwright living in Germany, who agrees to provide coded information to officials in his own country via anti-Semitic propaganda messages he writes and broadcasts by radio for the Nazis. In responding to the call to exploit his gift as a writer and actor for the patriotic cause, Campbell suffers the paradox that his use of language makes him adored by the Nazis and reviled by his own countrymen. He comes to the unbearable realization that his naïve use of language has caused him to actually be what he thought he was only pretending to be, a Nazi Jew-hater. The novel leaves readers with the chilling awareness of how history, to say nothing of personal identity, can be transformed by the way humans use and interpret language.

It seems likely that Vonnegut experienced something similar to the irony of Campbell's dilemma during his formative years. Stung by anti-German sentiment during the world wars, most German-American parents, including his, discouraged their children from speaking the German language. As a young enlisted soldier he must have been amazed by the paradox of his own capture, imprisonment, and abuse in Germany by what could have been his countrymen, an irony compounded when, as a prisoner of war, he was one of the few survivors of the Dresden firebombing by what actually were his own countrymen.

As Vonnegut has often said, his formal study of cultural anthropology at the University of Chicago influenced his interest in cultural relativism and his skepticism about absolutes. But his concerns with those who feel righteous about moral "Truth"—as he has said many times—obviously have earlier roots as well. In addition to being descended from a long line of Free Thinkers, he was deeply impressed by what he learned about the Bill of Rights as a high school student. His adamant public defense of the First Amendment underlines a motif threading through all his fiction: freedom of thought and expression are fundamental to human awareness and survival, no matter the risks these freedoms might create. For him, language is an intimate and curious aspect of the creative nature of humanity closely associated with consciousness or awareness. In this sense it has powers that resonate with the daemon or creative muse in classical Greek myth and thought.

So while the biblical—or any other—"Word" did not impress him as divine truth, the ironic intellectual and ethical problems that words create became important to his work as an artist, as did the profound philosophical and political questions language could both reveal and hide. As his talent in writing satirical fiction developed and his vision matured, his work dealt increasingly with the technical problems of how language—that human invention that creates rational order and meaning out of chaos—can also distort the clarity of our awareness. Through irony and satire he came to excel in making language reveal its inherent paradox: to function simultaneously with *daemonic* creativity or *demonic* destructiveness.

One of his most successful early efforts to show how stories can affect the way people perceive reality was *Cat's Cradle*, the 1963 "black humor" novel in which he created a new language and a new religion to convey how language and religion help to invent beliefs that provide meaning and purpose in the face of life's paradox. When the narrator begins the story with the quietly loaded statement, "Call me Jonah," Vonnegut launches a literary irony of several dimensions. One aspect is of course that of the Old Testament prophet who was punished for his failure to carry God's message of mercy to the Assyrians by being cast off a ship into a storm, swallowed by a whale, and then coughed up on dry land—a remarkable gesture of compassion. Second, the narrator's statement echoes Melville's *Moby-Dick*, a well-known story about human honor, revenge, and death in a battle against a whale and the mysterious powers of nature, which another outcast survivor begins to tell with nearly identical language: "Call me Ishmael." A third level is drawn from both these literary contexts, by putting Jonah or John, the fictional protagonist/narrator of a story about the day the world ended, into the same role as protagonists in these two powerful stories from the past. At the novel's end, John even wants to leave some "magnificent symbol" atop a whale-shaped mountain.

To add to the complexity, the narrator John's surname is never given, except to imply that it is a German name, most likely that of Vonnegut himself. (Thus, he foreshadows the style he introduces later in *Slaughterhouse*, of entering the novel himself as a character.) It also should be noted that the German form of Jonah is Johann, the first name of the great German author, Goethe. It is also the name of Johann Faustus, the actual historical model for Faust in Goethe's masterpiece of that name. (Not only does Vonnegut refer to Goethe on several occasions in his writing and interviews, but the title and central theme of his previous novel, *Mother Night*, is actually taken from Faust.)

As narrator of *Cat's Cradle*, John tells us his name is also the same as that of Bokonon, another Jonah (real name: Lionel Boyd Johnson), who was washed up on the shore of San Lorenzo Island where he established himself as a holy prophet and invented a new religion called Bokononism. John comes to believe in Bokononism because it seems to explain coincidences and help soften contradictions in his life. Thus the three named Jonah/Johns—the Old Testament figure, the narrator, and Bokonon—can all be seen as daemonic muses or masks of Vonnegut in their creative, authorial roles as writers or myth-makers. Likewise, he reminds us of the great biblical and secular literatures and themes of Western tradition that have all had a role in creating meanings that give comfort or direction to an otherwise paradoxical and absurd human life. Tangential to them must surely be the New Testament genesis story in the Gospel of John, which assigns generative divinity to the biblical word for the Christian world.

The narrator tells us he intended his book as a factual account of the bombing of Hiroshima with a title of *The Day the World Ended*. Instead, the novel unfolds another kind of apocalypse in which the world is destroyed by Ice-Nine, likely a metaphor of Vonnegut's experience of the Dresden firebombing (with the epigraph disclaimer that "nothing in this book is true"). In the story, this fictional world ends when the children of a great scientist find themselves on the tropical island of San Lorenzo where they accidentally release their father's invention of Ice-Nine which turns the earth into ice (rather than into fire as it had in Dresden and Hiroshima)—but not before the narrator-protagonist discovers the new religion of Bokononism that has given a sense of purpose to the miserable life of San Lorenzons.

The central theme of Bokonon's scriptures is drawn from Charles Atlas' comic book ads for muscle building through the exercise of "dynamic tension." Thus, Vonnegut satirizes the logic of the principle of opposites and makes his point: the purpose of a text, holy or profane, is to help strengthen the reader's sense of power and purpose in a world of accidents and contradictions, whether through building muscles or spiritual atonement. The narrator comes to the bittersweet realization that it is through Bokononist "foma" (harmless untruths) that humans can find the energy to play out the joke, the absurdity, the purposeless polarity that makes up the cat's cradle game called Life. (Perhaps the greatest irony of *Cat's Cradle* is that it eventually qualified as a master's thesis, giving Vonnegut a delayed but earned graduate degree in cultural anthropology from the University of Chicago!)

The inherent paradox of language and of life is an ironic theme and aesthetic central to the Vonnegut oeuvre. Insight into and resolution of this paradox was probably most clearly articulated in the 1973 novel, *Breakfast of Champions*, when the intractable abstract expressionist painter Rabo Karabekian defends his painting, "The Temptation of Saint Anthony," to a skeptical audience at an arts festival. Present in that audience is another guest of the festival, the fictional author Kilgore Trout, and none other than Vonnegut himself who "literally" appears as a character disguised by mirrored sunglasses.

The huge Karabekian painting is comprised of a green background bisected by a single vertical stripe of "day-glo orange reflecting tape," likely a Vonnegutian parody of the aesthetic concept of the "golden section," the geometrical proportion believed to be universally pleasing. In reading Karabekian's speech, one may also be hearing Vonnegut's own defense against critics who were by then beginning to be quite volatile about his nontraditionalism. He has Karabekian say that his painting:

> shows everything about life which truly matters, with nothing left out. It is a picture of the awareness of every animal—the "I am" to which all messages are sent. It is all that is alive in any of us—in a mouse, in a deer, in a cocktail waitress. It is unwavering and pure, no matter what preposterous adventure may befall us. A sacred picture of Saint Anthony alone is one vertical, unwavering band of light. . . . Our awareness is all that is alive and maybe sacred in any of us. Everything else about us is dead machinery.

Now read the description of the "fire-storm of Indianapolis" that another Vonnegut character from an earlier novel, Eliot Rosewater, envisions in a hallucination that derives from his "inexplicable guilt and anxiety." In *God Bless You, Mr. Rosewater* we are told that Eliot:

> was awed by the majesty of the column of fire, which was at least eight miles in diameter and fifty miles high. The boundaries of

the column seemed absolutely sharp and unwavering, as though made of glass. Within the boundaries, helixes of dull red embers turned in stately harmony about an inner core of white. The white seemed holy.

I think it is safe to say that this description, published eight years before *Breakfast*, gives a close approximation of the Rabo Karabekian painting. When we link it with a factual, eyewitness description of the Dresden fire-bombing quoted in *Rosewater*, Vonnegut's intent seems evident:

> As the many fires broke through the roofs of the burning build-ings, a column of heated air rose more than two and a half miles high and one and a half miles in diameter. . . . In a short time the temperature reached ignition point for all combustibles, and the entire area was ablaze. In such fires complete burnout occurred; that is, no trace of combustible material remained.

This horrific baptism by fire seems to be the ironic vehicle for an unexpectedly Platonic aesthetic—a vision of the form of life spirit or soul abstracted from "combustible material," that is, freed of the literary conven-tions, sensory illusions and truth-altering institutions that limit and distort. It seems to be Vonnegut's vision of what the daemonic life essence actually is, unlimited by biological or any other encumbrances. The irony is that it is apparently a vision Vonnegut has abstracted from his own painful experience of surviving what he called the "moral zero" of the Dresden holocaust in which thousands of humans perished.

That column of light, then, represented by "day-glo orange reflecting tape," may be his way of expressing the paradox that new life stems from primordial chaos—and that just as planetary life and awareness arose out of the cosmic chaos, so his own renewal comes from inventing new forms out of the turbulence of his experience. And, not incidentally, it is to express the irony that it was the disaster of Dresden that helped him gain this insight. This story, then, like the Karabekian painting, is to transform into an artistic aesthetic the tragic experience of the chaos represented by the Allied bombing of Dresden, which did indeed cause the purposeless, rapid combi-nation of all substance with oxygen, the holocaust of death. As usual with Vonnegut, however, there is a further irony: While death is what human life in its awareness attempts to avoid, inherent in what we call life is also the bodily process of dying, that is, a slower but similar process of oxidation. In short, we are born to die and doomed by our human evolution to a painful awareness of that paradox.

But there is yet a further paradox that takes this vision a step beyond what the Greeks celebrated in their great tragic dramas: that column of light representing life's consciousness was visible to Dresden survivors only because of fire and as a characteristic of it. That is, light is radiant energy that accompanies the oxidation process in combustion. Light—and the life that is aware of it—cannot occur separate from that process of oxidation. Or, as Jorge Luis Borges said in his *Labyrinths*, "Time . . . is a fire which consumes me, but I am the fire. The world, unfortunately, is real; I, unfortunately, am Borges." That is to say, Vonnegut celebrates that daemonic life essence of awareness represented in Rabo Karabekian's painting, but the origin of the image in the Dresden holocaust confirms his recognition of the ultimate paradox: the very essence that makes life awareness sacred is inevitably of those same transforming processes. Light cannot be separate from fire. We are the profane and consuming fire, and at the same time, the sacred light.

This paradox is similar to that described by psychoanalyst C. G. Jung when he spoke of the "primordial experience" of the poet as:

> the source of his creativeness, but . . . so dark and amorphous that it requires the related mythological imagery to give it a form. . . . It is nothing but a tremendous intuition striving for expression. It is like a whirlwind that seizes everything within reach and assumes visible form as it swirls upward. Since the expression can never exhaust its possibilities, the poet must have at his disposal a huge store of material if he is to communicate even a fraction of what he has glimpsed, and must make use of difficult and contradictory images in order to express the strange paradoxes of his vision.

Thus, we have Karabekian, the invented creator of the profound painting, who is, after all, drawn by Vonnegut as a cruelly insensitive and humorless man—in marked contrast to the beatific image of his vision. People in the bar where this artist gives Vonnegut-the-narrator his "rebirth" experience are themselves glowing—not from sacred light, but rather from the pollution of chemicals in their clothing created by the earnest (and paradoxical) productivity of their community. To abstract an immutable image of the sacred life essence as separate from the paradox of mortal life is likewise a humanly created artifice like Karabekian's painting and of the novel itself. It is created in such a way as to alert readers to its sacred symbolism but also its difficult and contradictory artificiality, and thus to the profaneness of its inventor. The epiphany Vonnegut celebrates is the awareness of primal life energy. His renewal comes from the creative ability to articulate that awareness, even if what he invents is limited and may be short-lived. To be a conscious participant in this creative process is a renewing experience to be cherished and protected at all cost—for the sake of life itself.

With this view, I differ only in emphasis with Kathryn Hume in her insightful discussion of Vonnegut's congruities with the Greek perception of cosmic flux. She emphasizes the distinction between the positive Heraclitean view of fire as divine and generative, and Vonnegut's view of fire as "the ultimate nightmare," but notes that "fire's visible element, purified and intensified, with its wavering and fluctuations gone, is light. Light is not so destructive. Light has associations with spiritual enlightenment, with rising above the self. . . . In *Breakfast of Champions* he affirms the identity of individual consciousness with this band of light."

In this affirmation, I think Vonnegut is as closely aligned with Borges as with Heraclitus, and perhaps even more so with the physicist and Nobel laureate, Ilya Prigogine, whose paradoxical "chaos theory" research focuses on the complex order that arises out of chaotic systems, an apparent contradiction between the biological sciences and 19th-century thermodynamics. Prigogine is among those exploring how complexity and life itself can spontaneously emerge in the face of the universal tendency of heat energy to dissipate (leading to the "heat death" of the universe). Prigogine reconceptualizes the Second Law of Thermodynamics (in a closed system, entropy or disorder always tends to increase) to argue that in turbulent systems, this entropic tendency is so great that it actually can power a nonlinear transformation toward self-organization. Prigogine says, "This description of nature, in which order is generated out of chaos . . . leads to the conception of matter as active, as in a continuous state of becoming."

In discussing the cultural ramifications of Prigogine's work, cultural critic N. Katherine Hayles says,

> The reconceptualization of the void as a space of creation has deep affinities with the postmodern idea of a constructed reality. . . . This reconstitution makes clear that the world as humans experience it is a collaboration between reality and social construction. . . . Prigogine's vision illuminates and validates the dialectic between order and disorder by finding analogous processes in physical systems. Moreover, it imparts an optimistic turn to such processes by positing them as sources of renewal for the universe.

Vonnegut points toward the collaboration between reality and social construction when he titles Rabo Karabekian's painting the "Temptation of

Saint Anthony," perhaps to remind us of Gustave Flaubert's play of the same name, in which the asceticism of the protagonist actually generates the illusions that tempt him. Finally, exhausted by these enticements, Saint Anthony is able to perceive in the ubiquitous chaotic flux the beauty of "being matter" (i.e., Prigogine's "continuous state of becoming")—the beauty of seeing and being part of the "birth of life . . . the beginning of movement" and to celebrate the absolute generative sensorium of his own body-mind. Likewise, Vonnegut seems to say that by embracing the paradoxical nature of our generative awareness (instead of trying to transcend it) we might live more humbly and gracefully with the ambiguities of life and death, and of the profane and sacred. Again, this may be why Rabo's brash personality is drawn as the opposite of what his painting celebrates. The paradox of Rabo is, I think, confirmed by Vonnegut's later treatment of this character and his paintings in his 1987 novel, *Bluebeard*, in which Rabo strives to achieve paintings that express soul, which he identifies as both life and death.

The rich ambiguity of the symbol in Rabo's painting of the unwavering band of light might also be more fully appreciated when viewed in (dare one say it?) the light of Goethe's *Faust*, which I believe figures as a parodic context to *Breakfast of Champions*. Early in the play Faust used the "triply burning light" or the sign of the Trinity in order to conjure Mephistopheles into materializing out of his canine form. Saluting Faust, Mephisto confesses his paradoxical identity—that he is "part of that Force which would do evil yet forever works the good." Which is to say, his efforts to destroy life result in the opposite of what he intended. Echoing the Dresden band of light and Prigogine's chaos theory, he says he has arisen out of the absolute primal chaos and, like man, he is:

> Part of the Darkness which gave birth to light,
> The haughty Light, which now seeks to dispute
> The ancient rank and range of Mother Night,
> But unsuccessfully, because try as it will,
> It is stuck fast to bodies still.
> It streams from bodies, bodies it makes fair,
> A body hinders its progression; thus I hope
> It won't be long before its scope
> Will in the bodies' ruination share.
> (II. 1350–1354)

That is, once consciousness evolved out of the cosmic chaos and became self-aware, it inevitably invented distinctions with language—differentiations between self and other, night and day, life and death, good and evil—which, with its enlightened ego, it took to be absolute. Goethe's "haughty" man (Faust) with his Light/consciousness has not recognized that he is inherently part of the undifferentiated primal source, the absolute Darkness; he suffers the illusion that he is distinct from that Darkness or that he can transcend it because of his consciousness, his intelligent ability to invent words to create reason. But his Light is "stuck fast" to the body and is subject to the cosmic paradox: consciousness by its very nature, cannot exist apart from body. Mephisto—perversely annoyed by the naïve arrogance of man and committed to annihilating his volatile paradoxes and tiresome cycles—complains that life keeps unfolding (the Heraclitean flux and Prigogine's chaos generating order) despite his efforts:

> I don't get far, when all is said and done.
> This stupid earth, this Somethingness,
> For all that I have undertaken
> Against it, still remains unshaken . . .
> And so it goes. Sometimes I could despair!
> In earth, in water, and in air
> A thousand growing things unfold,
> In dryness, wetness, warmth and cold!
> Had I not specially reserved the flame
> I wouldn't have a thing in my own name.
> (II. 1373–1378)

If Vonnegut's portrayal of the Dresden paradox is read in the context of *Faust*, then Mephistopheles whose flame represents death, and the Trinity whose "triply burning light" represents the creative life force, can both be synonymous with the paradoxical Dresden flame: all three derive from the primal cosmic void and have transforming abilities. But Mephistopheles is no more able to stop the creative flux than Rabo Karabekian (or Saint Anthony!) was able to live by pure awareness. The generative life/death paradox is central to both Goethe's and Vonnegut's work. Read in this light, Vonnegut's repetitive "So it goes" that occurs after every death in *Slaughterhouse-Five* may express cynical resignation, as many critics saw it, but could also be read as a celebration of the immutable life process, even if, in his view, that process is essentially purposeless. Regardless, like Goethe, Vonnegut seems always to have celebrated those who would strive on in the face of life's absurdity.

Critic Peter Reed perceived this early on. In his discussion of Vonnegut's 1962 novel, *Mother Night*, he argued that Vonnegut "does not submit to the darkness of nothingness as Mephistopheles does. . . . He recognizes that we are each a part of that original darkness, but affirms 'that supercilious light' in its struggles against 'Mother night.'"

Vonnegut's whimsical recapitulations of honored literatures like *Faust* affirm the continuity as well as the transforming cultural powers such archetypal figures have had and will continue to have. Humanity is unified and renewed—at least temporarily—by participating in this literary continuity with its generative transformations of language and "truths" that shape and are reshaped by human awareness and action. This seems particularly evident in *Breakfast of Champions* when he enters the novel's text to explain what he is actually doing. That is, Vonnegut as the "holy" ghost writing the novel also echoes the creative role of Goethe. He may even impishly have perceived himself as a spin-off of the actual historical figure who inspired Goethe and the many other legendizers of Faust: the 16th-century German magician and presumed companion of Satan, Doctor Johann Georgius Sabellicus Faustus, Junior. This "real" Doctor Faustus, a contemporary of Martin Luther, was a star-gazer and fortune-teller, as well as a teacher and professor, who dabbled in alchemy on the side. He was said to have spiced up his classroom performances by producing Homeric heroes alive, and supposedly once summoned up the form of Helen of Troy. Like many protagonists in Vonnegut's early novels, he was often accompanied by a dog, believed by Faustus' superstitious peers to be his satanic supernatural guardian.

Of course Goethe's version of that dog in his *Faust I* is the poodle transformed into Mephisto. In *Breakfast*, it appears in the epilogue when Vonnegut as narrator tells us he is waiting to intercept Kilgore Trout as he walks in the eerie center of a Midland City whose description resembles the setting for a Raymond Chandler novel. As Creator of the novel (and of Kilgore Trout, identified here with Vonnegut's father), his purpose will be to tell Kilgore his future and then to free him from any further use in his stories. That is, Vonnegut's patriarchal authority conflict as a driving force in his fiction has apparently been resolved. The scene is one of Vonnegut's funniest, as he turns his own suave private-eye imitation into slapstick. When he steps out of his rented car in a dark section of Midland City to address Kilgore Trout, he unknowingly alerts a fierce Doberman pinscher guard dog who is poised to attack him from behind a fence. The dog, surely a spin-off of the satanic figure in the old Faustus stories, is named Kazak, echoing the loyal space hound from *The Sirens of Titan*. The devilish dog springs, alerting the flight chemistry of Vonnegut the Creator, who leaps completely over the automobile and lands on all fours in the street. Fierce Kazak is flung back by the fence and, defeated by gravity, knocked senseless.

To see this scene as a parody of Faustian themes, one can recall that Mephistopheles lost his power over Faust to God because his magical enchantments failed to keep Faust from actively striving in life; in *Breakfast*, the satanic canine loses his power over Vonnegut—not to God, but to a (de)fence the author invents with language, and to the natural force of gravity. Furthermore, Vonnegut as narrator tells us he has invented a way to keep striving and to avoid suicide by bringing chaos to traditional literary orders, so as to create new fictions that can make life more humane and harmonious. In *Faust II* the heavenly ascension of the soul of Faust is by the power of divine love, whereas in Vonnegut's text, the Faustian narrator is bodily resurrected, if temporarily, by the automatic response of his own biochemistry triggered by terror, that is, by his awareness of danger.

But it seems that Vonnegut also performs another kind of resurrection by freeing Kilgore Trout, here the mask of patriarchal authority, from his psyche and from his literary form. First, like the historical Faustus, Vonnegut as mock magician does all manner of tricks to Kilgore, to convince him he is Kilgore's Creator. He says he could reproduce Helen of Troy before Trout's very eyes, even as the real Faustus was said to have done, and even as Mephistopheles did for Faust in Goethe's play.

Then Vonnegut tells Kilgore to "look up" at the apple he holds, possibly as a parody of the last scene of Gothe's *Faust II* in which "Doctor Marianus," the teacher of the mysteries of the creative force, admonishes heaven-bound penitents to "Gaze upward to that saving glance" from the Eternal-Feminine. But in Vonnegut's narrative, the divine saving glance is replaced by an apple, the obvious symbol of discrimination and knowledge— that seducer of Adam and of Faust—which he uses to satirize Goethe's and our insistence on images of divine truth and salvation. He tells Kilgore that the apple is the "symbol of wholeness and harmony and nourishment. . . . We Americans require symbols which are richly colored and three-dimensional and juicy. Most of all, we hunger for symbols which have not been poisoned by great sins." Vonnegut's apple is, I think, to remind us to be conscious of our persistent and paradoxical need to invent new works of art and bodies of knowledge to transcend our awareness of mortality and impotence, and to recognize that the epiphany we create with language is inevitably doomed to be temporary, given the ironic flux of life that awareness reveals.

Having freed the patriarchal aspect of his psyche, Vonnegut himself floats pleasantly through the void with the angst-ridden Kilgore Trout, surely suggesting a parody of "Pater Ecstaticus," Goethe's epithet for Saint Anthony, who likewise appears at the end of *Faust II*. Stage directions say Pater is "floating up and down," suspended in the ecstatic torment of martyrdom. Pater says, "Lightning bolts, shatter me! So the All may utterly/ Abolish the Nullity,/ Gleam the fixed star above,/ Essence of endless love." Vonnegut's understanding of that "gleam" is the light of life's essence: the awareness that makes creative and adaptive life possible. It has freed him from such martyrdom so he is now comfortably attuned to the nullity in which he dreamily levitates. In the distance he hears Trout call out, in his father's voice, "*Make me young, make me young, make me young!*" It is the voice of "logical" patriarchal civilization with its ecstatic torment and mortal need—if not for transcendence, at least for the power to find renewal and direction in the void.

Kilgore Trout, the incorrigible science fiction writer, has been Vonnegut's daemon and doppelgänger who has "kept striving" through a number of his novels. In *God Bless You, Mr. Rosewater* (1965), he makes his living working at a trading stamp redemption center, giving away harmless gifts. It is he who assumes a Christ-like benevolence to pronounce the sanity of "flamboyantly ill" Rosewater, the alcoholic philanthropist who went insane partly because of the social strain of loving other strivers against paradox: science fiction writers, volunteer firemen, and useless paupers.

In *Slaughterhouse-Five* (1969), he is Billy Pilgrim's favorite author of science fiction about people like himself who were "trying to re-invent themselves and their universe" to help deal with life's absurdity and war's irrational cruelties. Kilgore's stories spring up throughout the novel as mini-illustrations of how the ideas of science, religion, and politics become the lenses that alter human perception and shape values and "truth."

In *Galápagos* (1985), Kilgore Trout is the deceased father of the "ghost writer" of the story who was accidentally beheaded while working as a shipbuilder on the *Bahía de Darwin*, a Swedish ship wrecked on a Galápagos island. Despite outraged summons from his father who beckons from the "blue tunnel to the Afterlife," Leon Trotsky Trout inhabits the head of Captain Kleist (a Vonnegut look-alike), whose inept navigation caused the wreck—and the survival of a bizarre group of people who will evolve into a harmless race of small-brained, handless "fisherfolk." Leon Trout's irrepressible need for creative expression parallels the biological need to reproduce, both leading to the novel's thesis that how we perform the generative dance of life is largely a matter of luck, accidents, and genes.

In *Jailbird* (1982), Trout appears only briefly as the pseudonym of convict Bob Fender, a gentle and generous friend to all inmates, who is serving a life term for treason. Never mind that his "treason" was his brief cohabitation as a soldier in Korea with a beautiful Korean spy disguised as a nightclub singer. At that time, he was a shy, virgin veterinarian who had been drafted to be a meat inspector for the army, and who was set up to be the brunt of a joke by fellow officers who told the singer he was an elite commander of an atomic bomb guard unit. Now in prison for life, he has taken up writing science fiction. Walter Starbuck, the protagonist of *Jailbird*, tells us that Trout/Bob Fender wrote Walter into one of his stories about a judge from the planet Vicuna whose soul was flying about the universe looking for a habitable planet and body after his own planet was destroyed. People on Vicuna, who could easily leave their bodies, became "weightless, transparent, silent awarenesses and sensibilities . . . when they floated around without their bodies." The judge's soul floats into a jail on the planet earth, which he mistakes for a meditation center for philosophers, and ends up stuck in the head of aging Walter Starbuck, imprisoned on false charges of being a participant in the Watergate cover-up.

Stuck in the head of Kurt Vonnegut for all these years, it appears, is the same daemonic soul of awareness and sensibility that finds its apparently final inscription as Kilgore Trout in *Timequake*, Vonnegut's 1997 novel, which he insists is his last. In the Preface he claims this book is a story of how he failed to write a novel he now calls *Timequake One*. The protagonist, eighty-four-year-old Kilgore Trout, described the nature of the timequake as "a cosmic charley horse in the sinews of Destiny" in his unfinished memoir entitled *My Ten Years on Automatic Pilot*. This cosmic event occurred in the year 2001 when "a sudden glitch in the space-time continuum, made everybody and everything do exactly what they'd done during a past decade . . . a second time." A total of sixteen hilarious Trout stories and a play are drawn upon by Vonnegut to reveal the ineptitudes of human awareness, but also to set up a happy fate for Kilgore, who emerges as a tenacious model of hope after Vonnegut's literary career of misanthropic worry about determinism and random accidents. Kilgore becomes a hero through his humanitarian use of free will.

The timequake is Vonnegut's metaphorical device to defamiliarize the disintegrating cultural condition of America, in the hope that it might shock readers into an awareness of their careless disregard of human potential and indifference to the ideals of human dignity and unanimity in our society. Now an old man, Kilgore Trout is so cynical that when he is hauled with other homeless bums to a shelter in upper Manhattan (the former Museum of the American Indian, which has been moved to a safer location downtown), he makes a habit of dumping every story he writes into a wire waste receptacle in front of the fortified headquarters of the American Academy of Arts and Letters next door to the shelter. The academy's executive secretary is Monica Pepper. Those stories are read with delighted awe by her husband, Zoltan, a man she had paralyzed from the waist down in an accident, and who once plagiarized a Kilgore Trout story when he was a boy.

After "free will kicks in again," and unsuspecting folks on "automatic pilot" crash their cars and airplanes, or fall down at the foot of escalators, the only person who seems able to take control of himself again is none other than Kilgore! To mobilize people to put their free will to use and restore order, he shouts out a mantra that soon is broadcast over the media to the whole world: "You were sick, but now you're well again, and there's work to do." This mantra, which becomes "Kilgore's Creed," is too late to help Zoltan, the disabled plagiarizer, however. He is killed the instant the time-quake is over by a berserk fire truck that smashes his wheelchair into the steel door of the academy headquarters. But with that fortress now blasted open, Kilgore uses the building as a morgue and sets up a triage hospital in the homeless shelter next door, after organizing the bums into rescue teams.

Lest we get too optimistic about the beneficial use of free will at this point in Vonnegut's storytelling, we are favored with a flashback that reveals how Kilgore's father accidentally became a specialist in ornithology by discovering birds that were making themselves extinct or causing chaos by choosing easier methods of survival than those deterministic instincts of natural selection that had sustained their species for eons.

Never mind, it all ends happily. Happily? Perhaps for the first time in his writing career, Kurt Vonnegut has found a "gaily mournful" way to actually end a novel! Order is restored, and Kilgore is driven in widow Monica Pepper's armored limousine to the kind of retirement setting Vonnegut had wished for Nelson Algren decades earlier: the Ernest Hemingway suite of the writers' retreat Xanadu, in the summer resort village of Point Zion, Rhode Island. The retreat appears to be a reward for his heroic efforts during the disaster that ensued once the timequake finished its ten-year rerun and free will kicked in again. There he is welcomed by a loving extended family including members of the Pembroke Mask and Wig Club, the Xanadu household staff, members of Alcoholics Anonymous and Gamblers Anonymous, which meet in the Xanadu ballroom, and battered children, women, and grandparents who also have found shelter there and are grateful for Kilgore's Creed.

Kilgore's biggest achievement, however, is more subtle—Vonnegut tells us that he never lost his self-respect: "His indestructible self-respect is what I loved most about Kilgore Trout." This quality surely resonates well with Goethe's celebration of the stalwart Faust, ever striving in the face of demonic adversities.

The final reward for Kilgore is his role as the provider of sound effects in the last act of the Pembroke Mask and Wig Club's production of Abe Lincoln in Illinois by Robert E. Sherwood. It is an epiphanic scene that represents Vonnegut's celebration of the nobility made possible by humanity's capacity for awareness and language. Kilgore is to blow the antique steam whistle that signals Lincoln's departure by train from Illinois to assume the presidency in Washington on the eve of the Civil War. The scene allows Vonnegut to quote Lincoln's eloquent farewell message in which he recounts the ideals of the American Union. Then, in a rousing farewell, the crowd breaks into the singing of "John Brown's Body" as Lincoln gets into the car. The song signals our memory of the Stephen Vincent Benét poem in tribute to John Brown's anti-slavery heroism and in compassion for both sides of the disastrous Civil War. It is a moment not lost on the sound effects man:

> That was when Trout was supposed to blow the whistle, and he did.
>   As the curtain descended, there was a sob backstage. It wasn't in the playbook. It was ad lib. It was about beauty. It came from Kilgore Trout.

And after the play, a triumphant Kilgore gets to go to the cast party clambake on the beach, a party at which many of Vonnegut's own family and friends are present. There, proudly adorned in the tuxedo of Monica Pepper's deceased husband, he offers his and Vonnegut's star-gazing bene-diction to the uniqueness of human awareness in the universe: "Let us call it soul."

Thus, Vonnegut echoes the revelation first offered by Rabo Karabekian in his "Temptation of Saint Anthony" painting nearly twenty-five years earlier. Like Rabo and Kilgore, he has never ceased striving, nor has he ever betrayed his gaily mournful respect for the daemonic awareness that has driven his half century of literary effort to create aesthetic form and a humane culture out of the chaos of life's paradox.

Kilgore's Creed may have kept him going, too.

Chronology

1922   Kurt Vonnegut born on Armistice Day, November 11, in Indianapolis, Indiana. His grandfather was the first licensed architect in Indiana; his father, Kurt Vonnegut, Sr., is a wealthy architect; his mother, Edith Lieber Vonnegut, is the daughter of a socially prominent family. He has an older brother, Bernard, and a sister, Alice.

1929   With the Great Depression, the family fortune disappears.

1936–40   Attends Shortridge High School where he becomes editor of the Shortridge Daily Echo, the first high school daily newspaper in the country.

1940   Enters Cornell University as a chemistry and biology major. Becomes columnist and managing editor of the Cornell Daily Sun.

1943   Hospitalized for pneumonia and loses draft deferment; enlists in the United States Army.

1943–44   Studies mechanical engineering at Carnegie Mellon University as part of military training.

1944   Returns home before shipping out; Mother commits suicide by overdosing on sleeping pills, Mother's Day, May 14. Joins 106th Infantry Division; on December 19, Vonnegut becomes German prisoner of war after being captured at Battle of the Bulge. Sent to Dresden, an "open city" presumably not threatened with Allied attack. Works with other POW's in a vitamin-syrup factory.

1945   On February 13–14, U.S. and British Air Force firebomb Dresden, killing 135,000. Vonnegut and other POW's, quartered in the cellar of a slaughterhouse, survive. He wrote that they emerged to find "135,000 Hansels and Gretels had been baked like gingerbread men." Works as a "corpse miner" in the aftermath of the bombing; on May 22, Vonnegut repatriated. Marries childhood friend Jane Marie Cox on September 1 and moves to Chicago.

1945–47   Studies anthropology at the University of Chicago. Works as police reporter for Chicago City News Bureau.

1947   After Master's thesis rejected, moves to Schenectady, New York, to work as publicist for General Electric, where his brother Bernard is a physicist. Begins writing fiction.

1950   First short story, "Report on the Barnhouse Effect," published in *Collier's*, February 11.

1951   Begins writing full time. Family moves to West Barnstable, Massachusetts, on Cape Cod.

1952   First novel, *Player Piano*, published; sells short stories to magazines, including *Collier's* and the *Saturday Evening Post*.

1953–58   Publishes short stories, works in public relations, runs a Saab dealership, teaches English at a school for the emotionally disturbed.

1957   Father dies October 1. Sister Alice's husband dies in commuter train accident; Alice dies of cancer less than forty-eight hours later; the Vonnegut's adopt their three children.

1959   Second novel, *The Sirens of Titan* published.

1961   Collection of stories, *Canary in a Cat House* published.

1962   *Mother Night* published.

1963   *Cat's Cradle* published.

1964   *God Bless You, Mr. Rosewater* published and attracts serious critical attention. Begins publishing essays and reviews in *Venture*, the *New York Times Book Review*, *Esquire*, and *Harper's*.

1965–67   Begins 2-year residency at the University of Iowa Writers Workshop. Novels reissued as paperback become popular with college students, and attract serious critical attention.

1968   Receives Guggenheim Fellowship; revisits Dresden. A collection of short stories, *Welcome to the Monkey House*, published.

1969   *Slaughterhouse-Five; or the Children's Crusade* published and becomes bestseller.

1970   Takes up residence, alone, in New York City; a play, *Happy*

Birthday, Wanda June, produced off-Broadway. Serves as Briggs-Copeland Lecturer at Harvard University; Awarded M.A. from University of Chicago: *Cat's Cradle* accepted, in lieu of thesis, as a significant contribution to the field of anthropology.

1972   *Between Time and Timbuktu* produced for public television; *Slaughterhouse-Five* released as motion picture. Covers Republican National Convention for *Harper's;* elected vice-president of PEN; becomes member of National Institute of Arts and Letters.

1973   *Breakfast of Champions; or Goodbye, Blue Monday!* published; appointed Distinguished Professor on English Prose at the City University of New York.

1974   *Wampeters, Foma, and Granfalloons*, a collection of essays, speeches, and reviews published.

1975   Son Mark publishes the *Eden Express: A Personal Account of Schizophrenia.*

1976   *Slapstick; or Lonesome No More!* published; a critical failure.

1979   *Jailbird* published. First marriage ends in divorce; marries photographer Jill Krementz.

1980   A children's book, *Sun Moon Star* published in collaboration with illustrator Ivan Chermayeff.

1981   *Palm Sunday: An Autobiographical Collage* published.

1982   *Deadeye Dick* published; *Fates Worse than Death* published in England as pamphlet, by Bertrand Russell Peace Foundation.

1985   *Galápagos* published.

1986   Jane Vonnegut Yarmolinsky, his former wife, dies of cancer in December.

1987   *Bluebeard* published. *Angels without Wings: A Courageous Family's Triumph over Tragedy*, by Jane Vonnegut Yarmolinsky, published; the story of adopting and raising her sister-in-law's children.

1988   *Requiem* performed by Buffalo Symphony.

1990   *Hocus Pocus* published.

1997   Publishes what he claims to be his last novel *Timequake*. Brother Bernard dies.

1999   Publishes a collection of short stories *Bagombo Snuff Box. God Bless You, Dr. Kevorkian*, a collection of Vonnegut's thoughts on the after-life, published by Seven Stories Press.

Contributors

HAROLD BLOOM is Sterling Professor of the Humanities at Yale University and Henry W. and Albert A. Berg Professor of English at the New York University Graduate School. He is the author of over 20 books, including *Shelley's Mythmaking* (1959), *The Visionary Company* (1961), *Blake's Apocalypse* (1963), *Yeats* (1970), *A Map of Misreading* (1975), *Kabbalah and Criticism* (1975), *Agon: Toward a Theory of Revisionism* (1982), *The American Religion* (1992), *The Western Canon* (1994), and *Omens of Millennium: The Gnosis of Angels, Dreams, and Resurrection* (1996). *The Anxiety of Influence* (1973) sets forth Professor Bloom's provocative theory of the literary relationships between the great writers and their predecessors. His most recent books include *Shakespeare: The Invention of the Human*, a 1998 National Book Award finalist, and *How to Read and Why*, which was published in 2000. In 1999, Professor Bloom received the prestigious American Academy of Arts and Letters Gold Medal for Criticism.

TERRY SOUTHERN was a writer and satirist whose achievements included the novels *Flash and Filagree* (1958) and *The Magic Christian*—later made into a film. His screenplays included contributions to *Dr. Strangelove*, as well as having co-authored *Easy Rider*. Aside from his novels and screenplays Mr. Southern wrote numerous essays and reviews, and taught screenwriting at both NYU and Columbia University.

WILLIAM S. DOXEY is a professor of English at the State University of West Georgia where he is also the editor of *Notes on Contemporary Literature*.

JEROME KLINKOWITZ is a professor of English at the University of Northern Iowa. He has written over thirty books in numerous fields, seven of which focus on the life and works of Kurt Vonnegut.

RICHARD GIANNONE is a professor of English at Fordham University. His books include *Music in Willa Cather's Fiction* (1968), *Vonnegut: A Preface to His Novels* (1977), and most recently *Flannery O'Connor, Hermit Novelist* (2000).

JOHN L. SIMONS teaches English at Colorado College. His essay on *Cat's Cradle* first appeared in *Critical Essays on Kurt Vonnegut* (1990).

LEONARD MUSTAZZA is the Associate Dean and Distinguished Professor of English at The Pennsylvania State University, Abington College. His other works include *Forever Pursuing Genesis: The Myth of Eden in the Novels of Kurt Vonnegut* (1990), *Coming After Oprah: Cultural Fallout in the Age of the TV Talk Show* (1997), and *The Frank Sinatra Reader* (1997).

ZOLTÁN ABÁDI-NAGY has served as a Distinguished Lecturer in English at Texas Christian University. He has also held several positions at the Kossuth Lajos University in Debrecen, Hungary, among which are Chair of the Department of English, Dean of the Faculty of Humanities and Social Sciences, and a professorship in contemporary American literature and literary criticism.

PETER FREESE teaches at the University of Paderborn in Germany where he specializes in 19th and 20th century American literature. He has written extensively on Kurt Vonnegut.

WENDY B. FARIS is a professor of English and Comparative Literature at the University of Texas at Arlington. Among her publications are *Labyrinths of Language: Symbolic Landscape and Narrative Design in Modern Fiction* (1988) and numerous articles on Jorge Luis Borges and Carlos Fuentes.

DAVID H. GOLDSMITH taught in the English Department at Northern Michigan University. His dissertation on Kurt Vonnegut, published in 1972, was the first dissertation written on Vonnegut.

JAMES LUNDQUIST is a professor of English at St. Cloud State University in St. Cloud, Minnesota. He has written on Sinclair Lewis, Jack London, and Theodore Dreiser.

LAWRENCE R. BROER is a professor of English at the University of South Florida and author of a number of books on American literature, including

Sanity Plea: Schizophrenia in the Novels of Kurt Vonnegut; Hemingway and Women: Female Critics and the Female Voice; and *Hemingway's Spanish Tragedy.*

PETER J. REED is a professor of English at the University of Minnesota. His book *Writers for the 70s: Kurt Vonnegut* (1972) was the first book-length treatment of Kurt Vonnegut.

LOREE RACKSTRAW taught English at the University of Northern Iowa, and was a student of Vonnegut's in the famed Iowa Writers' Workshop. She also served as the fiction editor of the *North American Review.*

Bibliography

Allen, William Rodney, ed. *Conversations with Kurt Vonnegut*. Jackson: University Press of Mississippi, 1988.
———. *Understanding Kurt Vonnegut*. Columbia: University of South Carolina Press, 1991.
Bellamy, Joe David, ed. *The New Fiction: Interviews with Innovative American Writers*. Urbana: University of Illinois Press, 1974.
Berryman, Charles. "After the Fall: Kurt Vonnegut," *Critique* 26 (1985): pp. 96–102.
Bradbury, Malcolm. *The Modern American Novel*. New York: Oxford University Press, 1983.
Broer, Lawrence R. *Sanity Plea: Schizophrenia in the Novels of Kurt Vonnegut*. Tuscaloosa: University of Alabama Press, 1994.
Bryan, C. D. B. "Kurt Vonnegut, Head Bokononist," *New York Times Book Review* (6 April 1969): pp. 2, 25.
Burhans, Clinton S., Jr. "Hemingway and Vonnegut: Diminishing Vision in a Dying Age," *Modern Fiction Studies* 21 (1975): pp. 173–91.
Crichton, J. Michael. "Sci-Fi and Vonnegut," *New Republic* 160 (26 April 1969): pp. 33–35.
Gardner, John. *On Moral Fiction*. New York: Basic Books, 1978.
Hartshorne, Thomas L. "From *Catch-22* to *Slaughterhouse-Five:* The Decline of the Political Novel," *South Atlantic Quarterly* 78 (1979): pp. 17–33.
Hassan, Ihab. *Contemporary American Literature*. New York: Ungar, 1974.
———. *Paracriticisms*. Urbana: University of Illinois Press, 1975.
———. *The Postmodern Turn*. Columbus: Ohio State University Press, 1987.
Hearell, Dale. "Vonnegut's Changing Women," *Publications of the Arkansas Philological Association* 22, no. 2 (Fall 1996): pp. 27–35.
Hendin, Josephine. *Vulnerable People: A View of American Fiction Since 1945*. New York: Oxford University Press, 1978.
Hume, Kathryn. "The Heraclitian Cosmos of Kurt Vonnegut," *Papers on Language and Literature* 18 (1982): pp. 208–24.
———. "Kurt Vonnegut and the Myths and Symbols of Meaning," *Texas Studies in Language and Literature* 24 (1982): pp. 429–47.

————. "Vonnegut's Self-Projections: Symbolic Characters and Symbolic Fiction," *Journal of Narrative Technique* 12 (1982): pp. 177–90.

Irving, John. "Kurt Vonnegut and His Critics," *New Republic* 181 (22 September 1979): pp. 41–49.

Karl, Frederick R. *American Fictions 1940–1980.* New York: Harper and Row, 1983.

Klinkowitz, Jerome. *The American 1960's.* Ames: Iowa State University Press, 1980.

————, and Donald L. Lawler, eds. *Vonnegut in America.* New York: Delacorte Press/Seymour Lawrence, 1977.

Lundquist, James. *Kurt Vonnegut.* New York: Ungar, 1976.

Merrill, Robert, and Peter A. Scholl. "Vonnegut's *Slaughterhouse-Five:* The Requirements of Chaos," *Studies in American Fiction* 6 (1978): pp. 65–76.

Morse, Donald E. "Kurt Vonnegut's *Jailbird* and *Deadeye Dick:* Two Studies of Defeat," *Hungarian Studies in English* 22 (1991): pp. 109–19.

————. *Kurt Vonnegut.* San Bernardino, California: Borgo, 1992.

————. "Kurt Vonnegut: The Antonio Gaudi of Fantastic Fiction," *Centennial Review* 42, no. 1 (Winter 1998): pp. 173–83.

Mustazza, Leonard. "A Darwinian Eden: Science and Myth in Kurt Vonnegut's *Galápagos,*" *Journal of the Fantastic in the Arts* 3, no. 2 (1991): pp. 55–65.

Olderman, Raymond. *Beyond the Waste Land: The American Novel in the Nineteen-sixties.* New Haven, Connecticut: Yale University Press, 1972.

Pieratt, Asa B., Jr., Julie Huffman-Klinkowitz, and Jerome Klinkowitz, eds. *Kurt Vonnegut: A Comprehensive Bibliography.* Hamden, Connecticut: Shoe String Press/Archon Books, 1987.

Reed, Peter. *Kurt Vonnegut, Jr.* New York: Warner Paperback Library, 1972.

————, and Marc Leeds, eds. *The Vonnegut Chronicles.* Westport, Connecticut: Greenwood Press, 1996.

Scholes, Robert. *The Fabulators.* New York: Oxford University Press, 1967.

————. *Fabulation and Satire.* Urbana: University of Illinois Press, 1979.

Scholl, Peter A. "Vonnegut's Attack upon Christendom," *Newsletter of the Conference in Christianity and Literature* 22 (Fall 1972): pp. 5–11.

Schriber, Mary Sue. "Bringing Chaos to Order: The Novel Tradition and Kurt Vonnegut, Jr.," *Genre* 10 (1977): pp. 283–97.

Uphaus, Robert W. "Expected Meaning in Vonnegut's Dead-End Fiction," *Novel* 8 (1975): pp. 164–75.

Wilson, Loree. "Fiction's Wild Wizard," *Iowa Alumni Review* 19 (June 1966): pp. 10–12.

Wymer, Thomas L. "The Swiftian Satire of Kurt Vonnegut, Jr.," *Voices for the Future.* Ed., Thomas D. Clareson. Bowling Green, Ohio: Bowling Green University Popular Press, 1976, pp. 238–62.

Acknowledgments

"After the Bomb, Dad Came Up with Ice" by Terry Southern from *The New York Times*, June 3, 1963. © 1963 by *The New York Times*. Reprinted by permission.

"Vonnegut's Cat's Cradle" by William S. Doxey from *The Explicator* 37, no. 4 (Summer 1979): p. 6. Reprinted with permission of the Helen Dwight Reid Educational Foundation. Published by Heldref Publications, 1319 Eighteenth St., NW, Washington, DC 20036-1802 © 1979.

"The Private Person as Public Figure" by Jerome Klinkowitz from *Vonnegut in Fact: The Public Spokesmanship of Personal Fiction* by Jerome Klinkowitz. © 1998 University of South Carolina. Reprinted by permission.

"Cat's Cradle" by Richard Giannone from *Vonnegut: A Preface to His Novels* by Richard Giannone. © 1977 by Kennikat Press Corp. Reprinted by permission.

"Tangled Up in You: A Playful Reading of *Cat's Cradle*" by John L. Simons from *Critical Essays on Kurt Vonnegut*, edited by Robert Merrill. © 1990 by Robert Merrill. Reprinted by permission.

"From Formula Toward Experiment: *Cat's Cradle* and *God Bless You, Mr. Rosewater*" by Jerome Klinkowitz from *Kurt Vonnegut* by Jerome Klinkowitz. © 1982 by Jerome Klinkowitz. Reprinted by permission.

"Playful Genesis and Dark Revelation in *Cat's Cradle*" by Leonard Mustazza from *Forever Pursuing Genesis: The Myth of Eden in the Novels of Kurt Vonnegut* by Leonard Mustazza. © 1990 by Associated University Presses, Inc. Reprinted by permission.

"Bokononism as a Structure of Ironies" by Zoltán Abádi-Nagy from *The Vonnegut Chronicles: Interviews and Essays* edited by Peter J. Reed and Marc Leeds. © 1996 by by Peter J. Reed and Marc Leeds. Reprinted by permission.

"*Mother Night, Cat's Cradle*, and the Crimes of Our Time" by Jerome Klinkowitz from *Critical Essays on Kurt Vonnegut* edited by Robert Merrill. © 1990 by Robert Merrill. Reprinted by permission.

"Vonnegut's Invented Religions as Sense-Making Systems" by Peter Freese from *The Vonnegut Chronicles: Interviews and Essays* edited by Peter J. Reed and Marc Leeds. © 1996 by by Peter J. Reed and Marc Leeds. Reprinted by permission.

"Icy Solitude: Magic and Violence in Macondo and San Lorenzo" by Wendy B. Faris from *Latin American Literary Review* 13, no. 25 (January–June, 1985): pp. 44–54. © 1985 *Latin American Literary Review*. Reprinted by permission.

"Vonnegut's Cosmos" by David H. Goldsmith from *Kurt Vonnegut: Fantasist of Fire and Ice* by David H. Goldsmith. © 1972 by the Bowling Green University Popular Press. Reprinted by permission.

"Cosmic Irony" by James Lundquist from *Kurt Vonnegut* by James Lundquist. © 1977 by Frederick Ungar Publishing Co., Inc. Reprinted by permission.

"*Cat's Cradle:* Jonah and the Whale" by Lawrence R. Broer from *Sanity Plea: Schizophrenia in the Novels of Kurt Vonnegut* by Lawrence R. Broer. © 1989 by the University of Alabama Press. Reprinted by permission.

"Hurting 'Til It Laughs: The Painful-Comic Science Fiction Stories of Kurt Vonnegut" by Peter J. Reed from *Kurt Vonnegut: Images and Representations*, edited by Marc Leeds and Peter J. Reed. © 2000 by Marc Leeds and Peter J. Reed. Reprinted by permission.

"The Paradox of 'Awareness' and Language in Vonnegut's Fiction" by Loree Rackstraw from *Kurt Vonnegut: Images and Representations*, edited by Marc Leeds and Peter J. Reed. © 2000 by Marc Leeds and Peter J. Reed. Reprinted by permission.

Index